A
Vermont
Son – 4

Autobiography of Conrad J. Wells

Order this book online at www.trafford.com
or email orders@trafford.com

Most Trafford titles are also available at major online book retailers.

Cover Design by Ready Page Graphics
Design and Photography by Conrad J. Wells

Note for Librarians: A cataloguing record for this book is available from Library
and Archives Canada at www.collectionscanada.ca/amicus/index-e.html

Printed in Victoria, BC, Canada.

ISBN: 978-1-4251-8614-2 (sc)
ISBN: 978-1-4251-8615-9 (e-book)

*We at Trafford believe that it is the responsibility of us all, as both individuals
and corporations, to make choices that are environmentally and socially sound.
You, in turn, are supporting this responsible conduct each time you purchase a
Trafford book, or make use of our publishing services. To find out how you are
helping, please visit www.trafford.com/responsiblepublishing.html*

*Our mission is to efficiently provide the world's finest, most comprehensive
book publishing service, enabling every author to experience success.
To find out how to publish your book, your way, and have it available
worldwide, visit us online at www.trafford.com*

Trafford rev. 6/15/2009

www.trafford.com

North America & international
toll-free: 1 888 232 4444 (USA & Canada)
phone: 250 383 6864 ♦ fax: 250 383 6804
email: info@trafford.com

The United Kingdom & Europe
phone: +44 (0)1865 487 395 ♦ local rate: 0845 230 9601
facsimile: +44 (0)1865 481 507 ♦ email: info.uk@trafford.com

ACKNOWLEDGMENTS

Randolph (Vt.) Historical Society
The Herald of Randolph (Vt.)
Jim Cullum
Dick Monroe
Rudolf and Jean Day
Nathalie Wells
Barbara Lindquist
Joan Gray
Phil McIntyre
IBM Corporation
IBM Archives
Ralph Alfaro
My Wife—Marietta (Bunny) Wells

These people, and others not mentioned have helped to form another link in a chain which when added to the three previous publications, will complete the autobiography of 'A Vermont Son'.

Many attempts and much time was devoted to giving credit, courtesy for photos and/or documents. It's possible, the original photo owner could not be located for one reason or another.

All the photos or graphics about various IBM machines are referred to with the courtesy of IBM Corporation.

All the vehicles and products mentioned within this Book—4, carry Registered Trademarks whether an automobile, radio, television, machine, food or what ever else. Rather than continually note that a product talked about in a given topic is a Registered Trademark item, I prefer to recognize and exemplify that fact in a blanket recognition such as this. These products should not be recognized as an endorsement or certainly not in any way detrimentally, they are mentioned only to elaborate on the story of my life when and if I had the occasion to come in contact with them.

INTRODUCTION

Many names of past and former residents of Randolph (Vt.), appear throughout the text. One reason is that these people provided me with guidance, friendship and/or experiences. I didn't use any particular reason for whose name would be within the 4 books. I do regret I couldn't find space to include many more people that I would have liked to!

I've tried to hold down information about my two children to a minimum——I don't want their privacy to be as open as mine!

The topics are headed, so if you find yourself in a topic of low interest, just skip to the next one.

Within Book 3 and 4, much of the background of IBM was obtained from a Special 'Think' Corporate publication of 1989, some was personal exposure and a few instances from the 'grapevine' ——at the time as designated.

This segment will have a reduction in the amount of photos and graphics in order to provide for an increase in text. In trying to cover a period of forty plus years and staying within the same approximate number of pages as the previous segments, — something had to 'give' —

I have spent a lot of time and thought to all the topics, but my memory and the sequence of when in time they actually took place, may not be totally accurate.

And, again I mention that this book should not be used to establish dates, historic records or incidents of interest tied to a specific time.

Table of Contents
Book 4

viii

RECAP

If there was anything in this world I hated to do——it was to walk away from the employment of IBM. I've said before——I liked everything about the job from the machines to the versatility——I admit some customers got to me at times but no where near what the boss did, before I left!!

Before Management changed in Montpelier, I had the type of job where I looked forward to Mondays, so I could go back to work, I was so intrigued by what I was employed to do!!

As you read the subsequent pages——follow me in my trek. I DO eventually get back to being an individual who really enjoys life, the many jobs, the versatility of those jobs and the best of all——the new people I meet along the way!!!

FLASHBACK

DICK MONROE—— AND A WHITEWASH JOB

In the years gone by——all the farms used a whitewash which was a type of paint in the barn(s) in place of painting, just the area where the cows stanchions were—the milk house, maybe a shed or two. This was generally sprayed on which is easy compared to a paint brush, as most of the wood was rough.

I'm quite sure the spiders liked whitewash ——must have provided a nice background for their work and brightened up their 'living room'——or maybe the spiderwebs just showed up better! Seems like everywhere just off the walk way—— spiderwebs were always present, always fun to walk into one!

This specific topic deals with Dick working on Clyde Estabrook's farm and this day, he and (probably) Bob Estabrook were spraying in the barn and as they ran out of whitewash,they took a trip to the J. H. Lamson Hardware store in Randolph to buy more of the powder.

After entering the store, they were met by Bill Lamson. Bill was small and short, but always made a presentation as if he had just stepped out of a 'mens fashion' magazine——very clean, well dressed in a suit or sports combination and always with a smile. So they asked Bill for some quantity of white-wash (powder).

With that, Bill turned around and headed for the back stoop. On his way he picked up his work gloves and had them on by the time he came to a bulk container which held a white powder. Bill easily demonstrated he was NOT attracted to 'things' that weren't—— clean, canned, small or light (in weight)!

With a small shovel, he proceeded to fill a paper bag with the white stuff—weighed it and handed it over.

Back at the farm——Dick mixed the powder with water in a wash tub. For the benefit of those readers not familiar with a washtub———it's similar in appearance to a 10 quart pail—— silvery and galvanized—only its about two and a half feet in diameter and about one and a half feet deep. Very important item around a farm and used for anything from washing clothes, washing the dog and as a bathtub for kids up to a small or skinny adult! Picture yourself sitting in this and the water soon gets chilly when a pail of hot water is added creating an E-E-E-E-O-O-WWWW situation forcing you to jump out to a cold room!!!

Anyway, Dick mixed the powder and water —filled the pump unit Bob had —so he could start spraying again, when VERY soon—his sprayer worked hard and harder and simultaneously Dick could hardly move the paddle in the washtub. NOW—now they concluded that Bill had given them a bag full of Plaster of Paris.

Had to throw the pump out——and the washtub, with the paddle still standing straight up!!!!

HEADED TO CAPE COD

We packed our personal gear and the four of us headed for Cape Cod—Orleans Ma. to be exact.

I had been in touch with Jim Cullum and he said I could come down anytime ——I would have a job. This would be basically TV work. He had returned from South Royalton about 1952 and worked for a TV store— and in a few years had bought the business.

The store was named Musitronics and was located in a shopping mall along with a Supermarket and about 12 satellite stores on Route 6A in Orleans.

He and his wife had separated and he had the house he built, which was 3 bedrooms. Initially, we would live in Jim's house which worked out well.

We had left our belongings and furniture in the Springfield house and didn't plan to move them until the house was sold.

The store was a typical mall store with a lot of television sets and Stereo record players on display. The two most popular makes being Zenith and next would be Electrohome, a brand made in Kitchener,Ontario and I might add—excellent quality.

Other items in front were various and many musical instruments especially guitars and more guitars. Another item were Electronic Organs, about a dozen of them with the most popular brand name being Kinsman, made in Laconia N.H., along with quite a few used organs of various makes. New pianos were also in stock in high numbers with a leading brand name of Yamaha and a good selection of used pianos.

Jim's Father had quite a few new pianos on the floor also and it made no difference who owned what piano—they were all there to sell. At one time, after I had been there about a year, a semi drove up to the door which delivered between 25 and 30 new spinets and console pianos.

Of course, Ed and I delivered all pianos. We used a two piece rack with wheels which attached to each end of the piano—and which had handles on each end to make the job easier.

The store had a couple of insulated music instruction rooms for whoever was teaching.

One piano teacher was a woman whose name was Marie Marcus and was well known and respected, not only on the Cape—but all over the east coast. She was a jazz player and had taken lessons from 'Fats Waller'——a piano legend back in the days of the 1920's and 1930's. He had also composed many songs and was respected along with 'Jellyroll' Morton, Earl 'Fatha' Hines (and others)— and were household names in the world of Dixie.

At that point in time, I should have commited myself to a

4

few lessons from Marie——but I didn't do it, too many other duties to keep up with and now in my senior years——that topic becomes one of those— 'I should a !'

But regardless, piano, guitar and other music lessons were available.

The store always had many musicians come in during the day—and when they were in the store looking at the various instruments, the piano players always picked a Yamaha to sit down for a tryout.

Jim's father did a lot of piano work—tuning and rebuilding with the rebuild work mostly done at his house—next to Jim's house. So between the pianos, organs, TV sets etc, the sales floor was pretty well occupied and, of course, there were two or three display cases for other items especially musical items.

Mrs. Keenan, a semi retired senior from Illinois who now made her home in Orleans, was a very devoted sales person, a bookkeeper, and general gal Friday who was very apt to put in a long day just to keep busy, but also to insure Jim succeeded.

Jim was very busy especially in the summer months with his jobs playing string bass in various groups which included

Picture of Jim Cullum as described in text. Photo origin unknown

'gigs' in the evening, but also special events in the daytime such as weddings, anniversaries, private parties etc. He had established an excellent reputation among the numerous musicians who lived and worked the many establishments on the Cape.

These musicians came from all over the East coast to spend the summer and some even spent the winter months on the Cape. This was indeed fertile ground for all types of musical activities—especially well

Jim Cullum now using a guitar on Cape Cod. Photo - C. Wells

established and numerous high class restaurants.

Well known (in those days), musician Bobby Hackett, a trumpet player of the 1950's and 1960's would always recommend Jim work any group he would put together as would Teddy Wilson, a pianist who made his name with the Benny Goodman Quartet and whose photo is here with Jimmy and an unnamed drummer.

My job would be outside home service calls, antenna installations, new house wiring for TV and sound, custom TV and sound installations, commercial TV such as in restaurants, bars, cocktail lounges, Motel CATV (Community Antenna Television) wiring etc.——organ home service calls and sales deliveries, piano delivering and if any time was left over—bench servicing for TV and amplifiers etc.

Antenna installations were very easy here in comparison to Vermont, there was less snow, most ALL roofs were only one story with a relatively lower pitch —in most cases a single ladder would cover most antenna service jobs. This also was less dangerous for many reasons.

Musictronics in Orleans, Cape Cod Ma. Photo C. Wells - 1980

A fellow competitor, Ed Nemic who was self employed about 15 miles away would come in and help with antennas, deliveries etc. 2 days a week. so we would cluster many jobs around the extra help.

Later, Bunny got a job doing the daily book work and also took care of many customers in the front of the store, answered the phone and the typical many other duties.

Jim would come in mid morning, check the mail and here again, especially in summers, might have a wedding or whatever at 12 noon so he would be gone until mid afternoon or the whole rest of the day.

At times, the many TV's for service would increase and by the time 8 or 10 were lined up so no room was left——Jim could diagnose like lightning and in no time many sets could be cleared out. Problem was, many times his schedule was so tight it took too much time to get his attention directed toward the service bench!

I'm not going to get into a description of antennas and my various routine daily work chores——a lot of the chores here are duplicates of the TV business described previously

To minimize the duplication about TV, sales or service isn't any different whether its on Cape Cod or Vermont, so for that reason, I'll cut out all the routine work.

THE CONVEX MIRROR

Bunny's Mother had a convex mirror—as a matter of fact, this mirror was in the background hanging on a wall, in the photograph of her parents 25th Wedding Anniversary. This photograph was in Book—2.

It was a fairly common item (I guess), about 16 to 18 inches in diameter with a nice hardwood frame and with an eagle at the top, it was convex and I believe this style had some historical significance. But that topic is in a slice of life I'm not familiar with.

That mirror seemed to travel with us and really, to me, screaming for some tender loving care. So, one day, I took it out in the yard or garage, covered the glass with masking tape and then ———I sprayed it gold. Man, what a difference!!!

In a short time, I carried it in the house and rehung it on the wall———now it had a uniform color—it was painted gold and looked like a million bucks!

Just happened I did that job when her Mother was visiting and then the two of them returned.

NATURALLY, I pointed out the mirror being rather proud of the improvement and I was met with a humongous blast of shrieks and unlady like accusations! I had never heard my Mother in law carry on so!

Finally it came out—she had the frame gold leafed years prior and therefore she wasn't happy about my improvement at all!!!! Never did live that down!!

HORSE WITH A HANDICAP

Some of the entertainment in the decades gone by were the round and square dances on Saturday nights.

In the part of Vermont where I grew up, there was an abundance of 'dance halls' where round and square dances was THE place to be.

There wasn't much money on anyone's behalf, but in place of beer, there might be a few samples of cider and better yet——hard cider—stuff that had been nursed and 'cultivated' until the taste was just right , that is in the opinion of the 'nurser'!!!

Well, regardless 3 brothers from Brookfield (Vt.), decided they were going to the Saturday night shindig in East Braintree—just a couple miles away. And to have a little additional fun, they would ride their horses to this shindig.

After they had spent the evening among friends and sampling numerous examples of home brewed hard cider amongst other samples of whatever was offered (as was the custom)— —Henry suggested to Howard it was time to go home, so the 2 of them found Stub, the 3rd brother, and told him of the plan— —but he wasn't ready to leave.

They weren't going to wait, so they left— Stub said he would be along in a short time.

After Henry and Howard had been back to the farm and 2 or 3 hours had passed, this meant chores weren't far from being started.

Finally just as day broke, Stub came up the drive —riding his horse BACKWARD!!! The two of them went out to meet him—and who they found was thoroughly polluted.

As they helped him off the horse, Henry asked him where the Hell he had been and why he was riding the horse that way!!

To which Stub replied, " Some SOB cut the head off my horse and I had to ride all the way back with my hand over his windpipe" !!!!

PARENTING

While we lived in the Burlington area and then in Springfield with the two girls, Bunny and I talked about her getting a job.

She wasn't pushing to get a job and I wasn't crowding her to get one either, so in discussing the topic, we decided if I could possibly keep a roof over our heads, she would stay home and her main job was to oversee and to bring up the kids—— parenting.

We felt that the girls getting orders from other people—— instilling beliefs and desires as guidance from other people, might not always coincide with what we wanted the girls to follow or establish as certain rules to live by.

As we drove the initial trip to Cape Cod to start a new and different life—we decided to keep the arrangement as it was and for now, Bunny would continue during the day, as the main source for rules and upbringing. I could easily advocate that type of arrangement—but simply, that's what WE wanted.

However, that was in the 1960's. Since then, circumstances combined with a higher cost of living presents a different equation in the last dozen or so years. We didn't spend money on a way of life I would like my wife to enjoy——clothes and other THINGS.

We didn't have a new car every couple of years, we didn't go on bus trips, let alone cruises, we didn't have the latest appliances, didn't have an abundance of clothes etc.!! Those are generally the 'things'—the gadgets I'm referring to.

We did have two great girls, a lot of fun and we felt the girls would realize someday that fundamentals in upbringing would be more important in the long run than 'things'!! And skipping way ahead to the moment I'm writing this, I'm not going to evaluate this topic and whether we were right or not— that's for them to pass judgment!!

At the time, JoAnne was about 7 and Lisa was about 5, and were a product of 'family upbringing' belief. Once we get them both into school and after a few more years——then we could change the baby-sitter attitude and Bunny can work at some type of job (if she wants)——one where she can have some freedom during school hours.

MAKING ACQUAINTANCES IN ORLEANS, MA.

We soon settled in to claim residency in Orleans—Jo Anne went to Elementary School and Lisa wasn't quite old enough to start kindergarten yet, but close to it.

The people were friendly and I met many through work at the store and especially doing home service calls—and as I've said before it was harder on Bunny getting established than it was on me.

Sooner or later, we both made the acquaintance of Dr. Kelly—a long time resident and physician. I became very well acquainted with him and eventually when I had an office visit—

he and I had to exchange a few stories at his insistence. He would sit there, listen and most of the time the ashes on his cigarette would grow and grow until they finally dropped off onto his chest only to be there for a moment as when he got up—they would fall to the floor!!!

As a matter of fact, I had to visit another doctor in the area and during that office visit——he suggested VERY emphatically that I take Epsom Salts internally for some reason. When I got back to Jim's house, (where we were living at the time), and Jim called Dr. Kelly, who also was a personal friend. Jim told him the story and Dr. Kelly talked to me a few moments and suggested I bring in a 'sample' so he could have it analyzed.

Trying to follow his request, the only bottle I could find around Jim's house—was an empty 'soldier' with a scotch label on it! There was always an abundance of these around—so I specimined it and next morning took it to Dr. Kelly's office and with no one around ——I left it on his desk!! Later—after thinking about it for a few moments, I had to go back and ALSO leave a note—I certainly didn't want Dr. Kelly to think somebody was being gratuitous by leaving some scotch!!!!

Everything DID work out all right and I didn't take the Epsom Salts which I was VERY apprehensive about from the beginning.

WYCHMERE HARBOR

The owner of Wychmere Harbor in Harwichport, came in Musitronics and sat down in one of the wicker chairs in front of Mrs. Keenan's desk. Jim knew him well because of the number of music jobs he had done at the private Wychmere Harbor Club in Harwichport. We held our breath when he settled into the chair——truthfully, I was surprised he could even sit in it. And the reason was, ONE BIG MAN!! I won't say more, but the legs were straining to hold the weight.

Wychmere Harbor consisted of a LARGE main house right on the ocean, I'm sure started as a Bed and Breakfast. There was also a clam bar well known for its fried clams and other seafood specialties.

Later, he put up the private Wychmere Harbor Club—a separate building a short distance away and one that accommodated Members Only. All sorts of entertainment was offered including a shielded pool on the ocean side.

The reason he came to the store was that he was building a Motel—he wanted Musitronics to wire for TV and install the sets which totaled about 18 or 20.

The main house had an antenna on the roof which presently fed 3 or 4 bedrooms in that building. He also wanted his or the Master Bedroom supplied with a TV signal.

After the details —prices—TV makes etc. I started the work. I approached the Master Bedroom door and as I knocked, I had time to read the small sign on the door which informed everybody that NO ONE was to enter the bedroom. Not getting a response, I tried the door —it opened—and gingerly entered to find it empty. I proceeded to install a coax leadin from outside to the TV, which was on a large bureau. ALL the furniture in the bedroom was humongeous, solid wood and probably heavy as a Mack truck!!(Understandable— both occupants were quite hearty)!! I finished that room and as I left, I wondered why the caution sign was on the door.

Many a time, I had to get all the ladders off the truck to get to the antenna on the main House ——it was a two story house and the wind from the ocean was always strong.

More than once, in December or January the leadin would break —I don't care how well it was anchored——it would break a couple times in the winter when the wind blew the hardest! And, the antenna, (as it was originally installed), had a three foot tripod with a ten foot pole — I stood on the top of the tripod, it still took all my height and strength to repair the lead where it tied to the antenna.(Try this with a 40 MPH wind blowing and at 20 degrees!!)

Soon, the Motel was finished to the point the TV sets had to be installed. Ed Nemic and I had previously wired the individual rooms before the sheetrock had been installed. Now we were removing each set from the box and placing one in each room.

Before we finished, I took one of the new sets and headed toward the Master Bedroom and, again I saw the sign on the door. I knocked—after no answer, I opened the door just in time to see something scatter and run. I saw enough to know it was a raccoon and saw it disappear out a small scuttle hole which led to a caged area outdoors!!

That's what the 'No Enter' sign stood for and——in the future, more than once I had to return to a complaint of 'No TV' in the Master Bedroom. Then I would find the signal cable was eaten through or gnawed totally off!! One time the power cord was chewed off—I'll bet one of the two coons that did it got enough of a jolt to darken all his fur enough to match the circle around his eyes!!

Imagine, a high class Motel, eating place and a private club and the owner has a couple of coons for pets in the bedroom!!

One last thought, I would bet that Mother Nature knew each time I had to make a service call at the Motel—the wind was always blowing 20 or 30 MPH and right off the ocean, and believe me, as Al Gray used to say—"nothing between us and the North Pole but a screen door—and somebody always left THAT open!!!!!"

DICK DURLAND – 1964

One day sometime in 1963, I came home from work and my wife told me that Dick Durland was in Springfield (Vt.) Hospital. She didn't know why. His Mother was in that area, and we had briefly met her once or twice.

I would go back to see him as soon as I could. A phone call to the Springfield Hospital—which informed me I couldn't see him as I wasn't immediate family. Now, this set me back—why would not being immediate family prevent me from visiting him?

It wasn't only a short time before we learned he had Hodgkin's Disease and that explained the 'No Visitor' situation.

Although his Father was in Florida, we made arrangements for both his Mother and Father to stay in our house on Kirk Meadow Road as long as they needed a place to live. We weren't going to move our furniture and belongings out until we sold it.

The time frame worked out to be about 11 months at which time Dick passed away — March 16, 1964.

Needless to say that was a tough time—especially for his parents.

It was here that I learned how devastating Hodgkin's Disease could be.

Dick was a very talented well mannered young man with many fine qualities and many reasons to live—we'll miss him.

FLASHBACK

RODMAN SEYMOUR AND SANTA CLAUS—1940

On one occasion I was talking with 'Gus' Sivret—a long time acquaintance ——we touched a variety of subjects including the days when he was a member of the Green Mountain Drum and Bugle Corps (I wasn't a member)—this instance came 'to the surface'.

The Green Mountain Drum and Bugle Corps played many occasions at many different locations, towns and cities——its only natural that sooner or later, the group was in an unfamiliar city at Christmas time.

Many of its members were from ten years old up to about eighteen—this would be the minimum and the maximum ages. Its also realistic, the boys came from different backgrounds. This was a time when either loud language and swearing were big no-no's, (most especially language tainted by the presence of 'gutter language.

The boys were in Burlington (Vt.), at Christmas time and some of the younger ones were experiencing sitting on Santa's lap.

When it came to Rodman Seymour (approximate age of 10) and his time to sit on Santa's lap——he climbed up —got sat down and momentarily Santa said, "Ho Ho Ho—— and what would you like for Christmas—young man?!"

To which Rod looked up right at Santa and replied, " Jesus Christ ——didn't you get my letter?'

HEALTH STATUS

After I had been on the Cape for about a year, my health was now coming back and while I couldn't label it normal, I could see such an improvement,I was very encouraged.

I have no desire to burden any reader with a series of health problems so lets just say I finally broke the habit of being drug dependent. And by that, I don't mean illegal ones. But, I do mean— no longer was I popping pain pills for back problems. Doesn't mean I didn't need or want a Tylenol or two periodically for a headache or what ever—but at least I wasn't hooked on any medication, especially prescriptive pain killers.

MIND CONTROL

This is a topic I hardly even considered until I met a man from Hudson, Massachusetts and he was a sincere believer of mind control. He 'preached' this topic every time I saw him and to the extent it was becoming monotonous. I did believe some of his feelings, but NOT to his extent, and I also had a few servings of doubt!

I do sincerely believe that we have a conscious and a sub conscious mind. The conscious can be controlled and can also be controlling—it can rest, can stay in neutral but, it does do the normal thought processing.

The sub conscious is like an unharnessed engine—it runs all the time and can't be controlled. It as no morals or scruples— it just gallivants all over the place, similar to a leaf bud in the wind.

This is apparently where dreams originate—here this moment, gone the next. The thoughts have no continuity and most of the time don't make much sense. IT'S A DUMP—— anything in the way of its contents just float around.

An instance in relation to this topic happened to the acquaintance I mentioned before, who was a 'mind control' fanatic. He and I were opening about 3 dozen new TV sets and these cartons were held closed by big staples. He reached down inside and when he brought his arm back out——he caught one of those staples and put a 2 or 3 inch gash in his arm. It really startled me. I was ready to take him to the Emergency room, as he was bleeding badly.

While I was looking for a tourniquet—he said, "never mind ——I'll show you something relative to mind control." He sat on a TV box with his (bare) arms extended—palms up and didn't' move! I was concerned, I could see blood actually pulse and shortly the pulses lightened up, the blood slowed up and THEN stopped!! Even with an open wound!! Naturally I questioned what happened and he said through mind control, he had directed the blood flow away from the arm with the gash and into the other arm!! IF I HADN'T SEEN IT, I never would have believed it. We put some kind of bandage on it and he went his way! True Story!!

GETTING AUDITED BY THE IRS

As the year 1964 disappeared, and as usual in January of the following year, I started getting the easy part of filing an income tax in back of me. This involved going through the box of receipts for the previous year. As a matter of fact, I'm quite apt to do this January 1. I separate the receipts, cluster them and staple all the types together.

At the end, I make up a fact sheet for anything that may be deductible and will help me reduce the tax due, or better yet, increase the size of the refund check.

I must have mentioned to Mrs. Keenan at the store, I was stockpiling info for my taxes and she asked me if I was going to claim a deduction on my house in Springfield (Vt.), due to the fact I had rented it to the Durlands for a period of time.

16

I replied I wasn't going to claim it——really wasn't worth the hassle.

She was quite insistent that I should, so in the end——I did claim the income and I also claimed some operating expenses I was responsible for and paid.

I felt the same about my taxes as I normally did—nothing spectacular—right in line and reasonably accurate as normal. I finished the tax forms and sent them in.

A few months later, I received a letter from the IRS—— and it stated I was to be in Hyannis (Ma.), on a certain date and to bring my receipts to substantiate my deductions.

The day came and my wife and I were at the designated address and at the designated time. We were ushered into an office and as I sat down opposite the desk, I stated I had the receipts as directed. The examiner said they weren't really interested in the receipts——it was the deduction we had claimed.

I showed some puzzlement, then asked why this was so interesting to them. To which the examiner said I could not claim it because we didn't rent the house for a year—a requirement on rentals. We only rented it for 11 months, therefore it had to be disallowed and that meant doing the tax form over. I asked where we could get that done and he replied we'll do it over right here and now! This sounded simple enough and we were happy to get this in back of us!

So he started with a new form, adding the figures where they should be including the amount of the rental income. "Wait a minute," I said— "if I can't take the necessary deductions—I shouldn't have to claim the income"! BOY—that got his hostility up and he shot back with the statement—" I don't make the laws—I merely enforce them and the law says you have to report any and all income!"

With that, I knew when to keep my mouth shut—but I also at that point in my life, decided to change my beliefs——and at this time, that's about all I'm going to say!!

We finished the form, left and I wondered just where I would come up with the couple hundred dollars extra I would have to mail with the new form.

Needless to say, we did cover the base—just how—I don't remember!

A NEW HOUSE FOR THE WELLS'

Bunny and I, (along with JoAnne and Lisa) had lived in Jim's house about a year when we decided to look for a building lot. By now, I was familiar with the geographics of the area, and we wanted to stay in Orleans so that's where we concentrated looking.

Didn't take but a few weeks when a new subdivision was posted with lots for sale in South Orleans, on the road to Chatham, (which is Route 28). A total of 12 to 14 lots were available on Portanimicut Road just off Quanset Road. The price was 3750 dollars with town water. **THAT** made me cough, to remove that kind of money from the savings!!

I made an appointment with a local Bank and had a loan approved for a house on the lot we had purchased. (I may have been luckier there than what I realized at the time).

However, the lot we bought was one of two on a cul-de-sac and now, clearing the land was the next step. I chopped the trees after giving close attention to lot layout and selecting the house location. A fairly long driveway was laid out —one that would encircle the house.

Next, we picked a house from a local real estate office in Eastham. This would be a panelized Cape Cod style with a stick built second story to be added on site. Those materials were included in the base price. The house materials originated in Washington state, but the panels were assembled in Rhode Island.

The price of 5800 dollars included double glass for all the Cape style windows, and all the extra materials for the full shed dormer on the second floor. (Don't forget that 10,000 dollars then was a fairly decent annual income).

Also, 250 extra 2 X 4 studs were included for closet and partition framing inside, and I have to add, these (and all) studs were Douglas Fir—all straight as an arrow and practically knot free—planed and even had rounded corners to prevent possible slivers!

The trim boards all came prime painted. The price also included all framing to be done — the house was to be closed in and carpentry finished on the outside, including all the cedar shingles for siding and roof shingles, both in place.

The house was delivered just prior to Thanksgiving Day 1964 and the ground was littered with panels, bundles of shingles, trim boards, windows and a slew of other materials.

The cellar hole had been dug, the tree stumps had been removed that I had chopped. And the foundation had been poured.

Lindy and Barb had come to the Cape for Thanksgiving with us and as usual, Lindy was primed to help all he could for the 2 or 3 days they would spend.

I well remember coating the outside of the foundation with asphalt—it was cold enough so the asphalt was really hard to spread, that is until I used an available BernzOMatic torch on the outside of the 5 gallon bucket — didn't take only a few minutes and this stuff was steaming and then, thinned out to a point we could easily roll it on. We did the whole foundation in a short time! At that time, coating the outside of the foundation wasn't a building code requirement but I felt the extra cost was well worth the few dollars for the asphalt.

We placed the trim pieces and windows on saw horses and in one day had these all finish painted. This meant I didn't have to climb a ladder and do that job later!

Then——I ran into trouble—the contractor hired by the Real Estate office didn't show up day after day. He and his crew would work one or two days a week!! This was supposed to be finished by January 1.

Another trouble—the owner of the subdivision stopped me from progressing because he wanted to insure I was building a house 'appropriate for the area. He wasn't convinced even after seeing graphics of the house and sales brochure.

I had to hire an attorney to which he finally agreed. (About a year later, a cedar contemporary Ranch was built across the street from 'our' location)——talk about a structure that was inappropriate, this was the most ridiculous structure you ever could imagine. I wasn't very happy about that— to be honest, I was MAD as Hell and if I had a few dollars I could spare I would have 'slowed' that operation up—but at the time, I was totally occupied!

Another problem was weather— "no snow on Cape Cod— if there is, it will be gone in a day or two", so I was told by more than one person! Well, I can remember around Christmas we had about 15 to 20 inches. The four walls were up for the first floor, (minus the windows and no roof)— and I shoveled snow out each window opening! Of course, all the pieces that were on the ground, were covered and then —the cold weather. As far as I could tell, there wasn't much difference between Cape Cod and Vermont in temperature for the months of December through March of that year.

Finally after every excuse I could have heard—the contractor was fired and a new one took over. Ironically, his name was Conrad Willis and he was better, at least for a while, but by mid February, the work was slowing way down again. By this time, the house was up, the roof was on, the side shingles were being applied and there was staging bolted through all four walls. I wanted to progress on the inside and had already started the wiring and insulation.

I made an arrangement with an electrician in town to buy all the materials from him if he would provide me with guidance to insure what I did was in compliance, in case someone wanted to check this against state code. I nailed in all the boxes, ran all the Romex and installed the electric main entrance. Later, I would install the outlets, switches etc. He would do the entrance cable, connect my circuits to the entrance box and check my work—meaning, checking the circuit loads and outlet placements etc. This was a good arrangement.

I also did the same with a plumber—I did the work, he supplied me with the components for hot and cold water supplies, drains, and vents. He would also insure the work would pass any code requirements. Both the electrician and plumber were friends of Jim—thanks to him I could have those arrangements.

Time and time again, the work was lagging by the contractor—I heard every excuse from "gone deer hunting" to the "grandmother was sick". So as March was approaching I took a drastic step—I had to. I knew when June 1 came, my hours, my time and strength would be shortened due to summer residents flocking to the Cape and I had lot of work to do before I could move in.

If I couldn't move in by mid May, I might have to struggle until the fall when the population shrunk again due to the end of the tourist season.

So I went back to the Real Estate office (again) and told him that the scaffolding bolts coming through the walls were preventing me from sheetrocking and in 10 days, which would be March 10——any scaffolding bolt hindering me, I would remove the wing nut and allow the scaffolding to fall to the ground. If a hole was drilled through the sheetrock—I would deduct 500 dollars for each hole!!

This little 'act' got all the outside work done and all the scaffolding was removed by March 10!! I really hated to do that, but I was promised the house would be closed in January 1 and the work was now 2 months behind.

With the scaffolding topic settled, all the wiring was in the walls so I now turned to insulation, vapor sheeting, applying sheetrock and finishing it off by sponging the seams and nail holes to a finish.

I also went back to the plumber and ordered a boiler and the baseboard radiation, piping and controls. I had a lot of broken promises from Ed the plumber about coming to the house ——he never would show when he promised—actually, he never showed up at all—that is until one Saturday, late afternoon, he surprised me by coming around back of the house and in the cellar, where I was working.

We talked about one thing and another and he looked up at the carrier timber going the width of the house and literally jumped back!. "Who did your wiring here—I've never seen a house wired like that!" he said as he pointed up to the carrier.

I said, "I did, doesn't take much longer to lay the Romex out that way than it does to do a poor looking job." (I had taken the time to lay out all 8 'runs' of Romex so it was all parallel, straight and to 'drop off' each line from the top of the row)!

AND WITH THAT, I never had a problem again with him keeping an appointment—he was there when he said he would be!! And he even would call me once or twice to tell me he had to break his schedule! Apparently he was so impressed, that made him interested!

One night about 7 o'clock I arrived at the house to find a load of pea stone had been chuted in a pile in the cellar. I had ordered it so the concrete floor could be poured. With a round pointed shovel, I spread that load of 'stones' over the basement area of the house in about 2 hours. Some, I tossed to the approximate location, some I walked closer to where I wanted it to be but mostly, I just threw it. And near the end, I just leveled off where it was.

Here, I found one of my personal problems and that was the fact that a lot of work I did ——I did with nervous energy and/or nervous strength. I spread that entire load with nervous energy and vowed not to work in that style anymore. A few times I found I had reverted and had to correct myself. Working under that type of energy leaves you more exhausted than doing it in a relaxed form. However, I could imagine that type of labor could quite easily help shed some weight.

Since, I have convinced myself (and successfully), to work with a relaxed attitude—it's much better!!

When the heating materials arrived at his house, Ed the plumber called me so I could pick some of the pipes and baseboard radiation units. The boiler was delivered on the ground in back of (my) house. He said at the time he would give me a week and then come check the job out.

That was on a Saturday afternoon and here I'll say that Ed's kitchen looked like a supply store—he ate his breakfast cereal at the kitchen table surrounded by thermostats, high limit controls, zone control valves, bags of oakum and who knows what else!!

Monday morning the downstairs heat loop was all in!! Now I'm waiting for him to oversee connecting them to the boiler with the zone control valves, along with the domestic hot water connections. I had worked all winter with NO heat and I was anxious to get that boiler fired up!! Nights when I returned to Jim's house around 11PM, it took half the night to get 'thawed out.'

I know Ed thought there would be numerous leaks by either unclean joints or poor soldering. I was dying to get the heat working —it was cold all winter and the inside of a house is always cold(er). I did have the use of a kerosene space heater which belonged to the contractor while it was there, however, those things stink and they make a lot of noise—not only that, but if you get 5 feet away from the muzzle, it still is plenty cold!!

I worked on the house weeknights till about 11 PM and Saturdays from late afternoons till midnight along with all day Sundays.

So through April and May besides the downstairs sheetrock, I put on the pine wainscoting, and put down the pre-finished hardwood floors in the master bedroom, the (downstairs) hall and the living room.

When it came time to wire up the outlets and switches, my thought process had matured since Lindy and Barb's house in Vermont. The 3 way switches didn't slow me down only slightly, I solved those— even installing one or two 4 way switches.

Bunny helped with the stained and painted woodwork. I hung the doors, did the tile work in the bathroom—floor, tub area and walls.

I had hoped Ed the plumber, would install the wall hung toilet seat but, when it came time to do that job, he didn't want any part of it saying he always broke a corner off the toilet base. I had used 2 X 6 studs in the wall and now 'hanging the john' was up to me. I knew that inaccurate adjustments of the backnuts could easily allow a corner to break so, adjusting the bracket bolts VERY carefully brought success on that.

And next came the kitchen. Jim gave me a hand laying out the cabinets, counters etc. I had bought a table saw with an attached jointer.

We ended up building the cabinets by attaching the shelves and sides to the walls. The front frames were assembled with half lap corners and then attached to the shelves. Last were the cabinet doors, which were time consuming.

At this point, my friend, Harry Howard came down from Springfield, Vt. and did the Formica counter tops and some other finishing details.

I should say here, I'm not a cabinet maker and as with many of the tasks I tackled in building this house, the workmanship certainly was not top class, but it was acceptable. I had a strict budget and time frame to follow, which in most cases dictated

I would do many jobs I hadn't done before —pleasing outcome or not. I certainly learned a lot but some mistakes were made.

Finally, Ed the plumber came around and we finished up the heating loop by connecting the pipes to the boiler. I'm a little reluctant to say it, but we did have a couple of leaks in the joints he put together which were in the cellar, in wide open spaces—none of the other soldered joints leaked.

BUT, I was extremely cautious about my soldering due to the fact **ALL** of the baseboard joints were close to either studs or wood of some type. I used small pieces of asbestos board between the pipe and the wood framing because I was scared to death of starting a fire by careless actions or poor safeguards, and, doing it once is bad enough, let alone doing a joint the second time because it leaked. Also, the house was very isolated from anyone nearby, I had no phone, I was alone —during the evenings so, if a fire was started, it would be serious very quickly.

Strange as it may sound, even though it was cold there at night, I actually sweat at times, due to the tension of using a flame so close to the wood framing and envisioning a fire out there in the boondocks!!

Also, a leak means draining the system to the point where the water is gone from where you want to resolder, because the water hogs the heat— making resoldering impossible, unless you have a (high heat) Prestolite torch. Which I didn't. This extra step adds considerable time to the process, so it's easier and better to do it right the first time.

In the living /dining area, I used a 2 inch thick fiberglass ceiling which were 4X12 or 4X14 panels, a new product—but it was simple and quick to 'put up' and took a difficult job off the schedule. I also used 1 inch 2 X 4 fiberglass in the downstairs bedroom —but over time, these didn't work out well — they were so light, they would float up if the door was slammed.

Sometime near the end of May—we moved in and the pressure was off me just as summer traffic increased at the store.

AND, I might add—we had a stream of visitors until early fall, but we were pleased to have the company. The company also included Bunny's father, Bert and believe me, he could put some color in the atmosphere!!!

Bunny and I had the Master bedroom on the first floor—the two girls slept upstairs in rooms which needed some more work —like walls, doors etc!! The downstairs was 95% done and I might add the wind could whistle outside but there wasn't any draft inside!

Bunny and I woke on our Anniversary of June 27, to find the two girls had prepared a COMPLETE breakfast at the dining room table with all the right items for a breakfast fit for a king—not bad for two youngsters aged 6 and 8!!

Over time, I plugged away on the upstairs with walls for two bedrooms, a space for an upstairs bath, a couple of large walk-in closets and a hall.

A LOOK BACK AT BUILDING A HOUSE

At that point in my life, I would need a long rest period and away from any building project for a good length of time before getting involved that deep again.

The extra hours and hours were physically exhausting, (if you work normal hours of a regular job), — mentally, it was 'bloody maddening' —you were constantly thinking one day to a week ahead of where you presently were in time (deciding what materials to use and ordering those materials at the correct moment), also, there were dozens of items to think about, and emotionally, it 'gears you up so tight with the procedure—the routine —the ritual etc. etc. you feel like a yo-yo in a vacuum and the least little circumstance can make you 'hit the ceiling'!! AND, don't overlook the disappointments etc. when 'things go wrong'. AND, they do!!!

Years ago— that was the way many people gained a house, such as Lindy and Barb, Stan and Joan Gould did in the late fifties. Any time or way you could save on materials or ESPECIALLY labor — was a real plus. Recall the topic in a previous "A Vermont Son" where 8 or 10 people got together and with free labor covered a specific part of a house, and another weekend, got together again to do another section, or another major unit of construction.

But, as time progressed, an owner building a house, the process became more and more difficult. First of all, more and more cities and towns used building inspectors. It was their responsibility to ensure this house complied with, not only the State Building Code—but also with any and all local codes that pertained additionally. There is doubt, a nonbuilder by trade can now accomplish what the various codes require. Thirty years after I did this house, rules and codes had become VERY complicated.

Naturally, a small town in Vermont, New Hampshire or Maine didn't burden a prospective home builder/owner with the elaborate procedure that a town of thousands population in Massachusetts or Connecticut would. My point here is — somewhere along the line an individual just can't pick up a hammer and start building a dwelling.

How about the bank that's probably financing this house— they have certain requirements that have to be followed — they will write you a check for any reasonable amount you may need but, as it progresses, you have to work within their procedures and scheduled payment amounts.

By the time the 1980's came —it became a pretty good idea to hire an attorney to insure your interests are protected.

AND, by then, the builder had become a coordinator and his main job is to obtain the building permit, lineup the subcontractors, schedule the subs for a smooth integration of their work with others so ultimately the finished product comes about and at the designated time.

Another point here about an individual building his own house — and that point is this——is this individual going to perform all jobs that a subcontractor should perform and if 'yes'—is he qualified to do wiring and pass an electrical review of the work? The same for a plumber? The landscaper? Even the framing for safety reasons?

And if 'NO', will subcontractors be willing to do a certain segment and THEN be available when needed??? Believe me— its easy for a 'sub' to say he'll be available next Monday and then never show up! He really doesn't have much allegiance to you—you're only building one house. He's going to cater to other builders, who give him repetitive work!

The previous 2 or 3 paragraphs only scratch the surface on various topics pertaining to building a house — all of these topics vary in complexity and magnitude depending on where you live in a given town or city within various states etc.—so if you are still going to do this on your own—do your homework first and do it thoroughly!!!

So now, back to the Wells' house on Cape Cod. Fortunately, I didn't have to contend with multiple inspectors during the 1960's, there was only a building inspector, I guess— but I never saw him!

BUT—I had to accept the fact that the house I was working on — had many areas and places where it could have been dangerous. Places where methane gas could exist from poor venting in the plumbing—many places where carbon monoxide could prevail from incorrect furnace venting—not to mention a possibility for a fire in many places from incorrect or poor wiring procedures or chimney clearances. I was lucky —-actually it wasn't ALL luck, but the house was safe—would yours be safe, also?

One other point here is that I didn't want to do the outside work—it would take me forever to do shingles, trim work. Imagine either building a scaffold or renting one and then erecting it? Even if you do —imagine this—measure a piece of trim board and climbing the ladder to install it—then measure for the next piece—down and cut then back to install this one. Multiply that by a dozen-it's a very slow process UNLESS you have someone else cut and pass the pieces up to you!

So it was worth the price to me for the work to be done by 'others'. To work on the outside alone is a really tough job, frustrating and very time consuming.

I did hire the bulldozer work, the chimney work and some other relatively specialized jobs, like installing the septic system.

We ended up with about 17 thousand dollars in the land and house — not counting my labor AND this was a mistake!

Here's why:—working full time is demanding — working on a house is ALSO a full time job, and in doing both for that length of time nearly turned me into a basket case! However, most people couldn't reduce their job hours or not work at a job producing income.

Ideally, I should have worked at my job —4 days a week, and worked on the house 2 or 3 days a week, with each day about 10 to 12 hours regardless which 'job' I was working on. This still totals about 70 plus hours a week. But, in working both jobs, the total is nearly 80 hours a week—80 hours once in a while can be accepted, but 80 hours— week in and week out can really knock you down!

Now,—about pay. IF you could work only 4 days from an income producing job, let the house pay you for the remaining days you work on it. After all, someone else would get paid for working on the house—why not you? It's going to require a certain number of man hours, so write yourself a check each week for some of that labor!! AND, add that expense to the cost of the home. You're paying yourself for labor each week— but then add that cost to the mortgage and spread the payback over 15 to 25 years along with the other labor.

THE INCOME TAX SITUATION

SURE, you're going to pay income tax on that income, but, your main income may be reduced by a 4 day week—so it will probably even out.

And, talking about income tax—unless the laws have changed since the 1960's in regard to this circumstance—please be informed when you sell this house (if only a couple of years in the future, for simplicity) —you can't charge your nonpaid time as an expense in calculating the total cost of the house against the sale price. The only charges you can deduct are for materials.

Now, IF you pay yourself, you can now include your (own personal) labor cost(s) as an expense in addition to the materials against the sales price. Here again, these are items you should check out to minimize any chance of a tax hassle.

THE HOUSING CONCLUSION

With this under my belt — and with technology advancements—if I faced that situation again, what I would do is buy either a Modular Home or a Manufactured Home. There isn't much, if any difference—it's all so very easy, and so very quick with very little hassle. And don't kid yourself, these units are WELL BUILT and with LOW maintenance. The quality is tops and the materials are equal if not better than 'stick built'—bearing in mind some are better than others in both categories. If you want a 2 story or other than a rectangular shaped box—2 story units are available especially in Modular Homes as is 'L' shaped etc.

And with that—I'll close out the topic of building a house!

House on Cape Cod - Finished! Photo - C. Wells

SMOKING ENDED AND HOW WE DID IT

For July 4th weekend in 1965, Bunny,the kids and I traveled to Vermont and spent some time with Barb, Lindy and their kids.

As we traveled, naturally we smoked as we traveled both ways from Cape Cod to Vermont and back.

We ended our trip back in Orleans (Ma.), I had finished unloading the car and in the house, I sat down and lit a cigarette for a few moments of relaxation. No sooner had I lit it, I started to cough, I looked at that cigarette and swear that it made me cough—now, I had been building up to this,—I was now smoking menthol cigarettes and had been enjoying them less and less in the last few months.

Regardless, I went to bed and the next morning was no different than any other morning——but as I went to work and was down in the Eastham area, during the 'off season'——very few places to buy cigarettes, **and**, of course, I ran out.

For the next 2 or 3 hours ——my hand by habit went to my shirt pocket many times where each time, there were **NO CIGARETTES**.

I went the whole day without any cigarette——but **if** I had any in my pocket—I would have had one or more in my mouth and not even known it.

At home that night, I told Bunny I hadn't had a cigarette all day—because I ran out. She said she hadn't had one either, even though she had some in the house.

The next day, I loaded a thermos with hot coffee and I sipped this off and on all day, or threw a hard candy in my mouth —I still didn't have a cigarette and from that day forward—we never have smoked again in that 40 year time span!!

As I write this, over 40 years later we both are totally convinced it was ONE of the smartest changes we ever did!!

Before I let this topic go——here's a process I have used for years and one I'll elaborate on. Many people when they get stressed, need a cigarette to help overcome being 'up tight'. I have found that when this happens to me (since I quit smoking), I'll take 4 or 5 deep breaths. Before I quit smoking, I didn't feel any need to find an alternative—I felt a cigarette was the answer.

Now, I don't think it was—it's the fact that inhaling, the deep breaths —you take in more oxygen and this oxygen provides the calming effect. I've done this trick for years and it works for me,—IF it doesn't —take another 4 or 5 deep breaths. Also, after I quit, when I felt a real need for a cigarette, I would use this deep breathing idea. I know everybody is different— but try this and try it many times, it just might help in getting over the urge to smoke OR to rid that stress!!!!

A TOUCHY TV INSTALLATION

Sometime in the middle 1960's, Jim sold a TV and installation to a customer in Chatham (Ma.), and the house was very unusual. Owned by a man (and wife), he also owned a building supply center. This house, as you could imagine was something from the pages of Better and Homes and Gardens. It was finished to a head spinning degree with the best of materials of that time and very tastefully decorated inside and outside. Let's face it ——he's not going to finish his own house with anything less than the best!

This was about 1965, and for the years TV had been around, they had never succumbed to buying one. They were now making the plunge and while TV was fair reception from an outside antenna——it certainly wasn't much to brag about!

Partly for the reason of low signal and a couple other factors, we decided to install a tower in the back yard about 30 feet from the house—a tower that would only be about 30 feet high with a 10 foot pole sticking out the top. We would bury the line(s) coming to the house to minimize cuts with a lawn mower, tripping people up etc,and this would terminate at a panel on the wall in the laundry off the garage.

They wanted a TV set in the living room, another in the master bedroom and a third in the bath off the master bedroom, and all three were high priced sets.(The TV in the bathroom raised more than one question in my mind, but that's incidental)!

In a house under construction, this would be duck soup—
—however, this house was way beyond construction—it was
totally finished and well decorated. Believe me when I say
working on a project such as this causes a certain amount of
apprehension before you even get to the front door!

The bedroom and the bath coax line was installed with
some anxiety plus a little sweat, ——in the living room, the
customer showed me where the TV would be placed—about 3
feet in front of the built-in wall bookcase, so I measured,
remeasured and then measured again——to insure I would drill
up from the garage ceiling and INTO the wall giving a back to
the bookcase, also measuring the second coordinate to come
out at a given point in the bookcase area. The customer wasn't
aware of our plan.

The floor was a random width oak, screwed and pegged
with the screw hole pegs sanded to cover any 'irregularities'—
—it was stained with a reasonably dark stain and certainly
looked beautiful. Finally between Ed Nemic and myself, we
were convinced where to drill and come out in this wall where
we would attach a TV signal plate and then run a connector
lead to the TV set.

After several cautious moments of drilling we broke
through, so we left the drill right in the hole and went up to
the living room only to see the drill sticking up through the
floor near the TV! (How were we supposed to know the first
floor partition was offset from the garage wall downstairs by
about 3 feet——everything, including the garage walls were
sheetrocked)!

The 'Mrs' was sitting on the sofa across from the drill bit—
had stopped knitting and as I came into the room said, "MR.
WELLS, you came right up through the floor!!

She really didn't know where it was supposed to come up
so without a hesitation I replied, "GOOD, right where I wanted
it right beside the TV— so no one will trip over the leadin.
Now, I'll put a floor cover there and it will be perfect!"

By minimizing the circumstance and giving the explanation I did, that was how a mountain was reduced to a mole hill!

FATHER IN LAW COMES FOR A VISIT

The following Summer, Bunny's Father (Bert), came for a visit and ended up spending about 2 months. I really didn't mind especially when he did a whale of a lot of work around the lot. He came up from Florida and even though he was retired, he always had to be busy doing something!

He had a pickup with a camper in the back—a fairly heavy one and his first idea was we should take the camper off the back. Of course he didn't bring three jacks to do that chore, so he said I—I—I should have some idea on how to get that off.

Well, we worked and after more than 2 hours ——we did have it out and sitting on the ground in back of the house. We 'removed' it with only a bumper jack and, at the time, I made a mental note I don't want to do that again!!

We unloaded it in the back corner of the lot—and this is where he and his third wife slept.

He said he wanted to take a couple loads of brush to the dump (this was before it was known as a landfill). So, after a discussion AND a session on how to get to the dump using the back way, he acknowledged he knew how to get there, There was something about NOT using his truck with Florida plates and hauling brush in Massachusetts that might cause a stir——so he wasn't to use the main road going to the dump!

About mid morning, Bert walks through the back door of Musitronics, where I was busy in the service area. Thoroughly surprised, I asked him why he was coming through the back door of the store. His answer—— "I got lost—tell me again how to get there!" (OF course, now the directions would be totally different). So I went out the door and there sat his truck with a load of brush which came right through the center of town getting here—— AND he has one length of clothes line rope hold in it on ——tied under the gas cap!!!!

So, I directed him again toward the dump and he left.

That night when I got home, he told me a State Trooper had stopped him and wanted to know why he was hauling brush in Massachusetts with a truck registered in Florida. So Bert told him he came to visit his daughter so he could go fishing and since he had been here his son in law had worked him so much he hadn't even been fishing yet——and how he had to help out his daughter and son in law —whose poor as pee and didn't give him any time to fish etc, etc.

So, the trooper let him off with a warning!!!!

I think he made 5 or 6 trips to that dump—when he was finished, the lot looked a million bucks——incidentally, that's what he did in Florida, was landscape and general yard work.

There was another house going up about 2 lots away and Bert would go over and watch. Didn't take him long to get acquainted with the builder and offered to clean the yard of building debris and take it to the dump with the builder turning the offer down as his own men could load one of the trucks and do it.

Well, Bert suggested it often enough so the builder finally agreed to let him do it. Then the builder looked out and noticed the nearly full truck also contained a few 2 X 4's 8 and 10 feet long and other non throw away materials and told Bert, they weren't scrap. Bert replied he had to have some good pieces—he wasn't Santy Claus!!

So that arrangement didn't last even one load!!!

And another night when I got home, Bert said they were going to pour concrete steps next door so he asked the driver to throw on a little 'extry', "my son in law needs his front steps poured also".

Well that's a hell of a situation—I didn't want my steps yet—and for one reason is the taxes. Your house under construction isn't taxed full value UNTIL your front steps are finished, even if 2 years later and you still don't have steps!!

Also, I didn't have ANY forms built, so we had to work until midnight getting forms in place and— how much is throw on a little 'extry' ?—how much does that mean? and does the driver take him seriously? —and will he have any 'extry'??? AND, the biggest part is the fact, you have to fill the center part of the forms——it takes too much concrete to completely fill the forms, so you take up more than half the space with just plain old fill.

This means Bert and I took his truck to get some fill—I didn't know where to go, but he did and we ended up at the town dump backed up to a 10 foot bank of decent looking fill. So, we loaded the truck about a quarter full and then dumped it in the forms! (I'm not giving ALL the details to this little caper)!

Next day, the forms were filled and we had front steps whether it was time or not,—— and all I can say is that he meant well!!!!

And then there was the time he and Lindy took Lindy's boat and were fishing in Pleasant Bay. Having a good time— probably having a beer or two —yakking and so busy fishing — didn't see the fog rolling in and by the time they did see it, they were surrounded and couldn't find their way back to the launching ramp. They finally did, but not before it scared the peewadin outa the both of them. That little caper, I just as soon forget!!!

And, how about the time, Bert was about to carve a big turkey and he generally would dip the knife in warm water, the draw the back side across your throat while the warm water would run down giving you the impression he had actually cut your throat. So to demonstrate he did it to himself BUT, as the warm 'water' ran done——he had really cut his throat by forgetting to use the back of the knife and used the front — —which really cut and the warm feeling was his own blood as it ran down!!!!!

I have to mention that I think Bert's favorite NON ALCO-HOLIC beverage was Clorox—he used it for everything—washing his clothes—washing his truck—soaked his socks in it and even soaked his teeth in it every night. Said the teeth tasted fresh next morning and it killed all the crud!!

SELLING THE VW CAMPER

All the time the house construction action was taking place, the bills were coming in——so I decided to sell the Volkswagen Microbus, which I had converted to a camper. There was one problem——the rocker panels were totally rotted away leaving a jagged edge nearly the length of each side.

So, the way to combat that was to drop the price by a couple hundred dollars to allow for professional repair. It really was in excellent condition, not to mention the camper conversion assets.

I put an ad in the local paper and that drew 6 or 8 lookers. More than one asked why I was selling it so cheap and—needless to say I didn't sell it——at least that summer.

So we used it through the winter. Next year, Bert came back, so I said to him, one night, we're going to fix up the VW, so we can sell it.

I had on hand some metal transfer sheets I had obtained earlier from the Herald in Randolph and which they used to print the weekly newspaper——and these were just right to fix the rocker panels. They were aluminum sheets about 30 inches square which could be cut with 'tin shears'——so I cut a few patches and then with the use of a pop rivet tool, attached them to the body with the bottom(s) curled up underneath. A can of Bondo and a coat or two of matching paint and that transformed the 'old girl' into a dream vehicle!!!

I advertised it again and sold it to the first person to look at it, and for 400 hundred dollars more than I had asked the previous year.

Bert's cigar literally flew out of his mouth when the customer said, "We'll take it"!!!

JIM REMODELS HIS HOUSE

After Bunny and I had moved into our own house in South Orleans, Jim remarried and then he and his wife, Paula decided they would change his house—and I mean change it quite considerably!

He started with a 24 X 36 Ranch style which had 2 large picture windows on the end facing the east. One of these windows was in the kitchen area and the other was in the living room. There was a nice view looking down to the river —— which was affected by the tide—but the view was also a typical Cape scene as the river wound its way through the marsh. A boat could be launched in the area viewed from either of the picture windows, and then access the ocean, even though the ocean couldn't be seen.

Jim drew the plans and acted as General Contractor. The house had no garage, so a two car garage was added on the west side. A big transformation came when a crane was brought in and 24 feet of the house truss roof above the living room, became the garage roof. This was possible because it was a truss roof and the exact size was cut to fit directly on the garage. The remaining 12 feet of roof stayed untouched, but the 24 foot section of living room (where the roof was removed), was enhanced by modifying the walls to become two stories tall. This gave a huge effect, being 2 stories from floor to a double sloped ceiling!

The east end was modified by adding a 14 foot section for a new kitchen on the north side, which made possible a 12 X 14 master bedroom over the kitchen. This new second story room was accessed by an added staircase up to a balcony which allowed you to look down on the existing living room. And, to repeat, the living room was still the same size as previously.

Jim Cullum's house after remodel. Photo C. Wells - 1980.

This was an unbelievable change which really looked great and was accomplished by only expanding the original 'footprint' with the new kitchen addition. Granted, the garage could be accessed only by going outdoors—but the lot wasn't big enough, on the north side, to allow a garage to be added near the kitchen.

───── FLASHBACK ─────

HENRY HUBBARD AND HIS NEW SHOES—1940'S

I don't for the world remember how I heard about this topic and, I don't also know why I remember it!!

I saw Harvey Hubbard a few months back —I asked him if his father did this—to which he nodded in agreement and this pertained to when his father (Henry), bought a new pair of shoes—he would draw a couple inches of water in the bathtub, and then—stand in the tub, so the shoes soaked up some water.

His explanation was that when the shoes dried out, the shoes conformed to his feet much better—and also the toe part of the shoe had a tendency to curl up and he wasn't as apt to stub his toe!!!

At first, you have an inclination to snicker——but as the saying goes—He who laughs last—laughs best.

Maybe —just maybe, Henry was on to something the rest of us aren't???!!

Harvey was in the class ahead of me so when he drove some type of car to school I was always interested in what it was and what he had done to it—I speak about the Whippet, vintage around 1930 that I remember best of his vehicles. This particular one and I would imagine ALL Whippets—had a busy steering wheel! Dead center was a button, push the button was the horn—around the horn button was a bakelite ring. Turn this ring to the right were the headlights—turn it to the left were the parking lights—and grab this ring and pull up —was the starter!!

AUNT LUCIA — DECEMBER 4-5, 1930

This was a stage play presented in Chandler Music Hall in Randolph Vermont.

The cast was entirely from the town and apparently the men had to dress as women —— which in those days, was done only, as an amusing and comical presentation.

The playbill naming the cast —the stage photo and the name listing is presented by the Courtesy of Freda Rye and Joan (Rye) Gray – Thanks to them!!

AUNT LUCIA CAST

WALTER ORDWAY	EARL AKEY
BILL RIX	LOUIS MERUSI
MERVILLE GOULD	MERTON CARR
HARRY TILSON	HARLAND BASHAW
HENRY BACHELDER	ED MCINTYRE
BOB MAYO	GORDON LABOUNTY
PLIN MORSE	GEORGE RYE
HARRY HUDSON	STEWART JAMEISON
FLOYD HODGKINS	JIM NEILL
HOWARD SMITHERS	ROY BRAGG
THAD ALLEN	JIM WHEATLEY
FRANK HAGGETT	LEONARD PAINE
BABE SOULE	LAWRENCE LEONARD
HAROLD PHELPS	CHARLES ELLIS
PERCY ABARE	MERLE SOULE
PEGGY DAY	

AUNT LUCIA

The Great Collegiate Comedy		The Biggest Event Ever Staged in Randolph

Sponsored by American Legion
DIRECTED BY UNIVERSAL PRODUCING COMPANY

100 Local People as Characters **100**
DON'T MISS IT !   SCREAMS OF LAUGHTER !

All Star Cast Headed by Allan Hancock as "Aunt Lucia"

Jerry (Aunt Lucia)	ALLAN HANCOCK
George (College Student)	GORDON PECK
Dick (Football Star)	EUGENE MCGEE
Betsy (George's Girl)	OLIVE MAYO
Molly (Dick's Girl)	MILDRED S. BLACKMER
Ethelyn (Jerry's Girl)	ELLEN KAISER
Butter and Egg Man	PAUL HAYWARD
Collins (Dick's father)	ALBERT SALISBURY
Prof. Gaddis	DR. HARRY HAYWARD
Dean Howard	GLADYS WELLS
Dr. Seamore College Pres.	ROY JOHNSON
Mrs. Seamore	MRS. LESLIE MORSE
First Freshman	ALTON SWEET
Second Freshman	WALTER ORDWAY
Glee Club President	ARTHUR CHENEY
Fraternity President	DR. JOHN BLACKMER

Girl with Million Dollar Legs	James Wheatley
Athletic Girl	Charles Ellis
Spinster School Teacher	Henry Batchelder
Powerful Katrinka	Louis Merusi
Jigg's Maggie	Earl Akey
Giggles	Leonard Paine
Perfect 56	Harold Phelps
Vamp of Town	Floyd Hodgkins
Cleopatra	Stewart Jamieson
Bathing Beauty	Gordon LaBounty
Dancing Girl	William Rix
Corn Fed Co-ed	Howard Smithers
Bride of 1938	Percy Abare
Follies Girl	Merville Gould

AUNT LUCIA'S GLEE CLUB

Joseph Raymond	Leslie Ball
Ralph Wooster	John Maxwell
John Dumas	A. E. Day
James Hutchinson	Glenn Bailey
Allan Matthews	John Hutchinson
Robert Day	Fred Day
Hugh Seaver	Guy Lamson
James Sivret	Donald Salisbury
Stanley Judd	Eugene Batchelder

FLAPPER CHORUS

Sorority President	Roy M. Bragg
Peaches Browning	Horace Soule
Tillie the Toiler	R.J.Mayo
Baby Face	Harland Bashaw
Gloria Swanson	Harry Hudson
Campus Flirt	Frank Haggett
Studious Girl	Laurence Leonard
Gold Digger	George Rye
Hard Hearted Hannah	Ed. McIntyre
Clinging Vine	Plin Morse
Innocent Freshman	Jack Stehle
Clara Bow	Merton Carr
Conceited Junior	Harry Tilson
Teacher's Pet	Jim Neill
Beauty Winner	Thad Allen

SPECIAL MUSICAL NUMBERS

Out in the New Mown Hay	Girls' Chorus
Breezing Along	Girls' Chorus
Solo—Selected	Mr. Peck and McGee
Me and the Man in the Moon	Girls' Chorus
Who's That Pretty Baby	Flapper Chorus
Say It Again	Ensemble

Pianist—Mrs. Merle Soule

GIRLS' CHORUS

Frances Lamson	Eleanor Burns
Mildred Cone	Elaine Osgood
Dorothy Jacobs	Marion McIntosh
Myrtle Sweet	Ruth Jackson
Barbara St. Lawrence	Ruth Akey
Graceline Drew	Alpha Marcott
Merle Kidder	Eva Ruth Marcott
Joyce Bruce	Jean Wilcox
Velma Lewis	Izora Dudley
Beulah Miner	Regina Rowell
Gladys Newman	Mollie Booth

Priscilla Savage

SPECIAL BABY PAGEANT
"Take Me Back to Babyland"
Featuring 100 Children, Ages 5 to 7 Years
SPECIAL DRAMATIC READER
Ruth Mitchell

Chandler Music Hall, Randolph, Vermont
Thursday and Friday, Dec. 4-5, '30
▼ This Program sponsored by Merchants listed on back of this sheet. ▼
Show Starts at 8:15.   Admission, 50c.

A COMPANY CALLED CYBERTRONICS

One evening in the fall of 1967, I got a call from a man who said his name was Donald Hebert and he was calling from Boston. Wanted to know if I was Conrad Wells—the Conrad Wells who had previously worked for IBM.

I told him he had the right guy and then I asked him what I could do for him. He said he was the Branch Sales Manager for a company called Cybertronics which had opened an office in Newton (a suburb of Boston), and said he would like to set an appointment to talk about my future ——a future with this company. He said they were desperately short of service people and that's why he was interested in me. I said I wouldn't be very interested in doing service work of any kind in Boston. I was a country boy and the idea of carrying a tool case on the subway in Boston, from my behalf really wasn't creating an interest. He asked if before I totally rejected this idea would I come to Newton and talk more about it. I agreed to and we set a date.

When the day arrived, I found the office in a shopping center on Route 9 in Chestnut Hill (part of Newton). When I walked into the office, Don Hebert and another man were there—his name was Bill Mazur and he would be the Vice President of Customer Engineering from New York Headquarters.

We talked for about an hour and they told me about Cybertronics which was a 'third party leasing company' and which owned many IBM machines of the punch card type. There were branch offices in Manhattan, Union, (New Jersey), Philadelphia, Chicago, Denver and now would be opening an office in Boston.This was due to the fact they had just landed an account which would constitute nearly 500 machines covering the New England area and with a heavy concentration within Boston

I didn't know what a 'third party leasing' company was but for the moment, felt that asking for an explanation really wasn't that necessary to me. They explained what it meant and how it worked, which I'm going to step over at the moment—however it IS an interesting topic and one which I'll come back to.

They expected this office to grow as had the other offices etc.

They explained the geographics, the benefits, the course of business and I have to admit it did sound very interesting and they then offered a pay as a salary (not per hour), and which was over half again in size as to what I was now receiving. Here I should say that I was heavily trained and qualified on EVERY machine type that would be in the New England area, with the exception of one type—the 108, a statistical sorter. And here I had even been trained on a 101—the 108 was a newer model with a MUCH later technological level.

We finished the discussion with the conclusion I would consider the offer and which I had 5 days to make the decision This was a tough situation meaning I would have to sell the house on the Cape and relocate to somewhere more appropriate in geographics. I should add that relocation expenses would be accepted by them which would make the turndown a lot harder.

After a couple of talks with Bunny, we decided I should take the job and I then gave Jimmy a 2 week notice and prepared for the new company and new job.

I made arrangements with my sister to sleep in her den which was in Brookline (another suburb of Boston) for a flexible period of time. She and her roommate, Tina, were agreeable as I really wasn't going to change their way of life.

So, I started to commute up from the Cape Monday mornings—stayed for the week and Friday in late afternoon, returned to the Cape. During the weekend, I worked on the house so I could get it in condition to put it on the market. This meant finishing the upstairs——partitions, sheetrock, closets, heating, flooring and trim work. No finishing the second bathroom even though there was a room allocated for one.

During the week while I was around eastern Massachusetts, I studied the maps so I could determine what community we could live in. This took some work, but I pieced together a lot of information such as roads, highways etc. for access to the Chestnut Hill location. I soon decided I didn't want the 'South Shore' and equally I didn't want the 'North Shore'——what did make sense was from Route 2 going west down to Route 109 also going west, for one good reason and that was money,— also real estate costs.

From Route I-495 west put me in a favorable geographic area that appealed to me. The roads and access zeroed in on the Marlboro, Westboro and Northboro area, so I would test out the commute time, the distance, the different routes to satisfy all the parameters of the new residential location.

Didn't take to long to zero in on Northboro————Westboro was a more expensive community, with regard to real estate prices————Marlboro was more densely populated—Northboro was BINGO!! I didn't immediately start looking in Northboro until we were closer to a move possibility—anything I looked at now, would totally change before we were ready to buy.

It was quite a few months before we were to move—the house on the Cape went on the market —movers were contacted for cost estimates—and a few trips to Northboro to view a couple houses.

I was shown a house on a small pond about a mile from I-495, about a half mile to Route 20————and about a mile from Northboro center.

Bunny and the girls were on the Cape but I put a binder and an offer on the property with a contingency subject to her approval within a certain number of days. NOW, before anyone gets excited about the procedure—Bunny was not coerced into anything she was uncomfortable with. She agreed a house with a pond frontage would be good for she and the girls in place of a private pool, which we couldn't afford nor did we want.

This was an old house————needed many improvements— but the location was hard to beat. I could see I-290 under construction to the North. Also, I-495 was only 2 miles distant to the east, so without knowing it, we were in the 'Golden Triangle', (I-495, I-290, Route 9, and Massachusetts Turnpike)— an area of high activity for real estate and jobs.

Now the move was going into full swing, and which developed a problem, but one which I didn't have to resolve. We had 2 or 3 estimates for the actual move and this was controlled by Bill Mazur at New York Headquarters. He approved the movers which required 2 trucks—not semis which really doesn't make much difference on what or how many it takes to move us—it's the bottom line or cost. Only in this case, the estimate was about 60% of the cost—nearly double, which put it in a

*First project was to replace foundation on the pond side. Here I
learned to install blocks! Photo - C.Wells.*

higher dollar amount. Regardless, that was resolved, but it
required a hassle to do it.

So, the Wells family is now in Northboro (Ma.), and we're
all ready to get into the swing of living at a new location. The
house on the Cape was soon sold and that was all buttoned up
which now simplifies life a little!!

SOLOMON POND ROAD—NORTHBORO, MA.

The location was ideal for me geographically. It was at or
near two Interstate highways—near the Mass. Turnpike and
also Routes 9 and 20, both east-west local State roads.

Northboro was a 'bedroom community' and when we moved
in — (1968), there was very little industrial land and even less
commercial land. It was a well managed community headed by
individuals who volunteered their time and expertise in the
way of Selectmen, planning board, finance committee and other
vital capacities. I believe a population of 8000-9000 in 1967
would be quite accurate. There was no municipal sewage, but
town water was on most streets. Northboro didn't have the
Route 9 Commercial properties in comparison to Westboro,

except for a very short distance approaching the Route 9-20 intersection where these two roads cross.

The school system was highly regarded with a couple of graded school buildings and a Regional High School in conjunction with Southboro, our neighbor to the east.

In visiting Algonquin Regional High School many times— you couldn't tell if the building was 10 years old or 35 years old. The graffiti was absent, the walls were presentable, the fixtures were respected! Great looking facility.

SPAG'S IN SHREWSBURY, MA

When we moved to Northboro in 1967—the geographic 'get acquainted' process naturally, took quite some time.

I was traveling on Route 9 in Shrewsbury, when I saw a store that caught my eye. It was in the other lane of a split highway, so I moved over and took the first left which took me in back of this store. I found a place to park in one of the large parking lots.

As I went into the store, it certainly was different from most other stores I had been in. Naturally, I had been in country stores and this looked like a country store, I had been in large stores and I had been in large and larger department stores.

Spags was different——a store that had grown in the early 1930's with 25 dollars borrowed from his parents—Anthony Borgatti, better known as Spag had by this date—1967, grown to an outstanding retail 'outlet' and to a multi million dollar enterprise.

Through the years, Spags'made many upgrades and changes to the store on Route 9. For years, the main entrance was on Route 9 and into a building containing housewares, household goods, mens and women's clothing, paint, men's shoes and a small corner where keys were made. Continuing to a down ramp were vitamins, toothbrushes and dental supplies and dozens of everyday personal items were situated—off to one little corner were windshield wiper blades and arms and next were a couple or three cashiers so you could exit on a side street. Across and at the foot of the ramp—electrical supplies, electrical wire and fixtures along with light bulbs of all types. You could buy 23 feet of Romex or 11 feet of zip cord, if you wanted. Continuing straight were hand tools, hardware supplies and plumbing equipment. You could buy floor registers, hot air heat ducts—copper and steel pipe—cut to length. Across the store at this point were toys —toys —and more toys—you know near the outdoor furniture, auto equipment, motor oil, oil filters, electronics, books and bulk grocery items stacked against a large wall. Before you came up to about a dozen more checkouts and cash registers, were hand tools, garden equipment and more grocery items—bread, rolls, hot dog rolls, canned meats and more canned goods!!

In the late 1960's a few items were blister packed, but most items were individually packaged. For instance —toothbrushes—although individually packaged, you'd have to look through a box or a small barrel to pick the one you wanted. It was easier to stock this way and stock turned over really fast.

A garden shop was across the side street from the main store. Here were plants, fertilizer, lawn and garden accessories, bags of many items from paving to peat, cypress mulch to pea stones, ladders and items difficult to stock in the main store. You couldn't help notice ALL the trailers—older (truck) trailers past road usage and were used as storage trailers for stock in place of many buildings reducing tax costs——about 40 or more of them parked around the parking lot perimeters.

As the years passed by, he took over a small building at the edge of the main parking lot and converted this house to a sporting goods store——everything connected to sports. Next, an unused town school building was purchased and became 'The Old Schoolhouse,' the 25 foot entry was LOADED with certificates, photos and Spag memorabilia. This building specializing mostly in tools, (hand and power tools), more hardware and hand tool items, shoes, baby furniture, office supplies and office furniture, more clothes, photo supplies and film developing. Outside, were entry doors, storm doors, swing sets and lawn items, concrete items and lawn edging next to sheds for the yard!!

This operation was started long before Home Depot, Lowe's——Spags was the place to go AND for more than one big reason ——prices were very low, and selection was large AND ALWAYS changing!

Spags would buy in unheard of quantities —a trailer truck load of Life Savers, Romex, nail hammers—dozens to choose from, a truck load of Duracell batteries, paint and on and on it goes.

Spag, most always wore a big 10 gallon hat and rubber boots—barn boots that come up to the knee and it was common to see him working on arranging stock, and greeting customers!

His help, some had over 40 years of association with Spag's and I recall the total employees was over 200!! His bookkeeping department was in his house very close by and the saying goes ——for lunch, they ate around the dining room table, and I bet, in hot weather, were encouraged to take a dip in the family pool!!

His wife Olive, would fly the company private jet to National Hardware Shows—be it Chicago, Las Vegas or wherever. She and key employees along with Spag would be the buyers.

AND, later in the store, if you saw something you needed OR wanted—buy it when you see it —it would be gone in a few days!!! This was due to the hundreds of people making their way through the aisles—Christmas was UNBELIEVABLE!! WHY?—the stock! And the people!!

However, for years, there were NO bags—you grabbed stock boxes that were placed about in strategic locations, or you brought your own bag and another thing—no credit cards and ——the store didn't have a telephone!!

If you wanted a case of paint, or an item in bulk—you paid at a register and were given a 'pickup slip', then drove to 'Door 10' or the door as directed at the register.

When Stirco was putting up Lindy's house, I bought the electrical and plumbing supplies at Spags and the cost was lower than Lindy's wholesaler could provide them! For years I bought all my supplies for my house remodeling here at Spag's, especially plumbing supplies and electrical equipment and supplies

At the end of a selling season, items were donated to various schools, such as baseball gloves, bats etc., rather than store them for next season!

I have to admit—Spag's was a big part of my life from 1967 to about 1995. And, skipping ahead to about 1995, a major remodel took place by the addition of a new large main building— constructed at the rear— facing the one parking lot with a new main entrance, truck loading docks on a higher level — major change. Of course the long established hot dog cart moved near the new entrance— a cart that was said to sell as many as 2000 hot dogs a day!!

Spags store, his ability and methods were written up in many trade magazines. He was known to sell the biggest dollar amount per square foot of any store in the country. During the spring each year, he gave away hundreds of tomato plants and word spread like wildfire—Spags had tomato plants!!!!!

Spags took over the Canadian Club warehouse on Route 9, about quarter mile away and this became a supply warehouse and had dozens of trucks in the parking lot. Not until the 1990's did advertising say 'Spag's on any truck—didn't want it!!

Skipping way ahead, the previously named became competition , the marketing was copied by others and by the middle 1990's, Olive died and not long after, Spag died—— and his daughters tried to run the business. They allowed credit cards, they provided plastic bags. They worked long and worked hard, but the heyday had come and gone——NO ONE could have done any better and about 5 years after Spag died—in October 2002, the business was sold to Bldg 19 1/2

Its still there, but it now displays building 19 1/2 merchandising————SPAGS— THAT I KNEW, IS GONE!!!!

A PERIODONTAL PROBLEM

This is topic I easily could skip, but it is important enough I feel it deserves paper space. It is also a problem that brings with it an expense that certainly will get your attention—— and other symptoms which can not OR should not be ignored.

I noticed that I was having instances of poor balance, ringing in my ears coupled with other peculiarities.

For one reason or another, I felt my teeth needed some attention even though I did regularly visit a dentist—so my sister suggested I make an appointment with her dentist who was fairly close by. This was during the time we had made a deposit on a house in Northboro but we hadn't actually moved in yet.

After he had made a fairly extensive examination he said he wanted me to go to another dentist because I had a condition known as periodontal disease. Little did I know what was coming up— but after being examined by Dr Chaiken, a perio specialist, I was then given an extensive explanation on what was taking place.

I don't have any desire to spell all this out and in detail but the corrective process was going to involve a series of visits with my teeth and gums divided into four quarters. Each quarter required a surgical 'procedure' consisting of about 4 visits per quarter—that is to remove all gum tissue he called 'diseased' by opening the gums—clean deep within the area and then return the gums to 'normal position and allow healing. This procedure was going to cost about 500 dollars per quarter which naturally, would take a 2000 dollar bite out of the check book. However, I really had no choice and as each quarter was finished my general health improved, greatly.

I knew he used a number of Novocain shots for the first of the first quarter and being curious—I counted the shots on the first visit of the second quarter which came to 22!

I would like to say that this is a fairly common problem mostly in people with an age in the forties — gum disease — but can be minimized somewhat in some of the people by conscientious teeth and gum maintenance and regular plaque removal by your friendly dental hygienist. (Boy—what a sales pitch that was!)

This procedure I had —was pioneered by the Periodontist I had visited. It is not a procedure I would wish on anyone but should not be bypassed or ignored. I'm quite sure the procedure I received has by now been superseded or at least modified

BUT—look in the mirror and if your gums are red, as opposed to a pinkish color coupled with random gum bleeding— seek help—this could be a sign of infection and can affect you in many ways VERY detrimental to your health!!! NUFF SAID??

THIRD PARTY LEASING—CTI

I had never heard of third party leasing and was curious on how it worked, especially in the application I'm presently in. This is a process that is used with automobiles, trucks, machine tools, construction equipment and many more items— but, let's be interested in Data Processing Equipment at the moment.

In this situation, IBM manufactured the machines and leased these units to a customer. With tax laws written as they are (or were) with regard to equipment, these machines are allowed to be depreciated by IBM over time and therefore as the value is diminished—so is the purchase price. Also, all these machine types were VERY expensive to buy and also expensive to lease.

Simply, and as an example, Cybertronics makes an inquiry to N E Telephone (the user) to furnish the purchase price for a specific machine (or machines)——N E Telephone inquires to IBM and finds this machine can be purchased for the depreciated amount of (example) 2000 dollars. Normal purchase price for a new machine could be 25000 dollars.

IF, the purchase price is 'acceptable', arrangements are made and papers signed so when N E Telephone buys it from IBM—Cybertronics buys it from N E Telephone (immediately) for the same price. The machine never moves—it stays where it is and N E Telephone now leases it from Cybertronics for an approximate 20% monthly discount—— (the discount agreed to before the sale transaction), which is naturally less each month than it paid IBM for the same machine.

Cybertronics pays a monthly service amount to IBM who performs the service on the machine for the end user (N E Telephone).

The big difference here is that Cybertronics owns the machine—leases it to N E Telephone for 200/month. (Lease amount to IBM had been 250/month). Cybertronics pays IBM 100/month for a service contract. Cybertronics makes 100 dollars /month, part of which goes to pay for the machine, part is for expenses and part is profit.

Now, it does make sense for Cybertronics to do its own servicing which can be done much cheaper than to pay IBM for a Maintenance Contract (M/A), which was VERY expensive.

This machine performs the functions exactly the same as it did previously, is serviced exactly the same as it was,(by the same IBM Customer Engineers)—— and even though the machine was purchased by both companies for 2000 dollars—it still performs as well as a new machine!!

In actuality, all the machines within New England Telephone were bought from IBM and then bought by Cybertronics subsequently. The transaction was for about 500 machines which undoubtedly still involved hundreds of thousands of dollars, and no machines actually changed or were moved.

This was all above board—legal and accomplished with no one unhappy about the transaction. If you think IBM was coerced or resistant, they weren't' because there was a consent decree they had signed with the Federal Government. This consent decree was touched on earlier——however, another legal aspect of that decree was that IBM agreed to divest a (certain) percentage of machines owned , and which this transaction in a very small way, helped to fulfill that agreement.

STRANGE— isn't it???

And to go a step further——any complaint by a third party leasing company, with regard to 'unfair' treatment from IBM along this line, there was an arbitrator that could be contacted for the purpose of resolving any conflict! (I suspect this arbitrator was an employee of the U S Justice department—— but I don't know factually that was the case).

I always thought that was rather an unfair situation—but the Justice Department felt IBM had a monopoly on the mechanized accounting industry and while no one else would probably go into manufacturing products——it DID open the doors for other companies to provide hardware and services.

One company, MAI, was a national operation ——along with a couple others. There were more regional companies, such as Cybertronics (CTI) based in New York City, and another by the name of Unit Record Service Corp., based in Stoneham, Ma. which will be coming up in the years ahead.

I, as Service Manager for the Boston Office, tried to keep an open friendly relationship to any and all IBM personnel I encountered——either in management or any other capacity and——it seemed to work well.

CYBERTRONICS GOES TO COURT

I hadn't been associated with Cybertronics only a few weeks when a 'paper' was delivered to the office and which was a court summons.

It seems there was another company somewhere in Boston whose name was Cybetronics and had their name Trademark Registered. They didn't like the idea of another company using a name similar in sound and spelling the same, with the exception of an extra 'R', in the middle.

The judge agreed and Cybertronics had to change the name we operated under in Massachusetts and which was agreed upon to be CTI Leasing Inc., (a division of Cybertronics). So with that, the Boston office became CTI Leasing.

This really didn't effect me only to the extent my check was printed slightly different at the top.

So from here on, I'll refer to the company as CTI.

NEW YORK CITY ON BUSINESS

A few months after I had started with CTI, I was told I would be going to N.Y. City so I could be trained on the 108 Statistical Machine. Each N.E. Tel. Revenue Office had one of these machines, and down the road, I expected to be servicing at least one —maybe more.

This was to last one week—and I think I was one of 2 people to be trained.

And, the more I think about it, I'm sure I'm right in or near the same block — where I spent the night in an alley years before, delivering plywood for Fyles and Rice!!

I'm not going to get monotonous OR boring here on this machine and describe what happened there. After work hours the first day, I decided I would wander up Broadway as it was very near CTI Headquarters.

I poked along noting many 'things' that probably most people would ignore and by the same token, I also missed many a 'thing' that most other people would see. As an example, somewhere around 40, 41 or 42 Street, I decided to get something to eat. I needed some strength because I was booked at the Gramercy Park Hotel way back near 23rd Street, and would probably walk back there.

I found a place that had a menu stuck to the inside of the big window, so I went in and sat alone (naturally), in a booth. I really couldn't figure out from the menu what I wanted, so when the waitress asked me if I had decided, I pointed to an item and then resigned myself to wait.

The order finally came, and IT was the weirdest food I had ever eaten——looked OK, but tasted something like, I would assume a wet washcloth could taste like—— after soaking for an exceptional time in cold oatmeal and lard!!! A glass of warm orange juice would have helped to wash it down!!!

And then, I noticed quite a commotion out front—commotion being like fire trucks, with dozens of blinking and flashing lights, plus a few N.Y. City police cruisers sprinkled in for more color effects.

I didn't bother to get up, as I could see a little of this action from where I sat. Had to be across the street and nothing was going to be gained for my high curiosity. So, I finished not eating —but making the food on my plate disappear——Good Lord —what was that I ate?! Then I noticed on the check I was in a vegetarian restaurant.

That made me feel better, I at least now knew you can't grow washcloths —I don't care what kind of a garden this stuff came from!! And, I don't know to this day what it was.

So as I stepped up to the cash register to pay the bill, I asked the girl at the cash register what was happening outside—— and she replied, There was a fire upstairs (over the restaurant) AND, NO ONE got upset or even excited by that fact.

As I went outside, I had to step aside twice to allow a couple firemen to get by. THAT was interesting— I don't know what was burning—didn't smell much different than the food I had just paid for!!

AAHHHH—life in the city!!!!

GETTING UNDERWAY WITH CTI

One of the first tasks I found myself doing was to work in the (small) parts room of the Boston office. Somewhere in lower Manhattan is a group of hardware suppliers—for all I know it's right beside the famous Fulton Fish Market! Regardless where it is, there were a couple dozen boxes delivered that contained various and many screws, "C" clips of a dozen sizes and dozens of other hardware items.

Shipped from Cybertronics New York City headquarters were IBM parts ——boxes and boxes, and all of this had to be put in drawers, tagged and catalogued. This could be done just as soon as I assembled the racks that hold the drawers.

There is a section of Manhattan called Gramercy Park right in the same area and location as Cybertronics Headquarters, which was on 23rd street in Manhattan. This headquarters location was chosen down in the garment and financial district due to the daily need for money (in fairly large sums) so the equipment within various installations could be financed and the transactions finalized from the many sales proposals made each week. Salesmen for Cybertronics were scouting the cities for accounts where Sales and Service offices were located and now, Boston was one of those cities.

In Manhattan, New York Telephone was one of the accounts and had been for a couple of years——as was Metropolitan Life Insurance, New York Life Insurance Co. and numerous banks I don't even know the names of.

Back to Boston——it took me days and days to identify and tag hundreds of parts, place them in drawers and record the locations.We also had many parts books, reference manuals, operators manuals, theory and instructional manuals, and service guides pertaining to all the machine types we would be associated with.

When that chore was finished, next I would go to each installation in the New England area, not only to promote customer relations, but also to inspect each machine and create a history of features added to each, a service call history from the specific machine log book, and to evaluate each for mechanical condition, appearance, and specific complaints.

On days in mid week, I could leave directly for the account location, but on Mondays and Fridays, travel to the customer location and was in addition to the 90 mile commute from the Cape.

It didn't take Don, the Boston Sales Rep, to start landing more accounts in addition to the N E Tel accounts. This meant in each case, I would inspect the equipment, so if we provided this machine type as a swap from our own inventory, the extra features (if any) would be correct. And if CTI did swap prior to shipment from N.Y., IBM would inspect the unit before it was shipped and then accept it at the new location under IBM Monthly Maintenance Service.

One situation where this exact circumstance was taking place was at a large Boston bank. The room where the IBM machines were located was in the large curved building called Government Center, which was known as Scollay Square in years long ago.

The problem here was that CTI had gained this bank as an account and, in this case was going to swap the Accounting Machine now used, with a machine from the CTI inventory. The machines were originally put on the third floor by a crane—through a large window. As the windows were now sealed with restrictions preventing a repeat of that procedure, so now CTI is going to use the elevator to swap the IBM 407 out and the CTI 407 in.

While the elevator was too small to actually get the machines in—an upending 'kit' was ordered which actually raises the machine up on its end and then is wheeled into the elevator. When the first machine went into the elevator——the overweight alarm went off, which is a rather startling alarm! The elevator (guessing) was probably rated at 2000 pounds and this machine weighed close to 2400 pounds.

Needless to say, I didn't volunteer to ride on the elevator—so we pushed the button for the right floor and stood back while the door closed and then hoped it delivered to the right floor and, also the right floor height. I sweat that fact out—certainly didn't want the elevator to stop 6 inches too low—

and then have to put two more men in there for another 500 pounds—but we lucked out!! Both machines rode the elevator with no harm or complications and soon the swap was completed with CTI gaining another account in downtown Boston.

LINING UP THE DUCKS

Let's bring up a few items and give a short explanation on what is taking place.

The Branch Service Manager was Fred Korab who was transferred in from the Manhattan Office. He brought along a woman experienced with company policies and procedures, billing, dispatching, budgets and other clerical knowledge. I've forgotten her name, but she didn't stick around long——didn't like Boston etc. ——she went back to New York and after a short time, a replacement was selected by Don Hebert with a local gal named Irene.

All the equipment associated with the office was under an IBM Maintenance contract so at this time, there was no servicing done by the office as yet—however, it was the main objective to slowly remove them and have them serviced by Cybertronics employees—I, being one of them. IBM Maintenance contracts were expensive and that's the reason for a big push!

The big contract Cybertronics had was with New England Telephone which totaled nearly 500 machines and most were associated with the New England Telephone Revenue Offices. These offices had the responsibility of accounting for all the telephone calls made under their jurisdiction. Each New England state had a Revenue Office with a couple exceptions——Connecticut was a separate company, Southern New England Telephone Co. wasn't included. Eastern Massachusetts (Boston) with such a high number of telephones, had three offices called North Revenue and South Revenue, and another in Quincy.

My job at the moment (to repeat), was to travel to various customer locations—keep track of service response, machine quality, customer feelings and satisfaction—good will, in general. Also, to install or delete any subsequent features on any unit, to prepare machines for either installation or discontinuance, evaluate machine conditions etc. and make acquaintance with many operators, Supervisors, the Manager and Assistant Manager at each location. There were a few non revenue installations scattered around the company, especially in Boston— that also came under our jurisdiction.

This meant that I would put a good amount of mileage on my car which soon came to hundreds of miles per week. I started with a small station wagon with a slant six which was a fine solution to the travel.

Soon, I bought a used Volkswagen 'Beetle'. With the commuting mileage to Boston and back to the Cape, adding a day trip to 'who knows where'——the miles piled on and a 1000 miles a week was common. Of course, I was reimbursed for company travel.

CTI LEASING—BOSTON

The Cybertronics office suite was five rooms——a sales office for Don, a service office for Fred and a front office for dispatch and walkins. A spare room which I used when I was there, and a room for parts storage. Fred spent a lot of his time in search for more service employees.

CTI PROGRESS IN BOSTON

Although IBM was still heavily involved in the Punch Card part of Data Processing, the total business was changing. Cybertronics was a newcomer to the Boston area, it had been around for about 5 years in New York City and a couple other locations.

Another company called MAI had been operating since about 1960 and this was the big competition as MAI was nationwide. MAI stood for Management Assistance Corp.,was at least 20 times as large as Cybertronics, and had been aggressively gaining customers across the nation——which really surprised me. I didn't think there would be much competition to IBM as these are so highly specialized and tightly controlled products of IBM.

But—they had succeeded enough so they had their own rebuild/reconditioning facilities in King of Prussia, Pennsylvania, plus a nationwide service force. So much for my judgment!

I thought when I left IBM——I was about the only person that had ever walked away from the "Big Blue"——however as I eased back into this business, I found MAI had many ex-IBMers.

Part of my job at that time was to talk to anyone experienced in field service on punch card machines regardless of where they lived or who they worked for presently.

Slowly, Don Hebert signed on new accounts in the Boston and eastern Massachusetts area—especially now with New England Telephone as a local large referral account. There were a few machine swapouts—at least at first—so a sale only meant a new account was under CTI jurisdiction—but most of the machines stayed the same as did the service and service procedures. From the customer's standpoint, the monthly expense was reduced by 20% and now billed by CTI.

Not ALL machines at a prospective account were bought by CTI—some were either too new or rebuilt, so the depreciated value wasn't low enough, OR CTI had units in stock so it made more sense to put one of those back in the field and get a return in revenue. And occasionally, a machine would be direct shipped from one account to another and in this case, it was shipped to the Boston office so I could check it out and, if necessary, clean it up—even spray paint it to improve the appearance.

BRANCH SERVICE MANAGER——CTI

After 10 or 11 months, the present Branch Service Manager—Fred Korab, left the company to go work for RCA Computer Systems in Cherry Hill, N. J.

As he left, the V.P. came up from Headquarters and interviewed a half dozen people he had lined up to fill the vacancy left by Fred.

Irene, the new 'Gal Friday' suggested I put my name in and be interviewed. I really didn't feel I was qualified and to be honest, I really wasn't sure I wanted the job!

Let me backtrack for just a moment——as I became acquainted with the capacity of the Branch Service Manager AND the Field Service Manager in IBM——a cartoon developed in my mind and it was a chair, a swivel chair— and in that chair sat any individual within a Service Management capacity. The chair straddled a round bomb (of the type depicted in many movie cartoons)—and from the bomb were three fuses!! Three groups of people stood around the bomb and each had a lit match. One person represented the customer(s), another represented company upper management and the third person was the various service people under this manager's jurisdiction.

In other words, Service Management appeared to me as a no win situation——constantly trying to keep everyone happy and 'under the gun 'of these three groups of people. It's just a matter of time before someone blasts you out of the water!!

So, I had convinced myself ——WHO NEEDS THAT?

Just at that time —I received a call from Bob Rademacher, my close friend AND fellow 'Customer Engineer from IBM Burlington (Vt.), who was in Boston and he wanted to get together. We decided on meeting at the 'Hilltop Steak House' in Saugus (Ma.). This place was a well established HUGE restaurant capable of seating 1000 people and it serves the absolute tops in all types of beef.

In discussing my dilemma with him——I said I just couldn't convince myself I wanted to follow all the so called rules. Bob gave me a bit of advice so typical of him and here is what he said————

1/ "When you are in a management capacity —YOU make the rules YOU want to follow————in some cases, these will follow rules of other people, BUT in many cases——you make the rules that fit YOUR circumstances!"

and

2/ " When you're in management and certain responsibilities are given to you———Make damn sure you get an equal amount of authority! Do you know what you're called if you DON'T?

You're called a SCAPE GOAT!"

Now —think about that for a minute——let it sink in for a moment and it makes a lot of SENSE.

I drove home that night which took a good hour, liked the conclusions I came to——and the next morning put my name on the list to be interviewed and with a strong determination to win that capacity——which I did ——and then became the new Branch Service Manager for the Boston Office!

I really don't know if my qualifications were that 'great'— but the fact that I was there, the process was simple to promote me —regardless, it happened!

Sitting here now many years later, I can speak from experience and feel I'm qualified to offer the following information about decisions——

Management is mostly about decisions——many per day— every day! In a hurry, I learned that any and all incidents required a decision. THEN—I found out a quick decision was required in most cases so-o-o, you make a quick decision. SOME

The author at his desk at 200 Boylston St. Chestnut Hill (Newton) MA., a multi tennant office building with many stores on the ground floor. Photo - C.Wells - 1970.

will be good—SOME will be bad—you won't win them all, but you have to try really hard to keep the ratio slanted (by far) in favor of the good ones!!!!

And, no decision is the worst thing you can do——

There is a saying 'Halitosis is better than no breath at all'——what does this have to do with no decision? Naturally,—— ANY decision is better than NO decision!

However, this capacity wasn't all peaches and cream—I was now made exempt—I now don't get paid overtime no matter how many hours I may work —also I only get paid once a month! Now that takes some getting use to!!

This was near the end 1968.

We (and mostly I), finally found 2 field service techs, so a couple accounts came under CTI service in the Boston area, and then a well experienced man was found for the Springfield (Ma.), location—his name was Fred Adams from Albany, N.Y.

TRAILER TIME

The present time is about 1968 and here Bunny and I graduated from camping in a tent—to buying a new Yellowstone trailer. We bought this from Stan Gould in Randolph, who had started a trailer sales in Beanville. He had a few in stock and the one we chose was an 18 footer—single axle. We were elated and started to use this immediately.

At the time, we owned a 1965 Ford station wagon and had the trailer hitch installed on this—it had a big 390 engine and Stan felt that, should be able to pull the trailer.

MANPOWER INCREASES

We finally got a break on hiring a couple more 'Customer Engineers) or —as I prefer to call them—'Field Service Techs.' With Fred Adams joining CTI from Albany, this brought 2 more people—Max Schanze (ex IBM) and Dave Manning (ex IBM also). Both of these men were ideal in technical capabilities, personality traits and both became close friends over a period of time. Any problem from customer situations to technical—they could take care of.

We now had 4 well qualified 'techs'—Al, Fred, Max and Dave. Next, I had a relatively close neighbor I was acquainted with in Northboro and after giving him a Wonderlic Test was convinced he could handle the job—he was already mechanically experienced, but I could teach him enough electronics so he could handle Keypunch service calls. His name was Al Yellick—a very impressionable, well mannered young man and easily one I had no hesitation on him representing CTI at a customer location. So he used to travel with me when the circumstances were right, and I taught him fundamental electronics and soon, the events of travel started to pay off.

Two Jerry's were next hired—Jerry Madison and Jerry Kenny—these would work greater Boston locations.

THE WEBSTER - THOMAS INCIDENT

One of the accounts Don Hebert as Salesman closed, was the Webster Thomas Account. This was a wholesale Grocery Distributor in Everett. The account used the Tub File System where people pick IBM cards from a big tub file in conjunction with reading a customer order. Each product in stock is represented by a Card and at the end of the order, the cards are sent through an Accounting machine which prints the invoice.

In this case, the Accounting Machine had been received from CTI inventory and had been giving trouble in the few days it had arrived. 'Al' had taken most of the troubles off the machine with the exception of this last one and, which he had called me for service assistance.

I stood at the machine —ran a couple of cards to see the printed result, a second Al went to the Supervisors Office to ask a question and as he left ——I, for no reason tapped the start button and as the machine took a couple of cycles —I thought I heard an unfamiliar noise. Tried it again and it was fine——tried it the third time and there it was ——this time I knew it was an unnatural card feed clutch noise.

Al and I removed all the covers and then proceeded to remove the entire card feed off the base of the machine—— a VERY rare move which I had only once before had to do, indicating that the card feed clutch required very little attention.

After we spent enough time changing the clutch adjustments and ensuring they were correct—we replaced the card feed —tested the machine and it worked correctly and dependably. We turned the machine back to the customer and from that point on——Al's actions changed——I didn't notice it for a few days, but his mood and operation changed.

My conclusion was he took a dim view of me as a person or as a technician—I could sense this and— because he felt I showed him up——the biggest reason was that I had come upon the solution too fast! He felt it degraded him and my level of respect toward him! (If I had wanted to rub it in —I would have done so right then, but I didn't, because that isn't one of my characteristics)!!

A LARGE MILK (AND DAIRY) ACCOUNT

This account was a large distributor of milk and milk products including eggs, cottage cheese, eggnog, butter, etc. and of course, milk, cream, whipped cream and all its products. These were delivered to the door in a retail style within a widespread geographical area, but very heavily in eastern Massachusetts.

At this particular account, a few machines were swapped out and replacements were furnished by CTI from its rebuild/ distribution center in New York. By this time, Headquarters had moved from 23rd Street, Manhattan, to a larger one story building in Lake Success which is in eastern Long Island and right off the Long Island Expressway. This move ended the drive into Manhattan and all the city traffic.

By now, I was beginning to realize that machines coming from our own rebuild center were NOT to the quality I liked to see. The technicians at the rebuild did a good job on outside such as paint quality and cover fit etc., but had not been cautioned and guided to bring the inside quality up to (or above) par.

In the case of this 'milk and dairy' distributor, the most important, the largest and the most critical machine was an accounting machine. Unknown to me a couple of my Field Service Techs had been 'installing 'it and the first few attempts of the customer to use it, failed miserably and EACH time they tried it.

This brought a phone call from the customer to me and I was 'requested' to be at their company conference room at 3 PM that afternoon.

At 3 PM, I was there and the door was opened to a large room with an equally large conference table around which were at least a dozen men each in business suits. However, there was one chair at the head of the table NOT occupied——and it didn't take much in deductions for me to realize THIS one, was reserved for me.

As I was ushered to that chair, I was told——" Mr. Wells, in the 3 days your machines have been on location, the 407 has been down more than up and resulting in no production——so we're now 3 days behind on ALL schedules! Tell us what your plan is to achieve IMMEDIATE production with regard to the accounting machine!!!!! MAKE US FEEL BETTER!!!!"

And with that —there were at least 24 eyes on me, and at this point, I knew that a 2 minute soft shoe dance wasn't going to cut it neither was any type of card trick that I might come up with was going to make any one individual cheer ——let alone ALL OF THEM!!!

A quick assessment of the circumstances——I needed some time to check that machine out which could take a good 8 hours—— minimally.

After the meeting was finished —I called my boss in the New York office and told him I wanted a different machine shipped to this account. The BIG reason was that this machine was the old model AND the customer knew it—they would be unhappy no matter how well I fixed it and THEN——I went to the car,—pulled out my tool case and went to the Data Processing Dept—took off my jacket and before I started, called my wife and told her I didn't know how long it would be before I came home. Good thing —I was there all night!!

Why didn't I have one of the Boston men do this job? I really didn't' have a technically strong 407 Customer Engineer as yet. And, I felt this was too crucial ——too valuable to gamble.

64

Without going into a boring detail on what was wrong etc.
——take my word, it was just inaccurate work quality in adjusting some items to detail and ACCURACY.

When I finished, this machine would now pass ALL test
decks and do it correctly! Don't say I'm blowing my horn here—
—I'm not, BUT ——I do know that if specs call for a plus or
minus 1/2 degree tolerance—be accurate and set the item
within the tolerance of 1/2 degree!!! In doing so, that item will
NOT be a problem.

We did have an occasional downtime service call in the
couple of weeks after, while we were waiting for the replacement. And we did get this account 'settled' down and become a
satisfied customer even if we did have a bumpy start at the
beginning.

It was only a short time after, that a new Field Service
Tech was hired for the office and his name was Bob Gray. Bob
was an ex IBMer and regardless of why he had separated from
IBM—I didn't care, he could be a valuable man to me and the
office so I hired him. AND, BELIEVE ME, he was well trained,
well experienced, and proved to be a big asset. (He also was a
technically strong 407 man!)

Along with Bob Gray, we also gained Tony Staras who
proved to be a very capable man and who was a compliment to
the office.

Within a couple of weeks, the replacement machine arrived
and Bob Gray, with his wealth of 407 experience checked it
out—it was also the 'newer' model which pleased the customer's
operating and supervising people.

The office ended up with 13 Field Engineers even though
it's been 35 years, I can't recall a couple of the names, but now
we're in pretty good shape and are handling most of the local
accounts for service.

THE 360 SYSTEM

The 360 was the latest equipment manufactured by IBM and
again, was prominently displayed by customers within glass
walled rooms right in the lobby of many IBM customers. It was
very 'showy' and certainly represented a status symbol.

The 360 was a very versatile Computer System with the 'small' system known as a 360/20—then a larger model for medium and large users known as a 360/30 and the next, for large number 'crunching', known as the 360/40 amongst other models.

This System had been in the development stages by IBM for many months and was introduced about 1965. The release had come prematurely and even though the hardware was completed—the software had not been completed. The first 360 systems ran on 1400 System software while the 360 software was being completed and to be announced a few months later. For this reason, the 360 couldn't run much faster than a 1400 and caused a stumble on its initial debut. Many customers hesitated in replacing their 1400 until a realistic gain in processing time could be realized.

The rumor had it, that one of IBM's competitors forced IBM into an early announcement by unveiling a comparable system sooner than IBM was ready to release the 360.

However, IBM dumped its massive manpower and talent in finishing the 360 software which then succeeded in making the 360 fly.

This computer system (all models) and including the competition, was console operated—there weren't remote keyboards or access to computing, without sitting at the console.

I can remember reading some business magazine and recreating the topic—and that was around 1968. (I think its understandable I don't remember the magazine I read at this time).This went into great detail about Tom Watson Jr. pushing on this 360 System and with such foreseeable future for it —it almost flushed IBM down the drain, it was that big a step. Many others would have backed off—but not him, and his gamble eventually paid off—big time!!!

It was then well received and highly regarded— became a computer wonder and surpassed all expectations within IBM for demand. This really created a massive wave within the industry!!!

While the 1400 system was a huge step in the 'computer industry'—— it really could more accurately be called the 'foundation'. Other manufacturers were contributing to the demand and to the popularity of the 'Mainframe' Computers.

In my opinion—the 360 System was the real 'box' for the future. This was the real startler— the attention getter!

In 1968, Cybertronics (Headquaters) went to the market and purchased approximately 20 million dollars of 360 Systems. In a good business move, naturally they were put on lease before they were purchased. But THIS to me, was a good step in the right direction because it showed me Management was not only willing , but capable to progress to a higher level of equipment even if it was more expensive to accomplish.

OTHER MANUFACTURERS

We're now in the late 1960's and while the computer industry didn't bring about as many manufacturers as the hand calculator business did ——OR as many contributors as the pizza industry will in the future ——there was quite a sampling of manufacturers contributing to the computer industry.

One of the early entrants was RCA Corporation with Headquarters in Cherry Hill, N.J. and which was about to relocate to Marlboro, Ma. RCA had contracted to build a manufacturing campus right beside I-495 and near Route 20. This was less than a mile from where my wife and I bought a house. It was a very interesting construction process and one which I closely watched as I passed by, twice a day.

One building was a multi story office type which was finished first—even if it did take over a year. There was to be 2 more buildings and the second one was started immediately after the first one was finished.

Little did anyone anticipate a grand surprise in the months ahead.

We're about 10 years after IBM had introduced the huge 704 Mainframe and which I described way back, was installed at GE in Lynn, Ma. In those approximate ten years, the industry had advanced by leaps and bounds, and was now at a point where some thinning out might soon occur.

Wang Laboratories Tewksbury (Ma.), again right beside I-495, was constantly putting up additions to its building and

while Wang wasn't established as a Mainframe Computer Co.—
it was in the Data Processing industry, but machines with different goals.

Regardless, Wang was progressing so fast I'm sure that by
1970 the plans were solidified for a huge multistory building
which soon would occupy a site beside The Lowell Connector
and also I-495.

The real growth was coming from Digital Equipment Corp.
based in one of the old textile mills in downtown Maynard (Ma.).
A company that started around 1960 occupying a few rooms of
one old building and now— literally exploding into many buildings of the same complex—and also soon to be in Burlington,
Vt., Portland, Me., Manchester, N.H., Milford Ma., Westboro
Ma., Stow, Ma, and many places in between. Any building that
became empty, Maynard to Milford (Ma.),—soon was occupied
by some phase of Digital.

By the mid 1970's, Digital was entertaining the spot of second largest Mainframe supplier after IBM.

And there were two more——Data General at the intersection of I-495 and Route 9 in Westboro, Ma., with multiple
buildings around that intersection and lastly—Prime Computer
Corporation a Framingham based company —a company I know
very little about, but was another Mainframe manufacturer.

Not to be forgotten, but not based in the I-495 corridor was
General Electric——a natural for this company to be in the
Mainframe business as was Burroughs Corporation, Sperry
Rand Corporation and National Cash Register who had a name
change to NCR at some point in time, but which I don't have
the slightest idea when.

Of course, there were many other companies, small and
large that were involved with computers, but for one reason
or another never made national notoriety, or if they did it was
for a short burst only.

CTI SERVICE AT NEW ENGLAND TELEPHONE

As soon as we had 4 or 5 Customer Engineers, the main
goal was to take over service at least one New England Telephone Revenue location. Within the 4 or 5 men, we had expe-

rience enough to succeed and Bob Gray was on the staff which gave me a big shot of confidence. He and Max Schanze would be needed in a short time, which will come up later.

Also, Al Yellick was now capable and taking keypunch calls and while he didn't have a wealth of experience——he was very accurate, which was equally important. If he needed help, you could bet the ground he had covered was done correctly.

A lot of opposition was met at trying to take over service at N.E. Telephone.

In Boston, there were two Revenue 'Offices'. Both were located in one building at 245 State Street, which is at the corner of Atlantic Avenue— and almost across from the New England Aquarium. Although the Aquarium as it looks today wasn't there at the time, the location was being cleared and the building started.

This was an eight story building and CTI had machines on nearly all of the eight floors. North Revenue was on the third floor and this is where we first succeeded in taking the machines off IBM contract and used our own Service Techs.

The most serious and heavily used were 2 Reproducer (IBM machines) and even if these don't mean anything to you, just let me say why they were heavily used.

Every telephone call made in the geographic area of this office—if it required an operator (meaning a non direct dial call), this operator had to fill in a card that soon had to pass through one of these 2 machines——thousands of those cards per day 24 hours in 3 shifts!!

Before I walk from this topic for a few moments—every desk on the floor, if it had nothing else,—it did have a comptometer. The reason I bring this up, is the fact these are totally extinct and have been since the 1980's. Comptometers were a desk top calculator—it was about 12 inches square, and about 2 or 3 inches high, and the top was filled with numeric keystems. You could add on it and if, you're good with finger positions, you could multiply.

To add, you merely covered the keytops with your fingers equal to the number you want to add——repeat for the next number etc. —and you read the total on the numbers displayed at the rear of the base. To multiply, you place your fingers on the keytops signifying the first position of the multiplicand and you press down all the selected keytops equal to the number of times in the right hand multiplier. Then pick your fingers up, move one group of keys to the left and again depress the number of times equal to the tens position of the multiplier. Keep progressing to the left until your last position in the multiplier is used ——then read the answer in the number displays at the rear of the base——see how simple it was—— some people could really make those fly!!!

A PROCESS CALLED MARK SENSE

IF the telephone call was a credit card call, a reverse charges call, a third party call or any call INVOLVING an operator, who would then grab and complete this card by filling in various details with a mark from a special pencil. These marks will be 'read' by the machine where it will be ultimately fed to a computer for billing purposes.

I don't want to dwell on this topic, but ALL employees were 'graded' on the operation —starting with the telephone operator whose marking quality is 'indexed' against ALL other telephone operators within all revenue offices, and too many mistakes was cause for the operator to be called on the carpet!!!

If you can bear with me for a few moments, I'll show you how this all ties together and then affects the paycheck!! (theirs—not mine).

Any card not marked correctly for numerous reasons is then indicated by a pass through this 'reproducer,' which recognizes mistakes and identifies the operator causing the mistake!!

The count is compared to the other revenue offices and establishes a level for all operators within each revenue office. Once a month everyone from Revenue Manager—Asst Manager, Processing Supervisor, Telephone Operators etc. determines the current month standing with regard to mistakes and pay is adjusted for the next month paycheck.

For the paycheck reason, no one wants to do anything 'different' to jeopardize their pay check —this makes sense —it also makes the reason why CTI had to fight to gain a place to provide service AND KEEP it!!

SERIOUS TROUBLE FOR THE BOSS

The North Revenue installation supervisor didn't like CTI doing the service so if she got a call from the department with a machine problem on a night shift—she would call me at home, no matter what time it was.

Also, CTI was in a trial period and had been, for about 2 months. I knew we were making progress in getting the hardware back to reliable operation, but it was not an easy task. The machines were long from being well taken care of, so we were really trying to prove WE could be relied on.

A point of clarification here———don't get the impression IBM service was bad———it wasn't, but it also wasn't the quality it had been in the years gone by. However, at this point in time, IBM didn't rate this type of account as needing full throttle efforts due to other systems and hardware of greater importance. Another couple points of interest also come into play here———many of the 'older' IBM Customer Engineers already had retired and each month, more were being added to the list—which means the younger CE's didn't have the experience and also IBM wasn't training the younger CE's on the 'punch card' equipment due to a shift of demand to the newer Mainframes and peripherals.

Before I get to the center of this topic———bear in mind, all other Revenue Offices were maintained by IBM and IBM was considered the 'anchor'———the reference to which anyone else had to aspire to—whether it was CTI, MAI or any other competitor.

CTI, through the efforts of Max Schanze and Bob Gray, had rebuilt one 519 on location (North Revenue) and had done this job one weekend. Without getting detailed about the what and why—new feed rolls had immediately shown a noticeable improvement to 'lowering the rejects', apparently restoring concise travel through the card line. Worn feed rolls diminished in diameter if only by a few thousands also reflect to the circumference and THAT effects card travel!!

In doing so, this gave me a reason to believe this had to be performed also, on the other 519 at North Revenue. That fact, in conjunction with a couple other endeavors gave me a positive and optimistic outlook.

So it was a huge surprise when Don Sanborn (my N E Tel contact), called me to say a meeting was called at 185 Franklin Street, (Boston)—New England Telephone Headquarters building.

I just had a feeling that 'all is not quiet on the homefront'. As I entered the room I could feel Don Hebert and I were to be on the 'carpet'!! AND, as we found out, —for poor machine performance and not up to the quality level previously enjoyed prior to CTI service takeover! (Much of this was predicated on feedback from the Supervisor, who didn't want to have CTI service her account for any reason!)

SOMETHING not meeting the eye was taking place—— and the monkey was on my back to show how CTI could perform better and be worthy of retaining this account for machine service, by the next meeting in 2 weeks.

I was really surprised when Don Hebert said something to the effect ——that Con, as an expert, WOULD succeed in service at North Revenue.

So, I traveled to the other Revenue Offices with special attention to the IBM service history on 'their' 519 Reproducers. Bit by bit, and little by little, I started to realize that something such as a 'reference level' had changed.

THEN, I found that N E Telephone had changed the routine and thereby the application, by having their own System people add a "Column Split' feature to each and all 519's. AND they did it just BEFORE CTI had started servicing North Revenue.

Here's what I found—these feature changes had destroyed the old reference points and established new reference points so ALL machines (unknowingly) were producing results different from what they had established prior to the date that CTI had started to service.

ACTUALLY, North Revenue had its standing improved with reference to others and really lead all other offices—basically due to the new feed rolls, and the rebuild Max and Bob had completed!!

NOW, I had to document and statistically compare these records, so I could make a follow-up presentation.

At the start of the follow-up meeting —Don stood up and stated, "You will be pleased to know that Conrad has some information he will present and which will clarify the circumstances completely!"

I really didn't know he was going to present that in the fashion he did——and it could have been a little embarrassing —for them to find out they were wrong!!!!!'

Regardless, I presented the facts, explained it and asked for any questions ——without rubbing it in!

From that day on—CTI took a giant step in being established as the reference —CTI had now become the anchor and which strength grew more easily in the months to come.

We did retain the present service arrangement and a few months later, took over service for South Revenue when it moved to Braintree, just off Route 128.(I might add that I spent many an all night session in that building—sometimes alone on a specific 557 Interpreter failure, or a complex 519 Mark Sense problem).

I exited the building from that second meeting, it was during lunch break. As I rounded the corner I spotted a guy with running shorts—running shoes on. In a muscle stretch with his arms out, he was leaning into the building, limbering the calf and thigh muscles. (Physical exercise was just starting to become noticeable).I was about 10 feet away, and he stood up. I was feeling chipper as I had salvaged the CTI service situation, so as I came up to him I said, "Push against that once more ——I think I saw it budge!!!!":

He apparently didn't seem to think it was funny— he didn't laugh!!!

PRINTING ON THE CARD

Each telephone customer within all the Revenue Offices, as they was billed, had an IBM (punch) Card enclosed with the bill. This meant the two machines that printed at the top of the card ran generally 2 and 3 shifts a day, 6 days a week.

In retrospect, this type of machine wasn't designed to run to this extent, and sooner or later, a 557 in any account would suffer a major breakdown. Either a 'lifter arm' would bend, an intermediate gear would lose a 'tooth', or something in the drive and setup would fail and now, we have a serious problem.

More than once I received a call at home whether it was midnight or 5 AM and I would drive to Boston——245 State St. and find a 'horror show' which now required an 8 to 14 hour repair job.

I, personally responded to this account on this type machine, even though I didn't get paid and for one good reason. The other Customer Engineers were needed for prime shift service calls and I wanted them to be in reasonable physical condition.

I also had the most experience and could cope with these circumstances with a greater ease——so I thought!

I knew this was an involved repair and could consume hours, so it was my choice, at this time to accept this responsibility.

SOUTHERN NEW ENGLAND TELEPHONE

Near the end of 1969, George Lee, a resident of southern Connecticut was hired to fill a Sales Position within the western part of Massachusetts, all of Connecticut and even into Rhode Island. George was an employee of IBM years before, then MAI (another third party leasing cooperation) and now—CTI. He was well experienced with all the machines and equally well known in the territory he was to represent CTI in.

To give you an idea how naive I was —I met George in Springfield one morning so we went to some place for coffee and for me to get the plan for the day. George ordered a bagel with Lox. Now, I was around forty, and perhaps the wrong nationality to ever know what Lox was — a Bagel was known to me BUT not well enough to describe one—especially with Lox!!!!

We made some sales calls together over the next few months—its always a plus for a Salesman to be able to introduce the Service Manager—then the potential customer can meet the people he may be dealing with.

It wasn't very many weeks when George landed the Southern New England Telephone Co. The headquarters was on George Street in New Haven and all the machines were in one building there with one exception. That would be the 3 Keypunches in Meriden (Ct.) which were tied into coin counting machines.This is where all the coins collected from payphones were counted and records (Punch Cards) were made of each Payphone in the State. Quite a procedure to see all the coin boxes as they came in, coins counted and a card automatically punched for each pay phone. The place was big enough and the coins were so many in quantity— a Brinks Truck drove right into the room to cart the coins away!!

The total number of machines at Southern New England Tel (SNET) between the two locations was about 180. This meant another man had to be hired and was to be based in the building on George St. (New Haven). George knew a man he thought would be available.

He was contacted, interviewed and hired. 'Don' was well qualified and an excellent Field Tech (Customer Engineer). This guy had worked for MAI—had years experience and was an ideal person for the job. Never had one complaint about him and he was 100% reliable. Made my job in Connecticut easy!!!!

Soon George Lee had another account or two, so we had to hire a second man for the area and although not experienced on IBM machines, Don gave him OJT (on job training). This area ran very smoothly.

Here again, most of the machines stayed right where they were, with a couple exceptions, very few were shipped in from CTI inventory in Lake Success.

It was interesting to me that each coin collector employee was given a printout of 'his' route in the morning and a bunch of keys for the coin box of each payphone location. This route was generated by computer so no time was wasted going to a phone that wouldn't be nearly full of coins, nor would it be overfilled and jam the phone. In the case of multiple phones at a highway location, he would collect ONLY from the phone on the listing!! They weren't used evenly—therefore they weren't all automatically collected at one time!

CTI— SOLD

The day I got word that CTI had been sold, I was devastated—I just felt that this company had a good chance for maturing into a solid long lasting company, and this news gave me reason for doubt.

The company that bought us was Dasa Corporation based in Andover, Massachusetts. It was known as the manufacturer of an automatic telephone dialer and apparently had reasonable success at it, that is initially.

The telephones, at that time, were both dial and push-button type. This dialer had a memo strip about 4 inches wide— printed with red lines where telephone numbers could either be typed in or handwritten. On the back side was a magnetic strip. The idea was that you manually set the strip, so a name was aligned up in the center of a viewing window and at that point you magnetized the strip in back, by pressing the characters on the telephone. A red stripe running diagonally form 'A' to 'Z' was watchable so as the select button was pushed— a motor made the memo strip travel and its alphabetic position could be viewed. When the stripe aligned with the alphabetic characters across the viewing window—you stop and then manually advance the stripe until you come to the 'party' you want and then press 'Dial"—the magnetic strip is read and the number is dialed. All that to save time dialing either 7 or 10 digits!?!

Their headquarters (only) was in a building right on Route 28 in North Andover—a very impressive building previously the headquarters for an insurance company that built a new one nearly across the street.

It didn't take much to figure out that CTI had a great cash flow with minor indebtedness which made a buyout very lucrative on Dasa's behalf.

THEY GAIN———I LOSE!!

A short time after the sale was completed, and it was only a matter of days—the President of Cybertronics, Jim Hassett—

the Vice President of Sales, and the Vice President of Service, Bill Mazur (my boss) were all terminated. Happened so fast I never saw any of them again (with an exception, years later).

Regardless, I now have a new Boss who—I don't know. Oh, as far as that goes— I'll survive, and it didn't take long for me to find out that the Branch Service Manager of the Philadelphia Office was promoted to VP -Service, CTI Division of Dasa. His name was Dan and his last name escapes me, but I knew him but only slightly.

With this marriage of CTI to Dasa and over a period of time is where I became somewhat defensive, skeptical and indoctrinated to the games played in corporations with regard to egos, politics, covering your a— , and a few other increments of crud.

Part of that feeling emanated from the fact my shares of Cybertronics were now totally worthless as of the sale date. These shares had been given to me as a year end bonus, for each of the previous 2 years.

I don't remember how many shares there were, nor how much money they totaled. I'm sure it wasn't over a couple thousand dollars, but for the dozens of hours I worked overtime without pay, those shares would have made some of those hours a lot more palatable, especially with the number of times I was called to N E Telephone in Boston, at 2-3-4 AM and didn't return home from 6 to 20 hours!!!

So, the day I watched my 'stock papers' burn in a waste basket, really didn't give me an exhilaration!

Shortly, I had an executive at Dasa by the name of Bill Ziggenbien call for an appointment. At this appointment, we had a lengthy discussion on many topics. One of these topics was the current salesman in the Boston office and which I don't remember his name. Over a period of time, I developed an appreciation for Ziggenbien————but he was really the only one that cultivated admiration from my behalf!

About a month later, he came into the Office with another gentleman who was introduced as Gene Shapiro—it wasn't necessary to introduce him—I recognized him because I knew him, he came from Randolph, Vt. This world, at times can have the strangest coincidences—this is one of those! How ironic to have an office in Newton, Ma. and the Sales Manager and the Service Manager, both from a little town most people have never heard of !!

Bill Ziggenbien was a straight shooter, did what he said he would do and within the time frame. AND, he also respected my judgment and capacity.

UNFORTUNATELY—— within 12 months, I attended his funeral one afternoon on the North Shore. At an age under 50, he was gone. I'm sure it was cancer of some form.

CONTINUING EDUCATION AND COMMUTING

As I mentioned a few topics back, I hired Al Yellick and he was trained on the job. He was turning into a strong 'Customer Engineer' and now he needed additional training. Being capable of covering Keypunch calls had been accomplished, now it was time to learn an additional machine. I used that extra room at the office for more than one purpose——one of those purposes was for training, and here, by now, Al had been trained on reproducers(519), Sorters(083) and Interpreters(548-552). He was now ready for some field experience on these types.

I would snag a machine in transit like a 552 interpreter, 519 reproducer, 083 sorter, or a 557 interpreter and then teach one of the men this additional machine, even from scratch or in a few cases more extensive trouble shooting, or explaining some specific circuits to help diagnostic abilities.

We even had a 602A, which by now I could teach (and had to), even if it wasn't a full fledged 2 week course.

CTI was committed to a response time of 45 minutes—— from the time a service call is logged on the Dispatch Call Sheet, we had to provide a Customer Engineer to be at the site by 45 MINUTES!!

THIS, within the city of Boston could generate some stress—especially with traffic!

For that reason, more than once, I would jump in the car and cover a call myself, when I could detect a bottleneck for coverage—depending on the account, the distance and other factors.

I also used that room for a rebuild process——any machine that required cleaning inside and outside, replacement of parts, checking machine operation and finally, even spray painting. All of these tasks could be done providing a little discretion was used in creating no mess ——'over spray' with paint spray cans etc.

Anything that could be done and save on transportation costs, rebuild costs, or travel and hotel costs for training outside the Boston area was done in this extra room.

The Boston CTI Office was in a building that had an elevator, so most machines could be brought to the office with the exception of a couple of the large ones.

And while we're here— the building also had multi tenants which made it easy to be a tenant there—like an accountant across the hall where income taxes could be done, a barber, a dentist, stores such as a Supermarket, Friendly's for lunch etc.

In addition, it was right on Route 9, less than a mile from Route 128 so it was accessible to any direction, but it was about 30 miles from my house in Northboro, so commuting put me on I-495 for about 4 miles and then Route 9 through Southboro-Framingham Center and then the Golden Mile past ShoppersWorld, the big Carling Brewery and then Natick and Wellesley, which, in most cases, did take up to an hour.

Of course, in the afternoon your view was directly into the sun most of the way.

HOUSE REMODELING

In claiming our new home, this was the beginning of a long list of 'upgrades'—the first being to remodel the (only) bath upstairs. This well needed project was started within a couple months after we moved in ——the year, 1967.

The biggest drawback was the garage—and this was a mess. It sat almost on the ground and I didn't hold much hope to ever fix it——what that needed was to be removed. However, it did provide a cover for the car Bunny used—mine stayed outside in the drive which was wide enough to allow her car to pass. Good thing for Bunny's car, she really needed the dry floor for a run to get up the inclined driveway when snow came and it worked best to back her car in. We had trouble with the drive all winter long , especially with a rear wheel drive car.

Once the upstairs bath was done, I then had to work on the second bedroom by adding a six foot closet, add insulation, new wiring, new ceiling, and sheetrock walls. Each room I did, I repeated the process as I did in the second room and finished by hanging baseboard radiation in anticipation of converting the heat from a steam system to forced hot water in the months or years to come. This was roughly 1970.

Next came the master bedroom, overlooking the pond toward the west. Here, I installed a Bay window, which had 2 flanker windows at an angle to the large multi pane center window. I also used the entire north wall for twin closets totaling nearly 12 feet wide —both of which had bifold doors. I installed an 8 inch tongue and grooved pine board ceiling stained with gray Vermont Barnboard. With new electrical wiring, ceiling lights, wall to wall carpet and the baseboard radiation installed —this room came out pretty well—— and rather unique.

A year later we did the third bedroom, which was the smallest room upstairs—I would have been very happy to make the bedroom larger and the hall much smaller, but we couldn't do it—too complicated with the existing house design. We added a large closet and then the usual finish touches and that was completed.

The large up stairs hall——remained as is for now. This work put me into 1972.

In 1972, I saw an ad for a studio piano in Marlboro and after looking at it, I got a whale of a buy on a Yamaha studio (48 inch) black Studio piano from an engineer working at 'Digital Equipment'. He hoped to self teach but gave the attempt up. This was now in the large dining room on the ground floor.

Next came the porch on the pond side—which had four windows on the south side, four windows on the north side and six windows on the (west) pond side. All the windows were double hung style and I finished this off with solid walls at the ends and three sliding glass doors on the large wall. Total difference here, which was to be the living room and, again I used the pine board ceiling with a stain—, this was now beginning to be quite interesting. I really hated to throw the old windows out— especially as I had to keep paying for them on the mortgage, for years to come!!!

Up to this point, I had the entire outside for a project, however that could wait until I figured out what was going to happen to the garage. I was working on plans and we had a few ideas—but nothing set in concrete yet.

REMODELING THE NEIGHBORS HOUSE

When we bought the house in Northboro (Ma.) in 1967, our next door neighbors were Carl and Rita Daoust. Their 'house' was a summer cottage and was the second oldest structure on Solomon Pond. Actually, it was an old barn and Carl's parents and relatives had disassembled it, moved it to this location and then reassembled it as a summer retreat. This old barn was moved, so Carl said, before 1900. The house we bought was the oldest—we knew it was 'old' when we bought it!!

The family owned a convenience store in nearby Marlboro and what little time they had off, they spent the free time at the Pond. It was good fishing, a cool place to be as air conditioners weren't heard of yet and good fresh water to swim in.

When Carl's relatives died, he and Rita continued to spend time at the 'cottage' with the intent of someday upgrading it to a full time residence and then to use it in retirement.

Then came the day when Carl, his son in law—Danny Flanders, better known as Pauncho, another neighbor Paul Denusuik and myself were discussing what Carl hoped to do with the house. As it was, it was a poorly built place which 'sat' on telephone poles that had been cut and used as piers. These piers were scattered along the edge of the structure. They were creosoted and even that they had been in the ground for years, they weren't rotted enough to create problems—yet.

Carl said he had a railroad jack in the shed when the day would come he was going to use it to raise the building — raise it enough to excavate under it for a cellar. Someone said, "get it and lets see if this sucker would raise slightly and we'll know if it is going to work".

The jack was a ratchet type and weighed enough so just moving it was not easy! It was brought out of the shed, placed in an easy spot and the handle inserted.

I would say we're talking the year of 1969, maybe 1970.

THAT was the start of a project which would continue for months—many months. Once that corner was jacked up a couple inches, the jack was moved and another corner was jacked up a couple of inches. Before that day ended, the whole building was off the piers by quite a few inches!

None of us had any experience in raising a building, but at the rate we were going, we were gaining some very rapidly! At the end of day 2 (which may have been a week later)—it was off the ground by a foot and rather than drag this out a foot at a time, soon it was a good 4 feet—high enough to start digging the trench for the walls and the footings.

Paul was a welder and worked in Framingham. Over time, he brought back steel beams in his pickup and welded a piece long enough to use as a carrier beam through the middle of the house and one near each end. Now we could support the house farther away from the trench to be dug which made the job of digging easier. What we used for cribbing and blocks for piers—I don't remember, nor where they came from.

Carl dug the trench mostly alone, and when it was deep enough, he rented a cement mixer. I mixed the concrete and he and I wheeled it to the footings forms and dumped it. After a week, cement blocks were delivered and then, again I mixed some of the concrete and he laid in the blocks. This was all done in the early evening or weekends as we all had full time jobs.

Finally the walls were done—then the concrete floor was done inside and the house was lowered on the walls, with the steel beams now resting on the cement blocks. The beam ends were cut off and the wall 'pockets' were filled. The beams now gave a 'post less' basement usable as a family room.

Incidentally, while I'm telling about this house being raised etc.——I now look back at this 'job' and with MORE life experience, LESS enthusiasm and impulse, I would not be convinced this was a safe 'hobby' or project for anyone to get involved with. And with that said, I would NOT do a job like that OR, of that magnitude again!!

Believe me, this would be a hard structure to remodel. First it was built originally by a (common) style known in early 1900's as balloon construction——no sidewall studs—the studs were horizontal through the middle of the downstairs wall—the walls were matched boards that went from the bottom of the first story to the top of the second floor!

Secondly, there wasn't a square corner OR a plumb wall anywhere in the place! But, Carl and Pauncho struggled and a few months later it was ready to be wired—which I did. Carl helped run wire, but he didn't want any part of making connections.

Also the plumbing needed to be installed, which I also did. Carl didn't want any part of these items. It was still a few months away from being occupied.

Northboro had a building inspector, and one who I got acquainted with, but he was mostly interested in commercial and industrial buildings. Houses were pretty lenient—once the building permit was issued. The town was experiencing a rapid commercial/industrial flurry at that time.

As a guess, I would say the basic house size was about 20 by 30 or 32.

Carl and Rita ultimately moved in and it wasn't long before a deck was added to the pond side and a couple years later, Jim Flanders was contracted to add a new addition to the side opposite the pond for a kitchen. Jim was starting out as a contractor and this was one of his first jobs of any magnitude——and he did a really beautiful job!

They sold their other building in Marlboro which was a store front and a residence on the second floor.

At the Pond, there wasn't room enough on their lot for a garage, but there was a shed on the property line to store the normal outdoor tools etc.

Rita was a bookkeeper for a small trucking company in Marlboro and Carl was a custodian for the Assabet Valley Regional Vocational Technical School in nearby Hudson.

Carl took Bunny and I on a tour of this Regional Vocational Technical School one Sunday afternoon. It was so big we spent the entire afternoon walking and occasionally stopping in a room such as the automobile section. It was a Regional School for 7 surrounding towns.

GEORGE LINTON

One day Lindy and I were standing near the scales at the Coal Office at the edge of Salisbury Street in Randolph, when the north bound passenger train went by—slowed to the point where it finally stopped.

A few moments later I looked toward the (old) Esso station beside the Depot and said to Lindy, "Isn't that George Linton walking toward us?"

Lindy looked and replied, "I think it is."

I hadn't seen George for years so as he came up to us I said, "Hi George, I haven't seen you for months"—I knew he didn't recognize me—so I told him my name, then he knew me.

"Where you been, George", Lindy asked.

"Been down to the VA Hospital in White River Junction visiting my Father", George replied.

With this, Lindy and I looked at each other and for the same reason—we both knew George had to be in his eighties—and now he's telling us he's visiting his father???

"How old is your father, George?" I asked.

"He's 104'"George replied

"Your Father, George," Lindy said, "How is he?"

"Well," George said, "he don't do much anymore, his arm bothers him"!!?!

Lindy and I had a chuckle from that and after George left, we had a bigger chuckle, called a laugh!!

LINDY CREATES SOME LEVITY

Lindy then told me about a rather peculiar incident that happened inside the 'Coal Office' sometime earlier.

He was sitting at this desk facing away from the center of the office—doing some type of paperwork.

There was a counter and this counter was higher than normal—why I don't know but it was nearly chest high.

Lindy heard a rather muffled noise and turned around facing this counter and the middle of the room. Nobody was there at the counter, so he turned back to his work at the desk.

Then he heard another noise and this time after he turned around, stood up and looked over the counter. There on the floor, was George Linton and by now in the process of getting up.

What happened was that George came in the door and as he shut the door, his shoe laces were trailing behind, and he accidentally shut the laces in the door. When he stepped forward, his feet were stopped and he very slowly fell to the floor.

Lindy said it scared him to death that George had fallen down and he didn't even know it ——— now George is standing at the counter hardly able to look over it—he was very short. Anyway he said he was all right and not hurt, finished his business and went out the door!!!

Sprinkled over a period of time, Lindy had a couple of instances that he told me about and which, made me chuckle. I don't have any apprehension on telling them——Lindy laughed at himself as easily as anyone I've ever known.

He delivered some fuel oil to Mrs David Hedding on Forest Street and when it stopped pumping, he stamped the delivery ticket in the meter and took it in to Mrs. Hedding. The two of them talked for a few moments, Lindy left and returned to his office, near the Post Office. He hadn't been there only a few moments when the phone rang and Eileen Monroe, his gal in the office, told Lindy it was Mrs. Hedding and wanted to speak to him.

She then asked him if he had left a long rubber thing next to the road——and he replied not that he knew of ——then thought it might be well if he went over and checked. Once there, he recognized his hose lying next to the road——he had forgotten to disconnect it from the fill pipe and when he drove off, it had been ripped off the hose reel!!!! He said later, the worst part was traveling to Montpelier and spending the whole day getting it repaired—not to mention the cost, also!!

Lindy and Merwin Huntley (his helper at this particular time), were doing the annual oil burner and boiler cleanings along with inspections AND cleanings. Merwin had spent a few minutes with his torso stuck through the door of a boiler, and using a wire brush was cleaning the combustion chamber. It was a natural process for these chambers to become cruddy through usage, and it was customary to remove this crud and return the inside walls to the normal asbestos blocks.

There must have been an oversize door on this particular boiler, because Merwin was an 'oversize boy'! And after a few moments, Lindy suggested Merwin back out —and he would take a turn.

So as they traded positions, Lindy extended his arms and went in through the door opening, then proceeded to clean the chamber——stopping only to remove his glasses and lay them on the floor of the chamber—now he could see better in the short distance.

After a few moments, he was satisfied the job was finished, backed out, said something to Merwin and then slammed the door on the boiler and flipped on the burner switch. Said something else to Merwin, and then kneeled down to check the flame through the glass in the boiler door——just in time to see his glasses melt!!

As the owner of a small fuel business, Lindy, naturally did everything from filling fuel oil tanks——cleaning oil burners etc. ——during the winter he was also on call for oil burner service. So when the telephone rang at his house about 2 AM —the caller said, "Lindy—remember when you were here and cleaned my furnace?"

Lindy said he did.

"Well, the caller said, 'since you were here,—there's a squeak when the furnace is running!" Lindy said, "but that was nearly 2 months ago——you have a squeak and now you call me?" The customer said, "Well, I just happened to think of it"

Lindy said, "At 2 o'clock in the morning, you just thought of it?"

Customer— "I just wanted to let you know!"

So now that Lindy is wide awake—can't go back to sleep— decided he would go fix the furnace. So he got dressed and drove to the customer's house (couple of miles), and rang the door bell.

The customer opened the door and said, "Gosh, Lindy I didn't expect to see you here at 3 in the morning" and let him in.

Lindy said, "I just want to give you good service !!"

And with that, went down cellar and after a few minutes, took a wrench and pounded on the cold air return for quite a few minutes—saying to himself, 'if I'm not going to sleep——no one else is going to, either!!!!!

(He never did tell me if he fixed the squeak!!)

Sometime in the late 1950's or early 1960's, a bunch of us went to an Alumni Banquet at the High School on Forest Street. During a break, we came outside—a few sitting in a car—a few standing outside the car and a bottle was passed around. After I had sampled it, I passed the bottle to Lindy in the rear seat ——window was down. By this time, Lindy had a few samples and now had another. I had the bottle cap —a metal cap and without thinking much about it, I bent that cap just enough so it was out of round.

Lindy had just taken another sample as I passed him the cap and as he was talking, putting the cap on the bottle—or at least tried to! He tried again ——no go, so now he brings the bottle higher —and still the cap won't screw on. I started to laugh and then when he had that bottle about 2 inches from his nose and STILL couldn't turn the cap on, I had to leave I was laughing so hard. Naturally, I didn't want Lindy to see me laughing. I finally had to tell him why the cap wouldn't fit. GOOD THING he was in the car, and couldn't get out in a hurry!!

DASA CHANGES—BOSTON

Dasa also occupied an old textile building on Route 28 in Andover, (Ma), and which was previously occupied by J.P. Stevens Co., before most of the textile industry moved to the Carolina's, in the 1920's. This was a five story building with a lot of granite on the outside and typical hardwood oil soaked floors inside. An elevator provided good movability for either manufacturing, storage or distribution. There was also a couple of annexes of single story—— and a large parking lot.

For a few months, not much happened in the way of consolidation aside for a few management shakeups and personnel changes. Sometime, probably in 1970, it was announced ALL of the rebuild in Lake Success, plus sales administration, furniture, fixtures, stock machines and the balance of CTI would be relocated to Andover, leaving Lake Success empty. Didn't surprise me and truthfully, from a business point, it made economic sense.

The stock of these machines was increasing in numbers, as it was becoming more difficult to place them in accounts.

Most of the stock of machines, when received from the New York location were placed in the basement of the granite building when they arrived.

There was a brook running between this building and the office annex with a couple ramps up to a closed bridge between the two. I would guess there was at least 200 machines stored in the basement —that is as I stood looking over the floor from an elevated entrance with a few stairs going down to the floor.

Right now, I won't go down to the basement floor, as there is about three feet of water covering the whole floor. This is due to a spring freshet that made this small brook swell and ultimately flow over the banks!(My estimate this happened in the spring of 1971).

Of course, this ruined every machine there and if I had to guess—my guess would be that they were insured—and probably now a total loss!! Is your analytical ability parallel with mine?

BOSTON CTI-DASA

In 1971 and within the Boston office, I recall I had 12 or 13 Customer Engineers and my 'plate' was nearly full—considering all the accounts in Massachusetts, Connecticut and also a few in New Hampshire.

Generally, a typical Field (Service) Manager carries a maximum staff of 12 to 15 Customer Engineers. I was at that point right now and in addition, made customer calls, sales assistance, some teaching, office administrative duties and I could use a field Manager, but didn't have one.

88

If I had a situation any place, I would go there to prevent a calamity every time. This showed the customer I was aware, I was concerned and placed their interest at the top of my priorities. More than once, I left for Portland Maine or some other place, in early afternoon and returned ——probably late in getting home.

I remember one time I had to go to a fairly new building in Scollay Square (Boston). I don't remember the account name or the building name ——but waiting for the elevator, the doors finally opened and I stepped into the elevator.

VERY ERRATICALLY— the doors closed which immediately got my FULL attention— and then the elevator made a couple of lurches in the down direction and stopped. AGAIN, the doors tried to open —went about a foot and then closed again and I might add—ERRATICALLY!! NOW, I concluded I didn't want to ride this elevator!!

Again, without the elevator moving— the doors started to open very erratically and then I could see I was nearly 2 feet below the floor in front of me—so when those doors were open wide enough——out went my tool case and RIGHT BEHIND ——I literally dove through the doors also!!(I won't get into any words about me and elevators)!?

My choice of a location to live in Northboro, was really paying off—I could go North, South, West or East as a starting point and return home with ease, except for getting home from downtown Boston or Quincy, —traffic at times, was horrendous.

PAYBACK!!

I mentioned in one topic not far back that CTI had a couple accounts in New Hampshire. One account there was a woolen processing plant in southeastern New Hampshire——the name I don't recall.

This account was sold to be under IBM service and that would mean the IBM Concord (N H), Branch Office.

For one reason or another, the installation of the equipment was dragging, and especially the CTI 402-Accounting Machine.

It reached a point of stagnation(?), so I called the Branch Service Manager , who I knew and fairly well from my days of IBM Springfield (Vt.).

The day of the appointment, I was in the Concord office and was greeted by Bill P. and entered his office.

We had a few moments of reminiscing and then he asked what he could do for me. So I started to explain how this particular account was dragging in the installation of its equipment, when he interrupted and suggested he got the Field Manager for that account in so he could be a participant.

The door opened and WHO walked in??? Frank—— FRANK—my boss from Montpelier Office and who I had given my termination notice!! (Apparently he had gone from Boston Rebuild Center to the Concord Office as a Field Manager).

I hardly greeted him and then I took a chapter of operation from his own book——I reeled off about a dozen items JUST LIKE he used to when we met a Vlades Cafeteria in Burlington!!! (Remember that topic?)

And at the end of my volley—I asked, "And when can I expect this work to be completed?" I just know this all in front of his boss tied him up ——he always was gun shy about what he did.

And now as Jackie Gleason used to say, "How sweet it is"!!!

CABOT CORPORATION—CTI

Through the effort of Don Hebert the salesman, we gained the Cabot Corporation for an account. I don't remember the address, but it was downtown Boston.

The customer called to say that some equipment had arrived so dispatch assigned the action to one of the techs in downtown area.

Shortly I got a call from him saying the equipment looked more like it was dragged, rather than trucked from New York.

So I made a trip to the account and the 407 Accounting Machine looked horrible. The truck driver told the receiving clerk someone broke into the truck and vandalized the machine. Needless to say I was, I was ——never mind!!!!!

So now, a process is in effect ——covering the damage, paperwork on who pays for the damage, a machine ordered for replacement etc.—on and on it goes.

The more I thought about it, the more convinced I became it wasn't vandalized——I suspected the driver failed to 'tie this machine down'! Machines on casters roll around and, in this case, the machine weighed over 2000 pounds!!!

Since we had been purchased by Dasa—the transportation arrangements were now made from Andover. Other 'incidents' came to mind and then I became convinced, the shipping clerk at Andover had a 'padded van' trucker he was friendly with, who was doing the machine transporting now and obviously not experienced in machine transporting, ——also, CTI very seldom ran into the circumstances we were now seeing.

Within a week, another new account notified dispatch that a carpet was ripped in the lobby of a brand new building by a delivery of a machine with a broken caster!! This account was a Data Processing Service Bureau for the many Mutual and Stock Fund Accounts within the Financial District.

This was a new building the account was moving into and, in addition was changing hardware suppliers to CTI.

This building had imported Italian marble—special ceramic tiles on the floors, other expensive finishing touches and the lobby floor exhibiting an expensive Persian type carpet—— which got ripped!!!!

After damage control had been completed, I wrote an inter office memo to this guy at headquarters and I mean a scathing memo that was HOT enough to start a roaring fire! I laid it on him for his lack of follow-up, the numerous 'incidents and about the lousy service provided by his choice of transportation company and the 'guerrilla's' they were using for drivers etc.

A couple days later I had a call from THE transportation company on the North Shore and the owner or manager wanted me to meet him in his office and gave directions.

I met him and was surprised for two reasons— 1, when he showed me a copy of my memo, and 2, his office(s) and the way they were displayed gave me reason to believe his rates certainly must be VERY high!

I didn't back down on what I said OR how I said it, nor did I amend anything I said. When I left, he had given me a commitment to really improve their quality of service. I must have hit a nerve when I told him his trucks weren't carrying freight——they were transporting a one of a kind piece of equipment that is very difficult to duplicate—not to mention the time that's required to match the specifications!

And when I got to Headquarters in Andover I also read the riot act to the shipping guy about my memo being sent to a vendor outside of the Dasa Office, which is very discourteous——"make up your own damn memo"!!

HOTEL   HEADQUARTERS

Also in the same general area of Boston, and not many blocks away, we also gained the account of Statler Hotels. This was apparently the headquarters for the hotel operation and was in a building near the Central Artery—which is a divided 4—6 lane elevated highway through the middle of downtown Boston. The building was also near a Boston Fire Station. As I recall, the building was nearly 20 stories tall and had an outside finish of blue bricks along with other 'light colored' bricks.

The reason I'm pointing this building out is that a few months—maybe a couple of years before I'm now writing this — I was watching TV and the segment I was interested in, was THIS building was being prepared for demolition. The actual one hour show was a documentary on the use of explosives combined with the building implosion, instead of the usual 'wrecking ball' method of demolition. As the camera wandered through the corridors and rooms on many floors——it brought back memories of me walking some of those same corridors!

There was a lot of concern about the Fire Station and other buildings in very close proximity and damage that could take place by the controlled demolition——but, as I remember, there was no damage to surrounding buildings!

Once the pile of rubble had been cleared, a new and taller building was erected and I seem to think the name of which would be International Place.

Here today ——gone tomorrow!!!

DAUGHTER TO THE RESCUE

One day I was in the kitchen and she came flying down the stairs from her room. She whizzed through the kitchen and out the door headed for next door.

I asked her when she went by me in the kitchen what was going on but she didn't answer and she also didn't slow up, so I knew something of importance was happening!

I followed her out the door as she ran across the lawn, down to the neighbor's dock.

When she reached the end of the dock, she dropped right into the water (which was about 2 feet deep) and then fetched the little girl next door from the water!!

The girl was about 4 maybe 5 at the time. Naturally she was gasping, coughing etc. She sat on the dock and started to settle down.

She had seen her fall off the dock from her bedroom window which prompted the quick trip down the stairs and to the dock.

The childs mother never did give thanks for the deed—— and after a couple of days, I again praised her as did Bunny.

And this is a good place to also state that the biggest drawback I had to be living on the water, was the sight of seeing people skating on ice way too early, swimming after dark (and after midnight)—all kinds of activities in or around the water that I considered dangerous, but, apparently other people didn't.

And with that, I just had to resign myself that I couldn't assume the duties of a life preserver, especially when I'm a VERY POOR swimmer myself!!!

———— FLASHBACK ————

REVEREND FRED DAY GETS A HAIRCUT

One day, Rev. Fred went into George Rye's Barber Shop, —waited a couple of minutes, then was ushered to the chair by George.

As he sat down, George said, "Morning, Fred" —but with no return greeting from the Reverend.

So George rattled on as he normally did while cutting hair and in this case, Fred offered no contribution to the 'conversation'.

That didn't stop George, for the number of years he had been cutting hair in that very storefront,—he had seen all types of people—even had more than one go to sleep while this procedure was being done! (Actually, George had been there nearly 50 years)!

Soon, George was done, so he removed the apron, which to Fred was the signal to get out of the chair.

As George started to use the whisk broom on the shoulders, Fred spoke and said, "Not too short, George!!"

REAL ESTATE SCHOOL

In 1971, a thought that had reposed in my mind for months finally floated to the top of my list of things to do. That was to get a Real Estate License. It made sense—it was fairly cheap to pursue, couple hundred dollars plus a Bond cost, and fairly easy to do.

I enrolled in a well known school based in Brookline, near Boston. They had periodic training sessions sprinkled about the state. I enrolled in a night course about January in the Westboro area and which would take about 12 to 14 weeks. Duck Soup—I can do that even if I had an occasional interruption.

After the last class, I had to go to Boston and pass a State Test in order to get my License. In 1971, I could take a few extra sessions, and apply directly for a Broker's License, which was a step up from a Salesman's license. Couple of years later, you had to hold a Salesman's license for 2 years, and then apply for a Broker's license.

The Broker's License allowed you to talk not only price but to negotiate with any and all 'parties' to complete the sale. You could also locate a money source for a mortgage. As a Salesman—you couldn't do either of those.

My neighbor across the street in Northboro, was a State Representative, a lawyer, and had two offices——one in Northboro which sold multi line insurances and an office in

Westboro which not only was his law offices upstairs, but the Renco Real Estate Sales office was also on the ground floor. Bill Maurice was on the payroll as an insurance Sales Rep but, Bob wanted more action in the Real Estate office. He didn't feel the office was active enough and needed a couple more people there. Based on that, someway he found I was taking a course, and offered me a job in his Westboro office when (and if) I passed my State Test.

I didn't want a full time job selling RE——I couldn't afford it, there was no salary, only commissions. I still had a job and one with benefits, so no full time now.

I had taken the State Test and passed, so now I was a licensed broker. However, in a short time, I did take a job as a salesman to work part time, mostly weekends. This would give me some experience in sales, listing properties and following the transactions to see 'how it was done'.

I also made the acquaintances of many other people in the RE business from other sales offices and from different communities——that and getting acquainted geographically with the Central part of Massachusetts more so than I presently knew. Within that year, I listed quite a few properties and showed a few BUT——I didn't bring any income to the office or myself!

JACK ELLIS

During that time, I spent a lot of time with Jack Ellis from Westboro. Jack was a full time Computer Technician with Burroughs Corporation in Worcester and had over 25 years there. He really liked Real Estate, and he put a lot of time in. THAT'S the secret—a lot of time—you have to, in order to keep track of the listings as they are listed through Multiple Listing Service (MLS). AND, you should preview as many houses as you can so you can talk intelligently and factually about any house you MAY 'show'.

Jack was the greatest guy I ever knew in that he was always 'high', that is any time a customer was present. NO—not that kind of high—you wouldn't think Jack had a worry or a care in the world! Coupled with the fact he was very extrovertive, very knowledgeable about houses and house construction, knew the area and street names, not to mention he knew 'everybody'. But at times, I could see he was like anyone else in carrying household or children problems—but if a 'customer' walked through the door, he could turn his head around 180 degrees and in no time have them at ease in front of his desk! And this is a good place to mention that soon, his wife Annette and another gal Ellen Davis would join the Sales Team along with Jack, "Al" and myself.

Jack, and his wife Annette sold a lot of houses, even though we didn't get the traffic that a couple other offices did. Ellen Davis was a housewife and this is a good occupation for many housewives.

Soon we were working closely with other offices, two that come to mind—Bucky Rogers office in Northboro and Dorothy Hickox in Westboro.

One last item about Real Estate for the moment, the office was staffed during the day by another broker.

Being that Al was working full time, Jack and especially I would give him all the leads while we were in the office—so he could at least get a shot at SOME income and survive. After we had done that for a few months, it finally came to light Al didn't follow-up on ANY leads—it was against his 'policy' and apparently felt it was irritating to call a customer about a new listing—whether it was an office listing or an MLS listing!! Believe me —a giant threeway discussion took place when that came to light! In other words, if he didn't sell a customer a house the first time they met——you could consider that customer is gone——gone to another office. And—then the next office would follow up and ultimately get the sale!! I've pushed THAT button, which irritated me immensely—I'll change topics.

Jack and I soon joined the Worcester Board of Realtors and then started to participate in the many Realtor functions and which gave us returns in many ways.

PAYING THE BILLS

When our daughters were fifteen, we thought this was a good time to learn a little about bills.

Once a week, the paycheck or paychecks if there was more than one, all were reviewed. Up to this point I had been determining the amounts of money to go into the savings account(s), the checking account and any other place such as personal spending 'pockets'. Realistically, both Bunny and I needed daily cash as does everyone.

Now, before you get all bent out of shape about letting the 'kids' know how much you earn and also what and where you spend, think about the net result.

By bringing a fifteen year old into this financial circle—it gives her a working example that money doesn't grow on trees-it lets her know that good responsible planning is necessary to survive monetarily in these days, —it lets her help to plan for a purchase which could easily break the bank. It lets her see that a small amount of cash available is good insurance against any type of a financial emergency. It also lets her know that when she wants something bought for her and she is turned down——now she can understand there may not be money to make an 'impulse' purchase!

There's all kinds of benefits for a teenager to gain— by being part of the solution instead of part of the problem!!

This whole process became fun, —the participation, the financial solutions etc. and now ——being past fifty —she is one sharp cookie when it comes to finances—checking accounts—liquidity—bank statements —credit cards etc. and you can bet Mom and Dad are really proud of her accomplishments!

HOUSE——KITCHEN REBUILD

By the time good spring weather came around in 1971, the CTI office was running fairly smooth—I didn't have to cover nearly as many service calls ——I had my Real Estate license and did spend some time at Renco Realty on Route 9 in Westboro, however I had a few other items on my mind. I really wasn't paying enough attention to RE, but I was surviving economically so what's the hurry?

Right now, what I'm interested in is to work on the kitchen in our house. The present kitchen is really 'GROSS' as both my daughters would say. It was dark—one very small window in the door looking at the pond—and another similar door at the other end. It was dreary with ugly cabinets and in general, it was a disaster!

I had drawn detailed plans, including adding a half bath near the entry door—and talking things over with Bunny and on most items, we had made our minds up on finish work and appearance.

A local friend Wally Drohan, lived 2 houses away so I talked with him about some assistance. We agreed on pay, so that was taken of. He was a custodian with the local school system so he had extra time he could spend with me.

With that ——out came the prybar, a couple pinch bars, a nail puller and hammers. It didn't take long for the kitchen to be 'gutted'.

Bunny was working for a couple of welders in Hudson (Ma.) called Welderon so she didn't hear all the noise we made ripping the joint apart! All the trash was thrown in the yard and getting rid of it was no problem in 1971.

Soon we were at a point of running Romex, hanging electrical boxes, adding studs for the half bath and others as necessary, running the cold and hot pipes and drain pipes, installing a crank out window over the sink location. Over time we did the preliminary work on the ceiling and got the sheetrock up. Now, we're ready to sheetrock the walls.

The summer came and by July, we had the room sheetrocked and insulated——it now comes to the cabinets. This house to work on, was the hardest place you could imagine——not a square corner, or a plumb wall. And that is an item we corrected in many places especially where cabinets would be, if a wall was too far out of plumb, it would be corrected, even if it required to add a few studs.

With no kitchen all summer(and into early fall), we worked around that by cooking and eating in the travel trailer parked in the driveway.

I set my table saw in the yard near the kitchen door and started to do the cabinet side pieces and shelves and then hanging these pieces for the wall cabinets. We leveled the floor and built the frames for the base cabinets, by using 3/4 inch birch for all the side pieces for both wall cabinets and base cabinets ——anywhere they would show.

The faces of the cabinets took longer as I didn't have a router or anything but a tablesaw and a jointer. Here again, I used 3/4 inch Birch for a faceplate—then cut the door openings so no joints or half laps were needed. I used the Birch pieces left from the door opening cuts and using pine outside edge expanders——I now had doors which not only matched in grain, but also used pieces that would have been scrap.

By now, we're into September and the weather is starting to get chilly working on cabinets in the yard——but, finally it was time to stain and seal. The walls had been papered.

The half bath we added near the kitchen door, could wait until later to be completed.

One big incident happened when Bunny was staining and sealing the cabinets. The refrigerator was in the middle of the floor with a movers pad over it and I just finished the plumbing on the sink—told Bunny the plumbing was done and set the propane torch on the counter.

The new sliding door was installed on the pond side of the kitchen and was open with a small breeze coming in.

I grabbed the torch so it could be put away and as I unscrewed the top—there was a S-W-I-S-H ——and I had a fire in my hands! I dropped the torch which is now a ball of flames and then tried to pick it up to throw it around the refrigerator and out the slider. NO SUCH LUCK!! It hit the refrigerator and dropped on the floor and now the movers pad is on fire also! I yelled to Bunny to get out and quick——I couldn't pick the torch up—it was being fed by propane and I really thought the whole house would go!!!

I had an extinguisher right by the kitchen door, but truthfully I had doubts about it killing that torch.

I squeezed the trigger — one doze and the fire went out!!!

Do I have to say my skivvies got stained??!!

We were lucky and I can remember it like it happened last week. What actually happened was that the torch had a small pin flame—probably wasn't completely shut off but—the valve inside that tank didn't shut off completely either. When I un-

*View of kitchen center,
looking past eating area
towards Solomon Pond.
Porch was not present
until after the kitchen
rebuild was finished.
Photo C. Wells - 1996.*

*View of kitchen center,
looking east towards
Solomon Pond Road.
Added half bath is on the
left near entry door.
Photo C. Wells.*

screwed the top that allowed propane to escape around the threads and be ignited by the small flame.

The kitchen was finished—looked pretty good and we started using it not long before cold weather visited us. We did have to live with a profound burn mark on the new flooring where the propane torch dropped for a few moments while flames surrounded it!

Total cost to remodel the kitchen including labor costs and a new stove was under 2000 dollars!!

RENCO REAL ESTATE

After a year, I hadn't made but very little money —there was only 2 ways to generate money. One, obviously is to sell a house (or something) and the other is to list a house and even if you don't sell it yourself, but the office does, you get paid a fixed fee for listing.

In 1973 when I was working part time in Real Estate, the breakdown on any sale, the office took 50% and the salesperson took 50%. The office paid for all advertising the property, any office staff and expenses. The salesperson got paid for time and 'the closing'. If another R E sales office was involved, that office claimed 50% and the listing office took 50%—which now reduced the remainder to each selling salesperson from each office. The listing salesperson still collected a listing fee off the top. (The arrangement has changed drastically over the years following).

Every job always has a couple of negatives and the biggest one here is listings——finding a property to sell AND getting an agreement with the owner to sell it and then, a price. AND the price has to be realistic. Market price is defined as the price an owner will agree to sell at, and the price a prospective buyer is agreeable to pay, both with absence of pressure or duress. Many homeowners pick a price out of the air and this is what they expect to get. Doesn't work that way, and for the moment I'll bypass establishing a SELLING price.

The second year, I decided to really put some effort into this—more time and try to convince myself what I could realize through the effort. And I sold 12 or 13 houses—can't remember the details—had no reason to, but I do remember this was all weekend work with Saturdays getting interrupted at times, by CTI-Dasa responsibilities.

The office location was ideal for a Real Estate office, right on busy Route 9, better known as the Boston Worcester Turnpike—a divided highway from Boston to Worcester(and beyond) and highly commercialized most of the distance. However, location is good and important. AFTER the office is established——up to the many years it takes to become established, LISTINGS are more important! And these don't come by sitting and waiting! This is where success or failure will be determined!

STIRCO

Stirco is a coin phrased word I came up with about 1972. It comes from (ST)an Gould—(IR)win Lindquist and (CO)nrad Wells.

At that time we collectively decided to form a Corporation for the purpose of selling houses. Unlike a real estate office, we wanted to sell prefabricated or manufactured houses.

When we did this, Stan was working at Hughes Sporting Goods, Lindy owned the Randolph Coal and Oil Co., and I was working for Cybertronics in Chestnut Hill (Newton), Ma. We felt that we had the ability to represent more than one company that offered houses in a relatively new method, called Modular Housing, Prefabricated Houses or Manufactured houses——not trailers, as they were apt to be referred to. These would be manufactured in a plant and delivered to the site either as one and two completed units——or, in sections or panels.

We were representing New England Homes in New Hampshire and Stanmar Corporation in Sudbury, Massachusetts.

New England Homes was a truly Modular home, completely manufactured in a plant and trucked to the site on a special multiaxle trailer. Here, it was either slid to the foundation (site permitting), or a crane would pick half the unit off the trailer and place it on the foundation. These were at least equal or generally superior to a 'stick built', (which were completely constructed on location), in that materials were more closely controlled, labor was sheltered from the cold, or rain. Also, labor was quite apt to be a higher quality due to many ways the work was performed such as staging being unnecessary in a plant—and more ways to increase the efficiency of the process. In other words, labor was taking place in an atmosphere of comfort more of the time as opposed to outdoors in the rain, snow, wind or hot sun. Naturally, if a worker is working under pleasant conditions, his work quality should be at a higher level.

Stanmar was a different type of house——more like a 'vacation house', more contemporary designs, different interiors with wood beams showing, some open from floor to roof, lofts etc. These came as panelized, most were post and beam construction, which also allowed the structured beams to come all precut eliminating measuring and cutting under poor or questionable work conditions at the site. Stanmar homes were ideal not only for a primary home, but also for a second/vacation home.

The idea was that Stan would act as construction supervisor, Lindy could sell and install the heating units and provide an office/ sales space. If the action warranted later, I could join in the sales/administrative capacity as needed.

NEW ENGLAND HOMES

One of the first entries we made was a 2 bedroom Ranch for 'spec' at the corner of Elm Street (Sand Hill), and the south corner of Hargrace Drive in Randolph (Vt.), on a lot we owned.

This was a New England modular to which we felt a one car garage should be added primarily due to the winters. This would be a panelized garage spec'd by New England Homes, constructed at their plant and the sections joined after being trucked to the site. Lindy felt this house should have hot water baseboard heat with Stan and I agreeing. Once the foundation was ready, the house arrived and with that, the Sales Rep omitted noting that a crane would be required. This was corrected but not without time being lost—nothing too serious.

The garage arrived on a separate truck along with 2 men who bid in New Hampshire on the job to assemble the pieces into a garage. This was where Stan noticed a problem and pointed it out to the contractor. When he refused to cooperate—Stan called Sales and they became absent from the site!

Well, Stan was finally satisfied and then Lindy did his part by installing the heating system. Here I want to add, Stan was well qualified in house construction.

The house was put on the market and one weekend, Stan, Lindy and I were in the living room discussing a couple of topics. The heat was on, and one item being checked was the boiler and the heat, in general.

While we were there, a car drove up and parked in front. Stan recognized the gentleman walking toward the kitchen door as a good potential buyer and who was a local farmer. Whether he was just about to retire and sell the farm, or whether he had already sold it and needed a house to move to——I don't know, but as Stan said, he had been to look at this house more than once before.

He came in and was warmly greeted by the three of us and proceeded to look again. He had a checkbook sticking out of his shirt pocket and I would have been greatly relieved if he would buy this. I said that for a couple of reasons which I won't expand on. Soon he said, "This would make the Mrs. and I a good little retirement home—great location, town utilities of water and sewer—but the price is a little high!"

(We had just talked about the price and we had decided it was —if anything——quite a few hundred too low).

With that, Stan said, "This is Saturday, Monday the price is going up three thousand dollars, so you better grab the check book outta your pocket and put a binder on it now!!"

I'm sure I must have coughed unknowingly, but before I could do anything else—he said, "It is"!! And with that — whipped the check book out and wrote a deposit and handed it to Stan!!

Years later, when I look back at that house——it was a real winner!! Right in the village, town water and sewer, well insulated, garage, small and easy to heat, full basement, hot water heat and a great corner lot with minimum traffic!!

This man and his wife lived there for many years and I'm sure in comfort!!

STANMAR

Lindy and his wife Barb, had been in their house on Park Place about 12 years and it was now their desire to move farther out in the country. They had previously purchased some land on Braintree Hill and now picked out a Stanmar Model called a Prowed Space House to have built on this land. With the trees thinned out , there was a view southeast way down to Mount Ascutney near Windsor, ——Pico Peak, Killington southwest toward Rutland and directly east ——the ridge between Randolph Center and Brookfield (Pond Village) could be seen.

After the foundation was completed, the house arrived in many panelized sections in addition to many precut beams of humongous sizes,—— windows , doors, deck material etc. It still seems to me that a whole house on one truck is an unbelievable sight and, in this case, for the truck to get to the actual location in the woods with that load—was another scene of astonishment!

This came with a factory rep who oversaw the assembly of the house—and stayed until everyone was satisfied the balance could be handled correctly. Each panel was covered on the outside with mahogany Texture—111 and was prime painted. The real startler here was the open space way to the roof with no stringers——but a huge carrier timber at the peak which, with the walls, carried the roof load! The insulation was large 2 inch panels which were applied to the outside of the roof planks, then the roof shingles over these insulation planks. Also the circular staircase was different and interesting. The 2 fireplaces were built by Dick Piontek.

In the 1970's, this certainly didn't look like a typical Vermont house, being very contemporary in appearance. However now (thirty years later), it would be a very common second or vacation home as sprinkled throughout the state, and as time progresses, this sprinkle becomes heavier each year!

28' x 34', 3 bedrooms, 2 baths, 12' x 10' screened porch and sun decks — 1736 sq. ft.

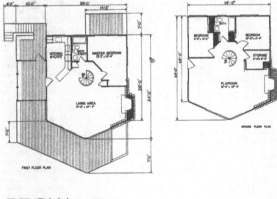

PROW

STANMAR LEISURE HOMES / BOSTON POST ROAD / SUDBURY / MASS. 01776 / (617) 443-9922

stanmar inc

THE SECOND STANMAR

We also sold one to be put on Brigham Circle in the village, one which Anita Rye still lives in. She and Allen Sprague were married at the time, and the style they picked was a Cape Cod with a deck on the south side with glass from floor to peak. This allowed a lot of sunshine to help heat in the winter.

24' x 32', 4 bedrooms, sun deck optional extra — 1096 sq. ft.

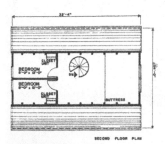

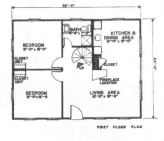

CAPE COD

STANMAR LEISURE HOMES / BOSTON POST ROAD / SUDBURY / MASS. 01776 / (617) 443-9922

When this one was delivered, the foundation wasn't ready yet due to an unusual amount of ledge at the site. Shortly, the foundation was poured, but in the meantime, the truck was unloaded and the entire house was stored in the double garages under the office of Randolph Coal and Oil Co. Lindy parked the 2 trucks outdoors for a short time.

This must have been around Thanksgiving—I came up from Massachusetts and was surprised the entire structure was in the garage!!

Kirby and Mercer did a fine job with the 'on site' work of assembling the parts. Lindy did the heating system, Donald Dustin did the electrical work. As time lapsed, the schedule became tight and then tighter.

In December, there was a heavy snow storm before the roof shingles were put on and the house went most of the winter without the shingles—just the felt paper as the roofing material.

Al and Anita had to be out of their present rented space by February 1, and about 45 days before that, this Cape was a long way from occupancy!

Bunny, our girls and I came up for the Christmas and New Year holidays and Stan, Lindy and I spent time getting this house livable. We all did what was necessary toward the completion. By now, Stan Kirby and Mercer were finished and with a great job——Don Dustin was finishing the electrical work and Stan was busy doing the finish work—kitchen cabinets, bath cabinets etc. AND THEN we ran into a problem.

I have to tell about this problem because if I live to be 1000, I won't forget the circumstances, which to me were unusual.

The town insisted this house be tied into town sewerage and not have a septic system. This meant running the pipe across the front of the next house before tying into the main pipe in the road going over the hill. This would be directly in front of Lindy and Barb's house on Park Place——it's a distance of close to 200 feet.

The trench was dug in December and the pipe installed way to the edge of the road. HERE—work stopped by the installer, Ralph Green, and was to be continued by the town crew—that is to open up the road, tie the line into the main sewer line in the road.

We now have an open trench next to the road edge and then the temperature dropped like a stone!!!!! I well remember the temperature to be 15 above during the day (around zero, or lower at night). The work being done in the hole was mostly by hand to prevent breaking the main pipe and Dick Hedding looked at me and said, "Who's responsible for the elevation of this pipe?"

I replied by saying, "I am in part to blame——why?" (I was there, Stan and Lindy were both working elsewhere at their normal job)

Dick then informed me that the new pipe was coming in at an angle from the house too low to make a connection to the main line—and it did look like it was too low —and by a noticeable amount. Here, I asked him, why not put a 45 elbow in there?

THAT, brought out a comment which I will exclude here!! And, it didn't take much observation to realize the cold temperature was not contributing anything positive to this circumstance! And with that, Dick and his two other men put the barricades up and said they were going to the garage. Before leaving, Dick said IF we come up with the answer they would be there till 5 o'clock—thawing out!!

Here it needs to have a sentence or two of explanation—— I felt this pipe coming in could merely run parallel to the main pipe just a couple of feet down the hill, until the elevations come out equal. I realize that means digging more in the road which was frozen, but at this point in time I felt it was better to keep my mouth shut.

Right here—I'll be honest—I didn't know what to do—except dig a deeper hole and crawl into it!!!!

With that, I went over to Hughes Sports Store where Stan was and explained our problem to him. He listened and said Ralph Green was supposed to put that pipe in at a half bubble off plumb(for the correct pitch to drain and the correct pitch to come out to the right height about 200 feet away)!!!

THIS knocked my socks off, I was hoping for something a little more accurate than "half a bubble" but, in the years prior, I recalled my Father saying— 'not to holler till I was hurt' and as yet, I'm really not hurt. (Ralph Green had taken ownership of Gordon Scribner's store and ALL the other parts of the business, including plumbing).

Then Stan said, " Go over to Mercer's house, get the transit out of his garage and set it up over the road drain pipe by Lindy's driveway—I'll be over in a couple of minutes".

I did this rather reluctantly, hoping no one would call the cops with a complaint someone is stealing from Mercer's garage!

As I was doing this 'chore', I was asking myself a few questions—quite a few questions such as——

Who's going to read this transit—(I can't),—and what to do with the reading? etc. The more I thought about it, the deeper I got into a hole——and how about that half a bubble pitch?—Isn't that a little inaccurate for Ralph Green to follow?

But, I did as Stan said and shortly he drove up—parked and headed toward the transit—now I'm mystified—I didn't know he could perform civil engineering duties. I held the 'stick' and after him peering through the transit——looked up and said, "That's right on the money" and in looking down the hole added," It's an optical elusion, if they keep coming with the pipe, it will come out just exactly right"!!!!!

Believe me—at this point I had a very high regard for Ralph Green and his ability to make this puzzle come together as accurately as that.

I went over to the Town garage on Central Street, explained to Dick the readings which seemed to satisfy him—presented him with a small aid to help him and the crew to stand the cold weather and with that, he and the other 2 men finished our sewer tie in, that afternoon!

Talk about luck— this was a pleasant case where the rabbit was pulled out of a hat!

Imagine, that pipe running 200 feet and then coming out —right on the money!!!!! **AND**, the **GOOD** job Ralph Green did to have that come right on the 'mark'!!! How **LUCKY** we were to have only an inch or two deviation at the end of about 200 feet ?!!?! At times, someone looks after us!!

STIRCO BUYS SOME LAND

At the time we put the Ranch on the corner lot of Hargrace Drive and Elm Street—we bought a tract of land on Sand Hill which was enough to put 4 maybe 5 houses, This was good land, in a desirable location and with town water and sewer.

I can remember taking this land and breaking it into buildable lots and trying to comply with lot requirements—frontage and sideline requirements, and still minimizing waste. It worked out all right and we held these lots for a few months with the idea of putting a spec house or more, or selling the lots and then selling the buyer either a Stanmar or manufactured home.

PINNACLE——RANDOLPH

At this time, a ski area in Randolph known as Pinnacle was being used extensively. It was in back of South End Auto with a dirt road about 1000 feet from Route 12. The tow was in and operating with a good sized crowd especially on weekends. This was not a difficult slope, just right for family fun.

One of us came up with the idea that a few Stanmar homes up there would bring in some renters or even buyers. After all, what could be better than to come out your door, put your skis on and glide to an uncrowded ski slope?

So we ran this across a likely place to get funded and pleasantly surprised, the funds were immediately available——not millions, but adequate enough so we could make a few sales out of it! Actually, the bank was very positive about this venture and for more than one reason.

Next step——get the ground 'perked' so a septic system would be known to work, (one for each residence). This test is generally done in the spring when the water table is the highest. This would indicate if it works then, it's bound to work with the water table lower.

The 'perk' tests were done and every place tested—failed!!! That area was full of springs—plenty of water, but no place for septic systems.

Scratch that idea. That was a great place, a great idea and a series of vacation homes would bring some new business to town. Too bad it didn't work!!

Stan didn't really want to progress with this and a couple other reasons dealt the death knell to Stirco of Randolph.

So we sold the 4 or 5 building lots we had bought in town and the three of us went our ways!!

CTI—DASA ENDS

In 1971, the Vice President of Dasa came into the Chestnut Hill office, sat down and then asked, "What if I decided to close this office and move it to Andover—what would your opinion be?" This is the man that made changes in CTI—big changes, with being a hatchet man taking first place!!

Well, this was a total surprise, but I replied, "From an economic standpoint, it makes sense, providing you have the room and from a personal standpoint, it wouldn't make me happy——as it will increase my commuting time on those days I head for the office, and I'll also increase my commuting expense.

"Well, you would commute ——wouldn't you?"

So now with the ball in my court I responded, "I would until I got sick of it—and then I'd probably tell you to shove it"!

He quickly smiled and as quickly, the smile was gone.

Didn't take only a couple days, I was notified the Boston office would move and that means instead of commuting 30 miles, I'm going to be commuting 45 miles and —20 miles of it will be on Route 128. Three solid lanes of traffic in that extra 20 miles, both ways. This will add up to an extra 30 minutes each way each day I go to Andover. At night, coming home, it looks just like a river of lights coming at you!

I endured this well into 1972. During that time, Dasa had sold the CTI inventory of 360 Computers —about 20 million dollars, and this brought quite a few of my field technicians into the office with questions about what was happening. With that transaction, a huge crack within (Boston) CTI developed. The guys got quite spooked about their future——— I don't wonder—so did I!

Six months later, the same VP called me up into his office and said, "I understand you're selling Real Estate—care to tell me what's going on"?

So, I told him I was ——on weekends, however it wasn't cutting into my CTI responsibilities—everything in my office was up to date with no ends open!

"Well, I don't like it —I don't want an avocation turning into a vocation, So I'll expect you will not spending any time in the future selling Real Estate, understand?"

So, as I stood in front of his desk, I replied, "Remember, when I told you I would commute until I got sick of it?"—— He nodded.

I continued, "I'm sick of it ——Shove it!!"

Now, before anyone thinks this was stupid—I had talked with Bob Reynolds about the full time job in the Real Estate Office—I had talked with Bunny over the past few months —I could tell this operation was coming unglued, the joy, the excitement, the fun to offset the occasional grind was disappearing. Actually, I'm very interested in having good people, good atmosphere, a challenge——some enjoyment and—naturally compensation within reason to what is expected from me. Take away one or more of these items lessens my desire to stay there. And now—I truly feel my freedom along with other attributes at CTI were disappearing——so I guessed I would also!

One reason we bought the house where we did, was the 'people' action, all the companies, the business climate in the general area. And the employment possibilities with all the companies around here.

SALES MANAGER—RENCO REALTY

Near the end of 1972, I made the move into real estate on a full time basis. The Northboro-Westboro area was not just warm, but hot and getting hotter with respect to houses selling.

A typical split entry ranch in Westboro was then selling for about the mid forties. In Northboro, the newest and most popular subdivision was known as Pine Knoll, offering houses in the mid forties also. The office had a tough time getting listings in that sub division, but we had access through a co-broke arrangement, so we weren't excluded.

Also by now, I was starting to get my feet wet in the commercial industrial part of real estate and in doing this, I had to get acquainted with industrial parks in Framingham, Hopkinton and Worcester areas. This was different and could yield a spike in income from a lease renewal when the initial term expired—if the tenant renewed for an additional term.

However, residential sales is where the meal ticket is still earned. So, I joined many others in showing house listings whether they were our own or someone else's. Real Estate sales was a good job for either Mothers or Housewives as they could work the flexibility into their routine. They weren't generally the 'breadwinner' ——a sale for them was extra money for the household. They could go for weeks and if a sale wasn't made— most still had a way to eat. But, there were many as the 'bread-winner' and naturally needed the income.

It was my hope to ultimately tie in with some builder, develop a strong relationship and not only act as a 'sales house', but also offer other services beyond just sales—but this takes time and lots of it.

In the months that followed, the owner wanted me to assume the capacity of Sales Manager, to which I was reluctant——but after talking with Jack Ellis and other members of the sales staff— I agreed to do it, especially after my 'terms' with regard to pay was changed enough to help follow up sales 'made by others'. Part of my responsibilities was to track all sales, help get sales guided through Attorney's Offices, locating financing with local banks and in all cases help provide effort and assistance to prevent a sale from coming unglued!

In this geographic area, part of this tracking responsibility would be, to repeat,— follow up with any seller's attorney. And which in a couple of cases, did not elevate my admiration for some members of that profession.

One office I called and the attorney asked me if I hadn't called with regard to a specific sale about 2 weeks previous and after I answered in the affirmative—I was told if I called again— when that specific file came to the top for action—he would just place it on the bottom and I would have to wait for it to rise to the top again, so don't bother him again!! 'Nice Guy'— so with that I called the seller and relayed 'his attorney's' instruction to me which covered me for any slow future action on a title search and deed prep on his property! I couldn't do much for the buyer. BUT—I did do a favor to future buyers in the way of a caution about his 'habits'!!(At times, this is a two way street!)

The Law office upstairs of Robert Reynolds was shared by Robert Gallagher—the two of them were a team. Also, Bob Gallagher was a member of the committee under the State's

Attorney General Consumer Protection Division and had jurisdiction for resolving any consumer complaint NOT resolved at the town level.

That office did real estate transfers, large and small legal discrepancies and even cases requiring the County Court with a full fledged trial.

So —the Real Estate office could sell 'the' house, the law offices could provide any legal services such as title search—deed prep etc. for the customer and then the insurance office could provide a Homeowners Policy (if the customer should choose these services). Couple that with the location—right on Route 9 where traffic was heavy, and many other businesses such as—— a large and well known Chinese Restaurant (The Honolulu), gas stations, Harry's Diner and Harry's Two, Chevrolet Dealership, golf driving range, a large Shopping Center—with Super Market and satellite stores, a couple of banks, car wash and about a half mile to the west, a large Colonial house presently used as an antique retail sales——only now, it had closed as the owner moved his business to Sandwich, on Cape Cod. This property now had my attention.

So I chased down the owner through the Westboro Tax Assessor's Office gaining his address and telephone and when I hung up, I had a listing on the property, and one which I'll come back to.

This property had been on the market for 8 or 10 months when I came to Renco full time. It was offered by the Dorothy Hickox Real Estate Office in Westboro—a long time business, much larger than Renco, but one which I very much respected.

Also, in this approximate period of time, Bob Reynolds called me upstairs and then proceeded to talk about some land a client had authorized Renco Realty to put on the market. This was Commercial land, right at the intersection of Route 9 and I-495. It was part of a large family holdings—had a humongous Colonial house on it, was about 8 acres and a choice piece of land.

Being right across the Interstate (495), and right in the lap of Data General, I soon was presenting this parcel to Data General. They were interested and an offer of 475,000 dollars was made against the asking price of 500,000 dollars——and as hard as I tried—I couldn't get a compromise —so it died. Not all deals were easy in 1972—even though many were made!

It WAS sold —maybe over a year later, some speculator from Texas bought it and over time a fairly large stainless steel office building was constructed after the big house was moved. This land became smack in the middle of numerous choice buildings. Nice try!!!!

BERGSON'S ICE CREAM SHOPS

Now that I had the listing on this big Colonial house on Route 9—what do I do with it? It was commercially zoned with a LONG frontage on the highway, there had to be someone that could be interested in this unique property.

One night about 3 AM —I woke from a sound sleep with the idea that Yield House in Conway New Hampshire might be interested —after all, the house was tuned to displaying antiques—wouldn't take much modification for it to display Yield House products, which were pine, some replicas.

The next day I called Yield House and ended up talking with the President and yes—they were considering a retail store someplace, their first one, and this location could be just what they wanted. He and others came and reviewed the property and it looked ideal. Less than a week later, the President called to tell me, they weren't going to continue—their business was expanding and they had to buy a mill that had just become available for manufacturing—so that died!

Then ——then I was inspecting a manufacturing facility in Northboro housed in a steel prefab building when I ran into a gentleman looking it over as a location for the Headquarters for his restaurant chain. We spent quite a few minutes and then I told him I had a location on Route 9 and he said the price was too high —knowing the property. I had the property listed at considerably less than that ——NOW he wanted to see it. He and his partner looked it over and we spent the rest of the day traveling to Sandwich to present the owner with the offer to purchase. It was accepted, as was an option presented to them for an adjoining parcel of land.

Wells Of Renco Brokers $110,000 Site To Bergson

WESTBORO, MASS. - The Clifford Hanson House and one acre of land on Rte. 9 has recently been sold.

Bergson Ice Cream and Food Shoppes of Needham purchased the property for conversion to its headquarters offices.

The reported sale price was $110,000.

Conrad Wells of Renco Realty negotiated the sale.

Courtesy of Bankers and Tradesman Publication

This house, after considerable modification of installing a new kitchen, sprinkler system and a new cocktail lounge became a top class restaurant and the Headquarters for Bergson Ice Cream Shops. (Most of their other locations were in shopping malls in the central and eastern Massachusetts).

The next year, they exercised the option of buying the adjoining land fronting on Route 9 and built a Bergson's Sandwich and Ice Cream retail store. This was great —the work was done one year and the next year a sales commission is collected.

ROAD SERVICE FOR BUNNY

During cold weather—about 1972, Bunny had the VW sedan and on the way to Worcester, the 'bug' started to run erratically and shortly ground to a halt. She was on I-290 at the time and had JoAnne and Lisa with her.

As she stood by the road, in a very short time, a wrecker pulled up and asked if she was having trouble. She said she was, so he told her he would drop this car he was 'towing' and would come back to get the VW.

About 15 minutes he was back —hitched on and before he went west —turned and took the 3 of them home, about 4 miles, by going back east.

When I got home from Real Estate and using the sedan—I called the garage where it was towed and was told it would be ready the next day by noon.

The next day at noon, I found the garage somewhere in Worcester and not in the 'best' section. When I went in, the girl at the counter said the car was done but didn't know how much the bill was. So I suggested she give me the key and I would call to find out the bill and then send a check. In the garage, I raised the (back) engine flap to inspect the work done.

When I drove down my driveway in Northboro, the garage owner was waiting in the kitchen—much to my surprise—however, I was prepared to pay him for the service. When I came into the kitchen—he jumped verbally all over me for taking the car. Didn't seem to make much difference his 'girl' had given me the keys and allowed me to drive off. Then he said he fired her for her allowing me to drive off without paying. AND THEN, presented me with a bill for over 300 dollars —including 100 dollars for the towing.

And to which, I refused to pay that amount, stating the total was way too much for the repair. He said he spent all evening the night before, removing the carburetor and then disassembling it to clean it and to get rid of the water inside.

I knew that wasn't true—I specifically looked at the carburetor mounting nuts and the outside of the carburetor for appearance, I could see where he washed it down, but he had not removed the carburetor—I could tell by the marks. I didn't want him to work on the carburetor anyway—it was all right as it was and sitting in the heated garage over night certainly took care of any water that had frozen. A can of dry gas would push any residual water through.

(Also, at this time or just before the incident, I was on the committee of the Northboro Consumer Protection Committee and I did know how to handle myself. The committee was a legal 'arm' of the State Attorneys General Office.)

Regardless, in the kitchen he again tried to collect the repair amount.

I told him I would pay a reasonable amount and 300 dollars was NOT reasonable, especially in 1972 dollars.

So, at that point, he threatened to take me to court.

I replied "I look forward to the day!" And with that — he left.

The next day when I was at the Real Estate Office, I went upstairs and talked with (Attorney) Bob Gallagher about the incident. Bob was also the appointed Regional State Consumer Protection Attorney.

Bob asked the garage owners name and when I told him— he looked at his paperwork and then said he had a case coming up that very day about another consumer complaint dealing with that very garage owner! So he wrote down ALL the information about my incident and took that to court also!

When he came back from court, he told me the case was dropped except the charges of the tow truck driver, who was an independent operator and not an employee of the garage owner. So I agreed to pay the tow truck driver his charge— after all, he did bring Bunny and the girls home and he also stopped on the Interstate to inquire if she needed help.

I'll bet that garage owner wondered how Bob Gallagher ever got my case information so fast and then used it to question his honesty in court the very next day!

And, I'll bet from that day on —he thought twice about how much he charged!

TRANSPORTATION

When we moved to Northboro in 1967, we had to add a second car to the household which was a 1967 Dodge station wagon. Now in 1973 with me working full time in Real Estate —I really couldn't show a house using my Volkswagen 'Bug', so after talking it over, we went to a well established dealer in Worcester and after a time, we decided on a used 1972 Chrysler 4-door Sedan. This was quite a car and I really had to talk to myself to be convinced this was necessary. But, Bunny would use it primarily and weekends I would use it.

By now, I had succeeded in selling a few houses and through these real estate transactions and locating mortgage money, I did have an opportunity to get acquainted with a few banks such as WCIS (Worcester County Institution for Savings), Peoples Savings Bank (both in Worcester), Westboro Savings Bank, Worcester National Bank, and some key people in those banks.

So I went to the Auto Finance section of WCIS and made out the paperwork. I don't remember what the trade was, but it could have been either the VW or the Dodge Wagon, nor do I remember the numbers.

I do remember sitting at the desk of the Finance Manager and him turning down the sale transaction because the Chrysler was used. I wanted to stretch the time, which was beyond the maximum the bank would go on the financing. As I write this —I would not be uncomfortable in that circumstance, but not remembering the facts, I'll assume I was!

As I was rejected, one of the Vice Presidents walked by who knew me (I'll omit his name) and asked if there was a problem. He was told the circumstances, looked at the finance manager and told him to approve the financing——he would accept the responsibility, and then added —if this man gets in trouble——we're ALL in trouble!!! So, I got the financing!!!

I have NO IDEA how or why he knew that amount of my background— but I took it as a compliment and let it go at that!!!!

We kept that car for quite a few years—and what a car, big 440ci engine, with ALL bells and whistles. AND YES——I did pay it off!

Minor incident—— later about 1979, Bunny, Lisa and I were driving to Florida in that Chrysler and around midnight we were passing through New York City. We wanted Lisa to see the World Trade Center on the west side of Manhattan and close to Battery Park. I stopped right at the base of the Towers—it was cold out and naturally dark (at midnight) when I smelled hot wires and a little smoke around the driver's door. In one BIG hurry, I had to unhook the battery and then pin down an electrical short in the driver's door window——we dam near lost that car right on the street!! However, we found the problem and eliminated it——lucky!!!!

SMALL HOUSE—GOOD SALE

I had a woman come into the office one day, and after the usual get acquainted discussion, we decided she should see a small house in Westboro on Milk Street. This was a contemporary Ranch with a carport, right near a shopping center and an intersection on Route 9. It was an ideal location for her, as she was in sales of some type and spent considerable time on the road.

I had just come back from Randolph Center, Vt., a couple of days before. We had a trailer and had spent two weeks at Lake Champagne in the central Vermont area. My wife was constantly reminding me to remove my shoes to let the feet breathe.

They did all right—— I sat out doors —read more than one paper and let the sun work on them, and before I knew what was happening—they had swelled up so big, I couldn't get any shoes on—even sandals!!

So now here I am, showing this very stunning customer a house with a suit on, necktie and a very business like presentation——barefoot!!! Now I know what an idiot feels like!?!

However, it turned out all right—she liked the house, she was qualified to buy it, and buy it she did!!!

CONVERT STEAM TO HOT WATER HEAT

The house we were living in, on Solomon Pond Road (and on the Pond), was originally a summer cottage. Sometime between 1900 (or before) and when Bunny and I bought it in 1967, it had been converted to a year round residence. A residence converted and a poor job at that. There was no insulation anywhere, not even in the attic and as I worked on remodeling a room, one of the items I did was to install insulation.

One very noticeable item of poor quality, was the heating system. It was steam heat with a boiler about the size of my Volkswagen and it took forever to get any heat out of it. During the winter, if the thermostat was turned up 2 or 3 degrees— it took a good half hour for the radiators to start whistling. And, this meant the oil burner was taking an equal length of time drinking fuel oil. I concede oil was cheaper in the late 1960's but costs and wages were still relative.

So in 1974 after talking with my brother-in-law Lindy, who was a fuel dealer and now owned Randolph Coal and Oil Co. in Vermont, I decided to convert the steam system to forced hot water—2 zones.

He came down one weekend, and the first chore that had to be done was to use a sledge hammer and break the many cast iron pipes in back of the boiler. This is where the steam condenses and is not necessary on a hot water system. I think Lindy was a little hesitant to break that 'loop'—this would be the point of no return. So to unburden him of any hesitation— I did one good swing and that produced a couple of pieces of cast iron, which meant we're now on the way!!

During the years I had spent remodeling rooms, all the baseboard radiation was connected and the pipes installed to the boiler location. This was a chore in itself. However, I kind of like challenges like those—think about it—plan it and then DO IT!

We installed the two zone control valves, the circulator pumps, a couple of controls—new thermostats and in short, hooked up the electric controls. I have to admit, the control 'hookups' required some study and I WAS grateful when we fired it up, we heard a normal burner sound instead of an explosion! We really had to make this thing work——couldn't go back to steam again.

It did work and I have to say there was no comparison between the types of heat. To me —I like hot water heat—— good steady full surrounding heat with no noticeable temperature fluctuations.

Lindy and I always seemed to have a good working relationship—and we always seemed to have some fun doing the work and then when it's done ——you do have a feeling of satisfaction which naturally is enhanced by the money saved. Don't conclude we didn't make mistakes—we did, but we still had fun. BIG JOB DONE!

HALF BATH FINISHED

When the half bath was planned near the kitchen, I asked a plumber I had got acquainted with while I was selling real estate to give me a quote on installing the drain pipe. He was working on a house we had 'listed'—and I felt he would give me a fair and reasonable price. So, later he came to the house— looked it over and then came up with a price of 1000 dollars to do the work.

Now—I didn't expect him to work for nothing and maybe to him, the price was reasonable. However, it didn't seem reasonable to me, so I excused him with the— 'I'll think about it'!

Lindy said for me to get the pipe fittings and he would come down and bring his Prest-O-Lite torch.

At this point in time, the Prest-O-Lite torch would be used for melting lead. And that indicates we're using cast iron pipe joined together. After the pipe is cut to length—the joint is filled with lead (in liquid form), and if the pipe is horizontal— a tinker's dam (a round non flammable rope like item) is used to keep the lead from running out so it can solidify.

Then the lead is tamped to compress it which will prevent leakage. It would still take a couple of years before we will see plastic drain pipe and fittings joined together easily by rubber couplings and stainless steel hose type clamps.

Talk about mistakes——we installed the pipe fittings and then found we couldn't get the last piece of pipe in place—

luckily, we noticed this before the joints were leaded——so we had to tear it out —and then reinstall it with a different sequence tactic!

Less than a month after the plumber's quote—it was done and at a cost of 25% from the quote from Joe, the plumber!

REAL ESTATE FAX

While I was working in the business of Real Estate, I noticed a lot of business came from the transfer of employees and for companies based in the Central Mass. area.

Many employees were transferred to this location from distances short and long. Some came from California while others came from any other state, there was no pattern and aside from California, no other state predominated.

Real Estate Offices around here, that had been around for years and those firmly established were picking up potential buyers referred from 'out of town' corporations. And now, there was more than one specializing in people being transferred, even to the extent of buying the house of a transferred employee and then putting that house on the market to sell OR offering a house in a different location to prospective buyers.

It was not uncommon for one of these companies to mail a photo and a listing sheet to designated RE Brokers, and/or Realtor Offices. Of course, this took time.

So let's talk about a prospective buyer coming into 'our' area. I felt it would be beneficial to 'send' about a half dozen listings and either separate photos, if the listing sheet didn't show the actual house. This would give our office a jump on the competition before the employee ever came here physically and would also offer a preview and samplings of properties for review for general prices etc.

Within a distance of one half mile, was a company called Alden Research, actually at the intersection of I-495 and Route 9. Alden had produced a Thermo Fax machine which could connect geographic points via telephone connections to do this application——with the exception of the photos.

I went to Alden Research and laid this idea to a man I was referred to and over the next few days we saw this application come to life. I had made up a couple of listings containing a house on each and could see this work there in Westboro. The machines they produced used Thermal Paper and the receiving machine actually burned the information into a special paper——these were used by the National Weather Service to transmit weather isobars to newspapers for printing weather forecasts, apparently popular at that time.

Unfortunately, technology at that time, wasn't advanced to the point where good, or rather acceptable quality was good enough—so not wishing to turn my time into a wild goose chase, I walked away from this application.

In the future, the computer jet printer, or a laser printer, either will work in a superb manner and would be known only as a fax, without the thermal. That's due to the fact, special paper is not now necessary—plain paper works like a charm!!!

INTRODUCTION TO A ROOT CANAL

In 1974 while I was at Renco Realty, I was having pain from a tooth and went to a dentist. I don't remember that I had a full time dentist—hadn't been in the area long enough and hadn't had any problems necessary to become pals with a dentist.

He looked into the mouth, did a couple of solos and then said he had an acquaintance he wanted me to go to Norwood (Ma.), which was a good 60 miles away. Would I go? —if so, he would make an appointment.

So on the day arranged, I traveled to Norwood and this endodontist came up with the fact I needed a root canal. Being 1974, an 'endodontist' wasn't a common profession in comparison with 10 years later. He explained what one was, that it would require 5 trips back to him and cost 500 dollars! Set back by this batch of whatever——naturally the 500 dollar tune stopped me cold. I said I would think about it.

When I went back to Renco—one of the Real Estate sales gals, Annette Ellis insisted I go to Tufts Dental School in Boston ——what ever the trouble— it could be taken care of there. And then she called—made an emergency appointment and in I went. Well, that's quite a trip, and to shorten this—I was assigned a student who took me to the 'endo' lab on Harrison

Ave. There I was seated in one of 23 chairs. He bypassed the usual checkin for I was really in pain now. Part of the procedure was to be fitted with a rubber 'dam' to isolate the bad tooth with a clamp on the tooth and a 3 inch rubber membrane, which covered part of my face. Then he had to get the instructor to inspect and approve before continuing.

When the instructor came and looked this over ——I could see it was the endodontist I visited in Norwood! I don't believe he recognized me!

To finish, this student performed the root canal and he did it without any pain. It worked out fine, but with the 3 or 4 trips and at cost of only 25 dollars total!! Of course, I did have to go to Boston, pay tolls and parking, but this started a long 'partnership' with Tufts which lasted for over 20 years.

OPEN MOUTH——STICK FOOT IN

About 1974, I happened to be in the Real Estate Office when a car drove up (and almost through the window). A woman got out and came through the door. In the car, I could see at least 4 heads and maybe five bobbing around— difficult to tell being chilly outside with all the windows covered with finger and hand prints, but by now, she was in front of me.

"What you got for a house in Northboro or Westboro for up to 25,000 dollars?" she asked.

So I replied, "Only one I know of is a Ranch in Northboro— brand new, really isn't quite finished yet, with a price of 24,999".

"OK, she answered——anything in Shrewsbury?"

So I reached for the MLS book of listings——and the reason I took the MLS book was that we at Renco Realty didn't have one listing in Shrewsbury at the time. BUT—I did know there was one house, (listed by another office) and as I thumbed through the pages trying to locate it and making small talk simultaneously ——I found it and as I laid the book on the desk open to the house I wanted, I stated—— "But, I don't think you want this one—it's a MESS, A TOTAL MESS!"

She looked at the book and said, "THAT'S MY HOUSE!!"

Needless to say, for a couple seconds, it was difficult to say anything with my foot sticking in my mouth!

Like a flash—I came back with the fact, the lawn needed mowing, the yard needed to be picked up—to get rid of the trash, gather up the toys etc. so it at least looks presentable in a picture!

With that, she tamed down and agreed maybe these should be done, then wanted to know if she could drive by the Northboro Ranch to see its location. The fact it was an exclusive listing with Renco I agreed, and told her where it was and off she went and as she walked toward the car —all the heads were still bobbing up and down!

Now strange as it may sound—I sold that new Ranch in Northboro to her, then I got the listing on her house in Shrewsbury and to top things off—I also sold her house in Shrewsbury to a friend if mine. It was a great little house, one and a half story Cape, hot water heat with cast iron baseboard radiation and also had a fireplaced living room—all for 22,000 dollars!

He cleaned it up, fixed it up —new kitchen, lot of cosmetic work etc, and he had a great starter house!

IMPORTANT COMMODITY GETS SCARCE

Everything seemed to be progressing quite nicely, listings were becoming more common, the sales staff had increased.

Annette Ellis, Ellen Davis, Jack Ellis and myself had expanded the operation. Two others were expected to come aboard shortly. We also had an office gal, Connie, who now handled the phones, wrote a lot of the ads and greeted customers.

Near the end of 1974, all this action suddenly stopped. I couldn't find any mortgage money to finance house sales with.

Finance money just dried up. I know that sounds impossible, but it happened and for what reason, I don't remember. Today or later, I probably would know and why—but whatever the reason, I don't recall now.

Anyone that had been in the business long enough to be 'established' with some healthy size of bank account could sit tight and this will probably pass, but newcomers such as Renco AND myself, this was a death knell!

There was also a gas shortage here at the same time and either one of these was bad enough, let alone having a double 'Whammy'.

I had three other people in my family dependent on me and I, along with Jack and Al said "Sayonara".

Dozens of Real Estate Brokers, Salesmen and Saleswomen fled the business. The only ones that 'weathered the storm' were the well established, or as the two gals at Renco were supplementing the family income, with the husbands established as the 'breadwinner'.

And this was typical of the many Real Estate offices in the area. They all were thinned out considerably.

INCIDENTS WITH BERT

A few topics back —I had an explanation about telephone operators which reminded me of my father in law —Bert— answering the phone in our apartment-(which was before dial phones) shortly after we were married in 1953. Back then— the operator would help you call a telephone number or whatever else it took to get a call completed. As Bert was in Bunny's and my apartment, and the phone rang—Bert answered it and I was close enough to hear the operator say, "Long distance from New York." To which Bert said, "Your dam right —it is!" And hung up!!

Another incident with Bert and in this apartment. Bert didn't like saying Good Bye, so as he was leaving for Florida he realized he left his glasses in the apartment, so at 4 in the morning he entered the apartment to get his glasses and then was on his way.

One problem——Tarzan, our Collie was there also and as soon as that door opened there was such a commotion in the kitchen. While Tarz wouldn't bite or draw blood—there was enough noise and action in the kitchen so the whole block must have wondered what was going on!

NO WAY was Tarz going to let ANYONE in that apartment— not with both Bunny and I asleep! BERT didn't try that again!

Bunny's Mother, Dolly wasn't appreciative of Bert's she-nanigans, and in many cases was quite cool to him and quite noticeable as we sat at an outside picnic table at Barb and Lindy's house at some family get together. The Wells, the Lindquists along with Dolly and Bert.

As usual, Bert had a mug of beer in front of him and the conversation came around to a bottle of Pelton's Homemade Horseradish sitting on the table. Now—take my word for it—Pelton's Horseradish was so powerful' I've actually seen Bill Pelton wear a gas mask while he ground it!

Anyway, Bert was always a showoff and in this case—it was his plan to take a teaspoon of horseradish in his mouth (which AFFECTS everything from the neck up)—then spit it out and neutralize —BUT as he took the spoon in his mouth, his ex-wife reached out —took that mug of beer and THREW the contents on the ground!! This left Bert with nothing to cool that horseradish down and we thought he would pass out right there! Someone got a glass of something to drink and he SLOWLY came back down to earth!

We laugh about it now—but it was scary for a few moments!

Bert had a great tendency to lean toward being accident prone—and when I worked with him, I would be doubly on guard to prevent a 'hurt' on my own behalf.

When you approached the house on Solomon Pond Rd. in Northboro down the long drive, there was a tree, a weeping willow tree about 12 feet high, in the very small yard we had. One summer when Bert was visiting from Florida——I had mentioned we were going to get rid of that tree—it was grow-ing too fast and always made a messy yard.

So—one day when I came home from work —the tree was gone!! Truthfully, it pleased me it was gone and tree removal around the late 1960's was not a problem—however, when I went in the house, Bunny was wearing an arm sling and when asked what happened—— Bert came in the house earlier and asked Bunny to help him for a few moments. He had dug around the tree and was going to pull it out with his truck. He wanted her to do something in the way of help getting the tree broken from the roots.   When it broke free——her arm was broken! I'm sure he felt bad, but Bunny had a terrible time trying to sleep—the break was very different and for days , she was in pain—big time!!!

One more———

Barb and Lindy in 1974, took a trip 'out west' and as a gesture, asked Bert to go along. I believe they had an Avion trailer at this time and without going into detail about how— and how much comedy Bert added to the trip—Lindy got a charge out of this.———

They had stopped at a combination gas station, convenience store, gift shop and meat counter. As Barb and he were looking down in the meat display case and edging along———at the end of the display case—Lindy felt a clerk was standing there to assist and without looking up—Lindy asked a question, then looked up. Behind the counter was Bert—white apron and all ready to custom cut or assist with the order!!! Naturally, Lindy was surprised to see this—but apparently, meat counter help there was scarce—didn't bother Bert to go around the case and then (being experienced as a butcher) proceeded to prepare the order!.

When they all went to the register up front—I think the owner asked Bert if he wanted a job!!

───────── FLASHBACK ─────────

PIERCE'S GARAGE——TEWKSBURY'S STORE

When I was about 8-10 years old and old enough to leave the property lines of my parents house, one of the nearby places I often visited was Pierce's Garage, on Main Street. This building was midway on Main Street hill.

It was a cement block building—but not the cement blocks that are so common—this was a cement block that had a molded face, not a typical flat faced block. It was constructed so a ramp went slightly up into the building from Main St., and on each side was a room about 14 feet square. The one on the left was the office and on the other side of the ramp was a room of equal size for parts.

Under the garage was a large sized space where about 10 or 12 cars could be parked. The entrance was in back of a small building which actually was on Weston Street and at that time was a Gas Station selling Gulf gas. Chet Pierce Sr., operated the gas station which included a canopy over the 2 gas pumps. This was about 1936—the garage was operated with his son, Chester (Jr.) better known as 'Dud'.

Up to this time, Chet (Sr.) and family lived in the big house on Main Street nearly across from the hospital, called Mari Castle. And, to digress for a moment—Mari Castle was built as the home of Colonel Chandler—the same Chandler, the Music Hall is named after. Mari Castle was built sometime after 1869 and prior to 1888. It was a remarkable house in many ways and in the early forties, I had the opportunity to go inside more than once on my way to the cellar to deliver coal for Randolph Coal and Ice Co. My job was to keep the chute clear by 'mowing away' the coal.

Up to this time, Allen's Garage had a franchise and sold the Nash brand of automobile. It's my belief, George Allen sold the Nash from the 1920's to 1936 at which time he dropped the franchise and started selling Studebaker cars and trucks. In making that move, Pierce's picked up the Nash franchise.

'Dud' occupied the office in the garage and with him at the time was Earl Akey who must have been a bookkeeper.

My young age allowed me to be impressionable and I liked to watch various procedures of getting cars inspected—brakes, horn, lights etc, and at times produced an abundance of 'traffic'. 'Dud' used to assist with bulb replacements, verifying the registration information, applying the sticker etc. During one procedure, someone provided an excellent and apparently loud example of flatulence and with no hesitation 'Dud' called out, "Horn works—try the lights!!"

In the garage, the chief mechanic was Glen Allen assisted by Frank Lamb.

It must have been a difficult job for both Glen and Frank——auto repairing in those days was totally different from what it now is. While cars were much simpler. even 'simple repairs were apt to be 'grunt jobs'. Examples——front end repairs and engine rebuilds were frequent, but no automatic transmissions, no electronics and no emission controls.

Up to about 1936, all popular cars had mechanical brakes which were seldom in balance. It was so common to see a car having the brakes applied and one wheel would lock up and as the tire shrieked—you always wondered how much the other 3 were contributing in the way of braking. Just imagine trying to get all 4 wheels to have equal amount of brakes with mechanical links to all wheels!!

By 1937, most cars came out with hydraulic brakes and then people would exclaim, 'Lord, I don't want to trust my life to little rubber hoses responsible for making my brakes work!!!"

BUT, the nice part of hydraulic brakes is that they automatically adjust so all wheels have the same amount of braking power. And, they were a big improvement.

The tools were scattered all over the place and the tools themselves were crude——no air impact wrenches, no air wrenches period, heavy and big floor jacks, lifts were scarce if existent, oil was changed using a creeper and one of those jacks— manually operated. Many places had pits, but Pierce's was on the second floor.

After the war, Allen Hancock had come to work as a salesman and by 1948 (maybe a year earlier), GMC and Pontiac had become the franchises. Pontiac in 1948, advertised "Built to last 100,000 miles!! THAT was unbelievable!! Nash had been dropped, which in time was to become American Motors.

Allen could easily qualify as one of the town's 'colorful' characters and displays of his 'dry humor' were frequent. He was a STRONG Pontiac man which I'm sure helped him to close some sales.

Dr.Bill Angell and his wife, Margaret always had a Buick for a family car.

So, one day Allen decided he would entice Margaret to buy a Pontiac. He called Margaret and set up an appointment as "he had a nice car he wanted her to try".

After she had driven it for a reasonable trial and they were sitting in the driveway back at the house, she said, "I'm very impressed with this car and I would like Bill to try it also".

As she said that, she looked at the steering wheel and asked Allen what that Indian insignia represented.

To which Allen said, "That stands for Pontiac".

She turned to him and said, "You mean this isn't a Buick?"

"No, it's a Pontiac!"

"Well, she said, "I don't want it if it is not a Buick!!"

I was in the garage when Allen came back. Here is where I'm sure I increased my vocabulary by some new and choice words I could use in the future!!(A good example of brand loyalty by Margaret, even if that wasn't how Allen referred to it!)

Also, after the war, the filling station had stopped selling gas (Chet Sr. passed away in 1937).

Reginald Tewksbury bought the building, removed the canopy and converted it to a 'corner store'. This was an early example of a fine small convenience store. He also kept the gas pumps and I recall him on many occasions pumping gas, (self serve was common—but still many people wanted their gas pumped by someone else).In addition to canned goods and staples, he had meats and would deliver.

Then he added a residence which was tied to the store where he and his wife Mildred not only lived, but brought up two girls—Jane and Sally. As they gained in years, the store became a family operation.

Much later in life, Sally married Murlan Cooper and after years 'on the floor', Reg and Mildred retired —Sally and 'Coop' took over the business. Jane married Ted Turner and they stayed in town also.

The store is now under the management of Mr. and Mrs. Ed Luce.

METROPOLITAN LIFE INSURANCE

While I was in thought about what to do for work, my niece's (Bonnie) husband Ted Peck, called me and wanted me to talk to him and his Branch Manager at Met Life. I did meet with the two of them, as a matter of fact, we had lunch at Bergsons (Main House) in Westboro.

Ted Anderson, the Branch Manager and Ted Peck, the Staff Manager explained the circumstances in becoming a Sales Rep for Metropolitan selling basically Life and Health Insurance. This didn't really light my fire, but they added that Met was entering the additional lines of Casualty Insurance— Homeowners, Renters, and Auto Insurance. This did create interest enough so I consented to work for Met Life and from the Lowell Office. Naturally this meant I would now be commuting to Lowell for training to start but I could contact prospective clients, regardless where they lived.

I was to be the first Sales Representative in the Lowell Office and in being so, I didn't have an 'Agency' assigned —clients that had previously purchased life insurance and now the 'Agent ' had either retired or left, so the policyholder had no one assigned and for which to contact. I— had to begin from ground zero and scratch for any and all prospective policyholders.

This was a rather unique arrangement——the pay. They would pay you 200 a week, 300 a week or 400 a week for a period of —I think, 60 days. During that 60 days you were trained on the products, the office and company procedures.

I had to take the Massachusetts State Test to become licensed as a Life, Health and Accident Sales Representative. This was pretty involved but I did pass the test. Failure would mean a retake. Of course, I had to travel to Boston one Saturday and be part of dozens and dozens of other test takers.

Coming back to the pay arrangement——during the time I was on salary—anything sold, the commission amount would go into a 'pool'. This pool would grow and grow with each sale. At the end of the 60 days, the salary pay stops and the pool amount is tapped and the first week pay is10% of the total in the pool. This becomes your gross pay——example, if the pool had risen to ——4000 dollars , your pay is 400 for the week. The pool is reduced now to 3600 dollars—next pay check is 360 dollars. Naturally, any sale commission is added to the pool amount——so it makes sense to keep that pool up, but if for any reason, you didn't sell anything that week, you still got a paycheck. Very unique, fair and acceptable way to get paid.

The bad news——if you sold a policy and after 3 months, the policyholder stops paying and drops the policy coverage— —you get charged back the commission amount for anything that lapses. So, now your pool can be riding high and in one week, can be a disaster if multiple policyholders 'go away.'

About six months later, I, and many others were in training again and this time it was for Casualty Sales—Auto, Homeowners and Renter's insurance. This took quite a few weeks and of course, this meant another trip to Boston for this test.

So now, I have another Massachusetts State License with which to sell Casualty Insurance in addition to Life, Accident and Health insurance.

MET LIFE INSURANCE AND JOHN ROGERS REAL ESTATE

After I had spent nearly a year with Met Life in Lowell, the mortgage money situation from the banks had been nearly resolved. I had a conversation with John Rogers in Northboro. He and his valuable 'partner', Eleanor Bullis, wanted me to come back into Real Estate and operate from their office In Northboro. John had bought an old house on East Main St. and remodeled it. They had two or three other sales people in the office and were now on the road to 'recovery' as money by now had become more plentiful.

This would work fine for me,—would give me an operating office, a phone to use and perhaps corral some RE business — also possibly some insurance leads which I always could use. Some buyers would be interested in mortgage insurance. So I started to use a desk at John Rogers Real Estate and I also tried to attend the office meetings.

In 1974, one hot item in Met was the IRA for retirement. This is a new Federally approved Retirement plan where individuals can build their own savings to be used for an addition to Social Security when a person retires, and in the meantime, by following guidelines, can deduct the premium amount from Federal taxes due. Other 'vehicles' could be used such as certain bank accounts ——but ALL had to be approved by the IRS, for an IRA.

At Met Life, we had an Endowment 65 product which was approved by the Internal Revenue Service and could be used as a 'vehicle' for an individual to buy toward an IRA. While very few permanent life insurance policies can be used toward retirement, this IRA approved E-65 allowed a greater amount of the premium to go toward savings with less for the insurance part. Also, the premium was tax deductible —so this made life more pleasant for me instead of 'pounding the pavement' to sell only life insurance.

For any individual that wasn't interested in the IRA E-65, Met also had annuities that could be used for an IRA——annuities were a totally different product, and had no reference to or contained any insurance. They also didn't pay but a piddling for a commission, which was bewildering.

Selling insurance had a tendency to give me mixed emotions—the hardest part of it for me was cold calling called prospecting. Ted Peck, the staff manager, could do this without an apparent bump in the road, but for months, I could easily sit there and just stare at the phone.

Finally, in analyzing it ——it's the apprehension of rejection that provides the lack of 'phone action', so with that, I developed a different outlook and attitude—then it became much easier!!

Even if became easier, that doesn't mean I was financially successful each week—as a matter of fact, at one point—I gave myself a stiff lecture while looking in the mirror one morning. I resolved that if I was going to do this for income —I was either going to do it with effort—full effort OR I wasn't going to continue. With that, I rolled up the sleeves and applied more AND better effort.

Simultaneously, Ted Peck had either come up with or learned of a sales tool in converting Family Plans that was very beneficial to the policyholder—equally beneficial to the spouse and a sensible sales tool for the Sales Rep. I'm not going into detail on how. One of the biggest obstacles to complete any sale is the lack of funding to pay for the additional premium. This sales tool eliminated that object by providing the income source—was totally legal and completed a win win situation for all, which is very rare!!

This helped me out and contributed to getting my feet back under me, however it is best used for sprucing up sales as it is quick and has a very low lapse rate. I had also built a presentation which yielded a closure rate of about 8 out of 10.

And while I now had defined benefits for myself and the family with MET, I still didn't have to spend much of my free time going to the Bank, for either a deposit OR withdrawal!

Since 1971, Bunny had a job as bookkeeper for a specialty welding company in Hudson, and about 1974 took a second part time bookkeeping job in Northboro for Regina Pierce at Pierce Oil and Gas on West Main Street.

But between the different sources of income we were keeping ourselves solvent and reasonably comfortable.

MOTEL PLANS

Our house was a 5 minute walk from I-290—a split highway that joins I-495 at one end, goes west and then does a gradual bend towards the south as it passes right through the heart of the city of Worcester (Ma.), and then joins near the Massachusetts Turnpike (I-90)—also Route 20 and Route 12 ——all in a small geographic area in the town of Auburn.

Back at the east end, the street we live on passes over I-290 and here we're pretty much in the country. The biggest and the only 'thing' there (at that time) was a gravel pit and within the gravel pit was a concrete mixing plant. The gravel operation is a short distance from the intersection of Solomon Pond Road and I-290.

In looking at the tax assessors maps in Northboro and Marlboro, one parcel of land unoccupied near the intersection was owned by E.L.Dauphinais Co in Grafton. So, one day I drove to Grafton and after entering the office, the man inside told me I would have to see Armand Dauphinais in the office 'out there'.

So as I entered the small office——there was one desk and Armand was at the desk. I told him I wanted to 'list' that piece of land —as I thought that would make an ideal location for a Motel. He thought for a few moments—the asked me," Who do you have in mind to approach for this motel?"

"I don't have anyone specifically——I would have to spend some time making some contacts"—I replied.

"So, why don't you build it and operate it yourself?"

Photo shows various and and many plans and details I had worked out over a period of 2 years. Photo by C. Wells.

With that, I gave him a quick answer, "I don't have the money to buy the land—let alone build a motel!'

"Why don't you come back——Saturday morning I'll be here and we can talk further about that plan," he asked.

So I was back there Saturday morning. Armand was in charge of the many trucks at this location, the 2 or 3 mechanics working on a couple of trucks in a separate garage, and the 'plant'—meaning the equipment present to 'make concrete'.

I also went back to this man for many Saturday morning conversations and during those visits found out there were nearly 30 trucks totally in this Grafton operation. Along with concrete plants in the Marlboro location, another in Charlton, one in Southbridge, one in Worcester, one in Nashua and another in Concord N.H.

Armand was also in charge of union negotiations, land purchases and (land) ownership. Armand's son Roger, did outside sales and some of the dispatching.

Armand's brother, Emil and his son Paul in the Grafton office, did the books and administrative work for the central Mass. locations.

Armand's brother, Al and son managed the concrete operations in Springfield and western Mass locations—one in Amherst, one in Northampton, one in Westfield, and the main office in Wilbraham (Springfield). Both New Hampshire locations were owned by the corporation, but operated by local management.

And to put a little more flavor in the operation——the company owned a multi store Shopping Center in Grafton and a large Shopping Center called Lincoln Plaza in Worcester containing an independent Supermarket, a theatre, R H White—a men's and women's clothing store, a Zaire Department store, a restaurant, Anderson Little men's clothing store, a bank and at least two dozen other small stores

Over the months to come, I would listen and be 'enlightened' by a series of stories and business transactions that I think I could write a book about——and most were very interesting. Armand and I got well acquainted and developed quite a strong friendship.

In the meantime, I started to develop a draft for the motel and then progressed to some actual and detailed blueprints for the building etc. It was a small building——54 rooms on two floors. Bunny and I would live on premises.

It was his plan to provide the land with his corporation and I as partners, then for a bank to provide financing for the building on owned land. I would operate it and make the mortgage payments on the package. This is where the 54 units had to be closely calculated to make this work. Here were many contributing factors I had to 'chase down', such as sections of the State Building Code, fire retardant construction materials and the big one—— one being that town water was available at the Solomon Pond Road over the I-290 overpass—which for a Motel was important—trouble was —it was Northboro water and to 'tap' into it for the Motel (which was in Marlboro)—required State Legislature approval!!! Town sewage was about 1000 feet away —here again I couldn't get across I-290 to reach it plus other factors, neither obstacle was insurmountable—just raised the cost —however, I could use well water and an on site septic system.

During the months I spent off and on going to Grafton Saturdays——I found out that he had a birthday coming up. Armand was the type of man that was always the giver. I had made a dozen plastic scale truck models as a hobby— and had attached a shelf over a bay window in my music room with these trucks on the shelf. Trailer trucks, dump trucks, log trucks and I had one scale model of a concrete truck —the exact make and model of the concrete trucks his Grafton company owned——Mack DM-600's. I painted it the colors of the Dauphinais trucks and then took it over one Saturday in a big bag—under cover. I had also made a clear plastic display case on a wooden base and anchored the truck to the base.

I brought it into the office and placed the brown bag on the desk———finally he asked what was in the bag and I told him it was a birthday present. When he pulled that case out with that truck in it ————he was flabbergasted— just couldn't believe he had been given this as a birthday gift.

Model of Mack concrete truck assembled, painted and cased as a replica of Dauphinais Concrete trucks, given to Armand Dauphinais as a birthday gift.
Photo By C. Wells.

I'll come back to the Motel and this truck in a later topic.

Each winter, he and his wife would go to Florida—near Ft Lauderdale where they owned a condo. I noticed that each spring when he returned, he would be 'slower' and I contributed it to being inactive for 2 or 3 months —he wasn't the type to be inactive—he liked action and lots of it.

THE AUTO TRAIN

In 1974, Bunny and I had planned a vacation for many months and the time is here to go. My belief is February of 1974, going into March. I can easily remember there was a gas shortage. Bunny was working two jobs—one was Welderon in Hudson, the other is a part time bookkeeping job for Pierce Gas and Oil in Northboro—this was a gas station, propane sales, auto repairs, auto inspection and Toro products, lawn mowers and snowblowers.

Bunny's car was filled with gas and the next day we headed out ——we had to be in Lorton, Va (just south of Washington, DC) by 2 PM the next day. This is the loading point for the Auto Train. Your car is loaded in one of numerous auto carrier cars and the passengers are in coaches.The ends of the auto carrier cars open and autos can be driven right through the cars on the lower and upper levels. After we arrived, it takes about 3 hours to load all the cars and the train leaves around 5 PM.

This was a unique and interesting experience. The farthest north the train could come at that time, was Lorton because the Vista Dome cars were too high for the bridges in the Northeast. The passenger cars were 'Pullman Style'—there were Private Rooms available but the Vista Dome cars had reclining chairs on the upper level. These chairs were very comfortable with foot rests and varying degree of recline—pillows were furnished. The roof of these cars were glass and you could watch the stars and sky at night. The girls had a double recliner at the front of one car with plenty of room for their gear. Bunny and I had singles, also with plenty of room. You bring an 'overnight bag' with you on the train.

There were two dining cars and you were assigned a car number and a choice for one of the three meal sittings. There were also 2 entertainment cars—with a lounge topside —even had a Hammond Organ and Player, while the lower level had a bar, sandwiches, snacks and a movie. The attendants were uniformed and the trip was a great relaxation. You go to sleep and by late morning you're in Sanford (just north of Orlando), Florida.

More than once, I sat in the lounge and looking toward the rear, you would swear that train was still in Lorton——each train I tried to count had about 48 cars!!

The Auto Train was a private corporation and operated on Amtrak rails on a lease basis. It did well for years and then ran into operational problems coupled with poor management and then quality went down ——finally Amtrak took it over and after a few years, has apparently raised the level to near original. For a while, you slept on bench type seats and the once or twice Bunny and I used it —I was disgusted. I feel the cars and the service by now, must be great again!

Once we 'detrained' in Sanford, we then had to really plan due to the gas shortage.

My daughter was working for Holiday Inn in Marlboro and through her job, we enjoyed the rooms of other Holiday Inns at discount —one being a brand new one in Winter Haven (Fl.), and others during our two week stay.

Naturally, we went to Disney World which had opened only a few months prior. I'm sure, Dad was more aghast there then either of the girls. I couldn't get over the construction of the buildings——the Monorail—the hotels— it was (and still is) a breathtaker. I just have to say Disney does things right—— the planning, the detail and the quality every where you look is certainly 'top shelf'!!

We had a couple of breaks with the gasoline shortage and while we spent considerable time waiting in slow moving lines—we DID get back to Sanford and in time to board the Auto Train for another enjoyable trip to Lorton ,Va.

The trip on Auto Train does cost slightly more than driving with Motel stays etc.—however there are so many variables, you would have to compare from a personal behalf—I liked the idea, once you're on the train—then all you do is ride!!!

Bunny and I used the Auto Train on more than one occasion—on one trip, we had returned from visiting Gordon and Sally Scribner in Melbourne and on the return trip, we stayed in a large Motel on Lake Monroe, in Sanford. This put us close to the train for the return trip to Lorton. That particular night ——it was cold —NO, it didn't get down to freezing, but it was close to it. The door on the room wouldn't close, but it left a large crack for the wind to blow in all night!! I'm sure the wind hit 60 to 70 (MPH), gusts all night!

To be honest, I was kind of glad to board the train the next day, just to get out of the breezes!

MET LIFE——STAFF MANAGER

Then I was promoted to Staff Manager, with the main responsibility being to hire and employ enough new Sales Reps to get the 'staff' total to at least 8 people.

Like most every other job in this country—it takes a while to get acquainted with the operation—paper work, forms, deadlines, pluses and minuses—you find out what you can do and what you can't do. There were some pretty stiff no no's and I can understand that.

Very soon after I was promoted, I had a couple of special meetings in Manchester,N.H. which required two nights, and two days of education. While there, I ran into my long time friend, Harold Rogers Jr. who was a Metropolitan Sales Manager from Brattleboro, Vt. We found enough time to get at least partially caught up on happenings since we had seen each other previously.

Any sales job or capacity generally requires a person to be aggressive, and a good life insurance sales person has to be aggressive to the extent of being offensive. At that time——I wasn't aggressive, it wasn't my nature and actually —I didn't like people who were aggressive. If you wanted to sell me something—show me the benefits, tell me the cost and allow me to make up my mind! And if the result was a 'NO'——no amount of hollering, yelling and putting your face right up to mine—— will convince me to change my mind!!

Right here, I can think of four instances (and all were close friends), where I could have displayed more effort in providing life insurance. Each of these was either a close friend, as I said, or I had a close working relationship with them. However, I didn't want to use my relationship as a 'closing tool'. If I had, and I repeat, IF I had, the spouse would be much better off financially today. AND, it makes me sad to say that.

Life insurance occupies a very peculiar spot in most peoples minds. It's not something you can wave in front of other people or friends in order to create even a little envy! It is a product you buy and in doing so agree to struggle and pay for over future years and in many cases, the many remaining years your earning power lasts. It 's not very rewarding when you buy it and all the time you own it —— you probably won't be around to see any of the rewards it does provide!

And that's all I'm going to say ——I don't want this to start sounding like a sales pitch!

So, let me tell you about one of the Sales Reps in Lowell— his name was Ernie, he wasn't on my staff. Ernie was the damnedest guy you could imagine. He might not come to the office until mid afternoon and when he did —would have 3-5 applications from all over the place. He had absolutely NO problem getting to talk to people—getting applications from people for life insurance!!

As time went on, I got better acquainted with him and I might add—I envied him and his ability to sell!! One time, I went with him even though I didn't need to—and after we finished an appointment——we came down from the third floor (without a sale) and he said, "Good, that gets that name off the list!" And I asked, "Why do you say good—I would say, darn (or something stronger)"!

He replied, " You aren't going to sell everybody you talk seriously to——you'll only sell about 3 out of 10, so—— get the ones that won't buy out of the way , then we'll get down to the ones that are going to buy!!!!" (That's how Ernie looked at rejection)!!

Ernie never ceased to amaze me —let me add a couple items about him—he came from Worcester Ma., and as a child hardly had any shoes as a kid—even in the winter. And he vowed when

144

The author at his desk after promotion to Staff Manager in Lowell, (MA) office of Met Life. Apparently somewhat bewildered in what is stared at! Note: dark hair and sideburns!! Photo origin unknown - date about 1976.

he got old enough to earn money—he was NEVER going to return to that quality of life. THERE'S HIS incentive!

One job before he came to Met Life, was selling baby furniture. One item was a combination high chair you could make into multiple objects useful for bringing up a baby. The biggest problem with these were getting them to the customer——so he used to carry a supply with him on the roof of his car — which by now was a Cadillac!!

In Boston, on Commonwealth Avenue was a car dealership, long and well established and known as Peter Fuller Cadillac. Had a large multi floor building and was probably the best known and the largest dealer in Boston.

One day way back in the early 1960's, Ernie had his phone ring and the voice asked if he was Ernie Mills, to which Ernie said "Yes and who are you?' He was told it was Peter Fuller and finally convinced Ernie it really was!! And Peter Fuller asked if Ernie had a violet colored Cadillac. Ernie said he did and to which Peter said he wanted to buy it! Ernie asked, "Why would you want to buy my Cadillac——you can get any and all you want—— and at wholesale?"

And to which Peter Fuller replied, "Because I want to get it off the road!! I've seen it on Route 128 and even had a couple customers—Cadillac owners— call me, offended at seeing a violet colored Cadillac looking like a truck going down the road hauling furniture on its roof —will you sell it to me?!!!?"

Ernie turned him down—liked that Cadillac—earned it and was going to keep it!!

Ernie was a hustler—always busy—he could get more done accidentally then most others can — on purpose!

1977— A YEAR FOR CHANGE

In 1974, my Mother was having problems with her health and now she was hospitalized with a serious medical problem——she had one kidney removed because of cancer and now I'm being told she can't stay by herself, that is, without someone who could oversee her and her daily routine. This created kind of a problem—I had tried to find someone locally to help out, without success and without going into details—— we just had a problem. I was the most likely to come up with an answer—being a Staff Manager at Met Life, I could leave periodically, but that certainly didn't mean every other day!

I inquired at the Gifford Memorial Hospital, which I think is the correct name for that time period, and here I was given a name of Merle Cannon. Merle was a registered nurse, and owned a place in Warren, Vt. called the Pitcher Inn. She had overnight guests, she served meals for temporary and permanent guests and, being a nurse was looking to oversee a couple of people in need of assisted living.

My wife, Bunny was tied up with our 2 daughters and was in Northboro—I had made a hurried trip north alone. With this circumstance, my sister in law—Barbara and I drove to Warren to check out the Pitcher Inn. She would have her own room, have use of the living room, sun room, kitchen at random—she could have her own TV even her own piano in a small room. All with a very reasonable and comfortable rate per month!!! This was a great answer to the present predicament—so Mother was moved to Warren as soon as she could make the trip.

Postcard showing the Pitcher Inn in Warren, Vt with the kitchen on the left end, next the sun porch directly behind the tree followed by the main house. Two unused buildings were converted to additional apartments—all connected on the rear. Postcard Courtesy of Russ White Enterprises, Rindge, N.H.

PITCHER INN—WARREN, VERMONT

While in Warren, she continued to have some medical problems, but not one of any seriousness for 3 to 4 years. During that time, Merle treated her like her own mother and became very devoted. If she was having a problem during the night, Merle would sleep on a cot right in her room which must have reduced some stress on behalf of my Mother. This was a situation in which I was helpless, even if I had been living in the area.

For Thanksgiving and Christmas get togethers, Lindy and I would travel from Randolph to Warren and get her—bring her to Randolph and then take her back to Pitcher Inn. The fact that this meant two trips over Roxbury Mountain in the winter could have certainly led to poor traveling, and most of the time it did, but for almost all the trips, there was only a couple where it was necessary to take the Interstate to Middlesex (Vt.), and then south on Route 100.

In 1977—she was again taken to Gifford Medical Center for complications of the kidney and the cancer situation and this time, she didn't return.

It wasn't many years after Mother passed—Merle Cannon also passed away — the date I can't give.

And, the Pitcher Inn had a fire sometime in the 1980's which not only destroyed the Main Street house, but also the 2 or 3 other buildings on Main St. which Merle had attached to the house. The buildings were originally stores, but were converted to guest rooms and in the rear, access was available so guests could go to the Main House and still be under cover. These structures were directly across the street from the well known Warren General Store.

PITCHER INN — REBUILT

The property sat dormant for a period of months — without a doubt, something was happening on the sidelines, but at some point in time, the equipment showed up and construction finally started. I have no idea who rebuilt the Pitcher Inn, but it WAS rebuilt and I might add, into a very distinctive Inn and eating place. Each room is unique in design, decorating and furnishings. It is now known amoung the elite as a quiet and private place to spend some time away from the photographers and news media. It also is known to support one of the best stocked wine cellars in the country along with food apparently prepared by well known and highly respected chefs.

If price is not a problem, and privacy is — try the Pitcher Inn.

MOTHER—AND HER WAYS

While this was a sad time —I can't help but look back and naturally remember some of the good times. As strict and precise as she was, she could also laugh at herself —poke fun at herself and 'break from the mold' enough to show a heck of a sense of humor. And I'll admit I probably have some of that humor, transferred to me AND for which, I am thankful. Her sense of humor certainly didn't lean toward the "Burley House 'style — "Heaven forbid" —or ANYTHING but the straight and narrow——Here's an example of a typical 'predicament'

Every time I came to visit (from Massachusetts), it wouldn't be long before she would tell about not sleeping nights—"Why!———I didn't sleep ALL night long"!! Long after this had become monotonous, I suggested she talk to the doctor about it on her next visit. Which she did AND to which he suggested she have a small glass of wine before she went to bed. WELL—this startled the church organ player—but she finally enticed someone to buy a bottle of wine from the Bethel State Liquor Store. NO WAY would she venture across the threshold of a place such as that!!

Here, I might add that she had an afternoon nap—every day at 3——NOT 2 —or 4——BUT 3 PM, she had a nap!!!

Well—she sampled that wine before she 'retired' at 9 PM.—and again the next night—and for 4 or 5 nights with no effect. Maybe —she figured —maybe she wasn't taking it early enough, so she started to take it a half hour earlier every 3 or 4 nights to establish the ideal working period.

NOW—I make another visit and in discussing this and when reaching this corrective step—I asked her what time she was now taking the sample and she replied, "2—in the afternoon!!!!!!" And then added she couldn't see where this wine did anything for her sleeping at night. So I asked her how the 3 PM nap was —— "OH, I have a wonderful nap"!!!

OR the trip she would take ———

She would drive to Framingham Ma., once, maybe twice a year and by herself to visit her brother, even into her seventies. So, one day we were talking about a trip and she said she had a terrible time going through Fitchburg (Ma.), "they, were always changing the way." I asked her how come —all you have to do is follow the Route 12 signs, (Yes,—its the same Route 12 that goes right through Randolph —How much simpler can you get?) "OH!—I don't follow the route signs"!

"So," I asked, "Why don't you follow the signs?" To which she replied, "I don't need to ——I KNOW the way"!!!!!

As a kid, I could get so irritated by her low amount of common sense, but somewhere along the line, I realized what she was trying to do was make me (and my sister) 'good people'.

If you have ever walked into an automobile parts store, perhaps you have noticed the various (and many) parts catalogs held in a counter display ——— I used to envision my Mother had a book just like those and these were the books of rules that I was getting indoctrinated to, as I grew up. There was a rule for everything——anything anyone ever did —there MUST have been a rule in that book!!

More than once as the three OR four of us entered a restaurant, a public building or a private home——if I had a hat or cap on,——as soon as I crossed the threshold, she would reach up, whip that hat (or cap) off and hand it to me by closed hand forcibly sticking it against my stomach, to which I always either coughed, winced or (both) and held my stomach in pain—— "Just a reminder —Take off your hat—It's just courteous!" (She WAS right—but I never had a chance!!)

NOW, **as a full fledged member of the old geezer club,** I look back—compare my up bringing in the world as I write this ——— I am, and will ever be, indebted to my parents (and especially to my Mother) for providing me with the guidance for this trip through life and equipping me with the fundamentals of how to cope, and handle so many of the circumstances I have already encountered and new ones I still may encounter in the future.

And, before I let go of this topic, she had to show us the new picnic table she had just bought and said. "Now you and the family can come up and we can have a picnic!

At the time, I was 34 years old with a wife and 2 children, so I though that a 'test' here would be fun (and appropriate especially at my age) so I said. "Well, Mother, I kind of like to have a beer at an outdoor picnic".

With that she said, "You can't sit at MY picnic table and have any beer"!! And she was dead serious!

MISHAP TO THE VALIANT

Part of the time I was working for Met Life in Lowell, I covered the ground with a 1964 Plymouth Valiant. This was the darndest car——it certainly wasn't a beauty BUT, this thing ran and ran and ran!

I had well over 150,000 miles on it and time and time again it always got me home, which generally was from 10 to 12PM, cold weather and all. It was a little tough on freeze plugs and over time I had to replace all three on the Slant six engine.

I used to get it serviced at Ray Braman's on Route 20 in Northboro—he and Jeff Congdon did good work and at a reasonable price. And occasionally, I did some work on it——they didn't mind and I always worked around their schedule so not to hinder them from earning an income.

There was one item about working around there I didn't like and that was the fact they were very careless about exhaust fumes. This became very noticeable when I was replacing the brakes on the Valiant. About half way through the repair, I noticed I was being affected—just how I don't remember but I struggled to finish the job which took about another hour. When I left I had a wicked headache and other symptoms. I laid in bed—couldn't move my eyes comfortably and I also couldn't move my head. I put a call into my Doctor who said if I didn't improve by ten o'clock I was going to the hospi-

1964 Plymouth Valiant as its condition and presentation is slipping as it has about 175,000 miles. Photo C. Wells about 1976.

tal. Fortunately, by ten o'clock I did improve——won't do that again. I enjoyed working on it up to this point, and had fun while there —apparently they were used to it——not me!!

One night, Lisa had taken the car and around ten, I got a phone call and she said the Westboro Fire Department was at the car parked at the Westmeadow Shopping Mall (in Westboro). She was upset —the car had a fire and she didn't know what to do. So I went to the Shopping Center to pick her up and look at the car.

Where all the wires come through the firewall—there was a large plug and this must have developed a short. The wiring under the dash started to smolder and before the battery was unhooked—all the wiring under the dash had 'cooked'!

Next day Lisa and I went to the car ——I jumped the ignition, got it started—so I drove it home.

Then she and I spent a few days —replacing all the dash wiring to the firewall plug. But it took some time using the correct size wire and also, using terminals on the wire ends. Nothing under the hood was hurt.

The Valiant ran for many months after that, not only for Lisa when she used it——but including many trips to Lowell and back for me—great car!

MET LIFE——PROGRESS

In 1977, my activities had changed once I was in the capacity of Staff Manager. I spent more time recruiting —looking for people to become members of my staff. I had hired a couple and progress was being made in that area.

I took a course called "Life Underwriters Training', which was taught by Ted Anderson, the District Sales Manager for Met in the Lowell Office. And I might add, he knew his 'stuff'. There were sales people from other Insurance companies such as Prudential and New York Life as well as Met Life. The course took eight or ten weeks and was held in Chelmsford. This covered how life insurance was used in business applications, estate planning and other stages of usage. To be honest, it was interesting and by now, I was running into circumstances where I needed the additional education.

Photo origin unknown

However, most nights, I didn't get home until at least 11 PM and during the day I was at a disadvantage in comparison to most of the sales people—they could go home sometime in the afternoon—I couldn't, it was too far and didn't make sense or economics to do it. But I would duck out of the office in early afternoon to gain a little 'quiet time'! So the days were quite long, but it was only 4 nights and 5 days a week.

And to back track slightly, we were now qualified and licensed to sell Casualty coverage's—Auto, Homeowners, and Renters in addition to Life, Health and Accident coverages. And now, most of my home sales calls were with a Staff Member (recruit) and helping him to become established.

The accompanying photo is yours truly teaching(?) a class of Lowell sales people in a room at a hotel near I-495——the subject of which now totally escapes me.

T M J—A HORROR SHOW

Three letters of the alphabet, why would those three letters spell—horror show'?? Well, there was a time in the 1970's, I couldn't have told you. But in 1977, I was about to find out.

This is another topic that may be deemed unnecessary—however if anyone one person reads this and is given enough information to gather the incentive to find some relief—my attempt here will be successful.

I had been going to Tuft's Dental School in Boston since 1974. I had been through the routine three month 'cleaning,' (numerous times), and which yielded a tooth that needed a filling.

This appointment was for work on that tooth and the 'new' dental student that had been assigned to me had nearly finished work when he put a carbon strip in and had me bite to show for correct tooth height. When asking me to bite and move my jaw to the right —I replied I couldn't do that, he then said move it to the left. Again, I said I couldn't do that either and then I added, "I'm more concerned why I can't move my jaw to either side than I am about you getting that tooth height correct"! That got his attention—so we got into a conversation about jaw and various symptoms.

When I told him what I had been experiencing for about 3 years and that Tylenol or Bufferin didn't reduce the pain —— now I really had his attention. The following symptoms are what I had been living with —and hoped someway I could find some way to relief:

1/ Headaches— from the neck up the back of the head, also tight muscles up the sides across the temples.

2/ Jaw 'clicking'

3/ Ringing in the ears (tinnitus)

4/ Equilibrium instability

And with that, he started making inquiries to various dental instructors and department heads to establish what the problem could be.

Soon he came back with a suggestion that I be given an appointment with Dr. Vincent Schaefer, a dentist that comes in from Cape Cod one day a week.

The appointment was made and at the given time, I was in the chair of his cubicle with him staring into my mouth.

He stopped, and then said he was sure I had Temporomandibular Joint Dysfunction————**TMD**. This is also designated

TMJ and is caused by the jaw joint. I had no idea how this joint could cause all this pain and grief.

So with that, he took a small electronic unit out of a case and sat it on the dental tray, then proceeded to apply three Gel Pads —one on each side of my face at the jaw joint and one on the back of my neck. He explained the joint had generated itself a position where the muscles are 'locked'. This is keeping the neck and head muscles in a false position and creating the side effects such as pain etc.

I had a plate in my mouth at the time, which was removed, then he tuned the electronic pulses to short bursts —one about every 2 seconds and suggested I read a magazine he gave me during the 60 minute session. **READ**? How can you read when your eyes blink so hard every 2 seconds they actually close??

After the time was up—he then mixed an acrylic material and adhered it to the plate —making me a spacer between the upper and lower teeth, so the jaw was limited to the correct amount of vertical travel, also to prevent the jaw from 'closing too tight' and thereby stretching the jaw muscles causing spasms and a 'lock'.

At this point—why am I taking this space to put this topic on paper? Because, while I was going through this predicament—-**very** few medical people knew what **TMJ** was, let alone what to do about it. **And**, here is the really strange part—even though this is a bone related problem, meaning the jawbone— —it's considered a dental problem by insurance companies and even the medical profession. To complicate it more, very few, **if any** dentists at that time, knew what could be done for treatment as a cure —or even how to talk about it.

I was lucky in finding this Dentist who basically was experimenting with **TMJ** and had this electronic unit to help him.

Another point—I found that experimenting with different pillows helped. As I sleep mostly on my side—I found that if I didn't allow the pillow to support the head below the ear might ease the resulting head and neck pain. This minimizes the possibility of having the jaw influenced to an 'unnatural' position.

My big point is—how many other people have a **TMJ** problem and are going crazy trying to find an answer——I wonder!!!

Some people have had surgery performed on the jaw pivot—
—but, that would be the last resort.

As this is being written, the subject has now become better
known and some dentists **NOW** can work on this topic. For
example, there is now a separate department for **TMJ** at Tufts
Dental School in Boston, and a place where confidence is given
to a **TMJ** patient that there is a good probability for relief.

After he had fitted these spacers to my 'plate', he said come
back in 2 weeks and let's see how you're doing.

Within 2 hours——2 hours—I felt an unbelievable decrease
in the pain—even the transition time was comfortable. Little
did I know what the future would bring, and for the moment
let's leave the **TMD** (dysfunction or disorder) subject.

KEVIN EATON

Being an autobiography, I haven't devoted much space or
time on any topic other than what has pertained to me, my
family or a topic some way connected to my family.

This topic strays from the usual and certainly is worthy to
be included. Back in Book—2, I devoted many pages to Clifford
Eaton and his parents while I was employed by them. Cliff and
Ann had 3 boys, Kevin, Brian, Jim and a daughter, Patty.

In December, 1977 Cliff had a few cattle and being this is
December, they were in a barn on the 'back road' between South
Royalton and Sharon (Vt.). As Cliff and his wife were going to
be gone for a few days, Kevin was taking care of the cattle.
One night he had finished his chores and headed south paral-
lel to the railroad tracks of the Central Vermont Railroad and
where he could cross the railroad tracks to reach the village of
Sharon.

This night, as he got in his truck and headed out , the
weather had been and still is snow, and lots of it——driving
and blinding snow with huge flakes. It had been snowing
heavily long before and during the time he spent in the barn
and by now, it was dark. Soon, he was nearing the RR crossing
near Sharon Village and as he approached the crossing, he took
the precaution of looking both ways and proceeded to cross
the tracks he had been driving parallel to. With absolutely no

warning, he was broad sided by one of CV locomotives, which was undoubtedly really moving—and with multiple Diesel units pulling dozens of freight cars. The number of locomotives really made no difference ——a broadside bunt by just one locomotive, let alone multiple units, is trouble—BIG TIME!

Before the train could stop, hundreds of yards were traveled, plowing and throwing snow and when it came to rest—— the truck was a mess and Kevin couldn't be found. Finally a policeman or trooper found him under the truck and buried in snow. The police checked him out and declared him gone. A short time later the South Royalton Rescue Squad arrived and one of the Rescue members recognized the truck, found the driver and as he frantically removed snow, Kevin opened his eyes, recognized a friend and said, "Hi, Paul"!

Kevin was taken to Dartmouth-Hitchcock Hospital in Hanover, N.H. Here, he was diagnosed as probably never to walk again and after weeks of recovery, arrangements were made in Colorado for specific physical rehabilitation for injuries of this type. During his stay in Hanover, Cliff daily massaged his legs and feet for weeks and weeks. Finally, one day, saw one toe twitch.

To end this true story, he was discharged from Hanover, and within a few months, walked and while I can't say he doesn't have any complications to his life, which he probably does, he at least lives and works reasonably normal, every day!!!!!!

RANDY—(MY NEPHEW), LOSES HIS BILLFOLD

Randy (Lindquist) likes to fish——as he says" A poor day at fishing is better than a good day at work". So when he had an opportunity to go salt water fishing off the coast of New Hampshire, he jumped at the chance. This IS a true story.

I don't recall ALL the particulars, but he was one of 8 or 10 people aboard a charter fishing boat. They left from Portsmouth N.H. and headed toward open ocean which would be about 10 miles off shore.

After they had reached a good location, they all started fishing. Someone had a good bite and shortly asked Randy for some assistance with the pole.

'Singing School' A Hit 30 Years Ago

By Miriam Herwig

One of the most outstanding hometown productions ever to draw talent from virtually all the community was presented nearly 30 years ago at Chandler Music Hall. Its noble fund raising purpose was to buy books and equipment for the Randolph Village School, which at that time housed the high school as well.

Randolph was bursting with talent in 1951, when the PTA presented an old-fashioned singing school on May 4.

According to the WRV Herald for that week, "It has been a long time since there has been a complete sell-out of tickets for a program at Chandler... but that was the case Friday... No tickets could be bought as early as Monday... and chairs were put in the back that accommodated a few anxious ones." Great credit was given Mrs. Henry Chase, "general director, script writer, chief inspiration, and

originator of the whole show."

The stage setting of blackboards, benches, teacher's desk and old-fashioned costumes gave the proper atmosphere, and Donald Hayes served as visiting singing master.

Names of prominent townspeople peppered the cast, which boasted a quartet of Drs. Wilmer Angell, John Blackmer, James Woodruff, and Ranson Tucker as the Tonsilettes.

Still fondly remembered are Bob Day's rendition of "Mother" and Gladys Wells' tap dancing and singing "I'm a lonely little petunia in an onion patch." Janet and Hugh Whitham rode a tandem bike as the chorus sang, "Bicycle Built for Two."

Rudy Day made a hilarious wife for school janitor, Red Dalton, and Rev. Leonard Pillsbury played the censoring preacher. And he might, with the Flora Dora Girls including Eleanor Drysdale, Della

Rogers, Theresa Fullam, Eleanor Hedding, Betty Rogers, Janet Whitham, and Virginia Hancock!

Specialty numbers and duets, solos and quartets followed each other to the delight of the audience, culminating in a skating scene as the "snow" fell and the chorus sang "Walking in a Winter Wonderland." "Snowballs" were thrown out to the audience under flickering colored lights, making a "very lovely finale," as the Herald stated, to one of Randolph's most memorable evenings.

It seems that everyone, parent or non-parent, was eager to help in some way - in the pit orchestra, as a stage manager, selling candy or tickets, if not in the large chorus itself.

Included in the cast, the orchestra and on the committees, besides those already mentioned, were: Myra Wood Adams, Elizabeth Barnes, Ina Boyden, Grace Stockfish, Alice Parker, Mildred Blackmer, Dora Tabor, Arthur Cheney, Wendell Smithers, Frank Howe, Merle Soule, David Cox, Homer Brown, Edward Rose, Robert Hancock, Wilmond Parker, Helen Savage, Gladys Bond, Lyndell Wood, Midge Howe, Eugenie Barcomb, Priscilla Ouimette, Dot Patch, Virginia Hancock, Phyllis Morrow, Lucille Bryant, Dot Sivret, Marguerite Waite, Ruth Milo, Ree Shapiro, Maud Dustin, Alice Angell, Harold Lary, Leo Paige, Bob Dustin, Cliff Patch, Clyde Esterbrook, Hugh Bovingdon, Leonard Slack, Dorothy Perry, Lem Leonard, Larry Leonard, John Lamson, Doris Bell, Mabel Leonard, Avis Murray, Abbie Mitchell, Jacqueline Smithers, Margaret Angell, Ruth Bovington, John Murray, Harold Baker, Henry Chase, Percy Rice, Philip Hodgdon, Elizabeth Cutting, and Billie Coffin.

PTA president Henry Chase was happy to report that the profits of $330 were used to purchase a jungle gym for the school year and $7.50 was given to each of the 10 rooms.

The show was such a resounding success that it was repeated with an audience of 600 on May 17. Later it was presented in Henniker, N.H., with a New Hampshire cast.

The photos that accompany this article were among many which were produced as publicity photos by Cliff Patch.

The "Old Fashioned Singing School" had been Randolph PTA's finest hour, and many a participant would confide that he hasn't had as much fun since. 5/7/80

Herald article about a Chandler Music Hall presentation in 1950. Courtesy Joan Gray / Freda Rye / Mim Herwig - Herald

Randy wrestled with the line and finally won out. As the 'catch' was brought along side the boat —Randy reached down either to net the catch OR to grab 'it' and the line together.

As he bent over, his billfold in his shirt pocket fell out——he stopped what he was doing to watch——watch as it slid under and out of sight in the big, broad Atlantic!!!!!

I would bet that he probably had dungarees on —tight dungarees and that's why the billfold was in the shirt pocket.

I don't think he had much money in the billfold, but he did have the typical other items——credit card, drivers license etc. which now needs to be replaced AND which is more of a hassle than a problem.

Sometime about 5 years later, the phone rang at his parents house and the calling party was asking for Randy. This caller wanted to know if Randy had lost his billfold to which Randy replied, "Yes, I did lose it about 5 years ago in the Atlantic Ocean off Portsmouth, New Hampshire—why do you ask?"

The caller replied, "I was trolling in the Atlantic and from what you say, apparently in the same general location, and I pulled a billfold out with my hook stuck in it"!!!

They made an arrangement to meet so Randy could get his 'lost' billfold back and which also still contained some money along with all the other items!!!

NOW, think about this for a moment and then think of the odds of this happening————why didn't that billfold sink to the bottom?——why did a hook penetrate the billfold?—Why didn't the hook just glance off? —Why did the hook face the right way so it could penetrate the leather?

All these questions, but it really doesn't matter much— the billfold WAS retrieved and it WAS returned to Randy!!!!! AND, this story hit the newspapers, I guess way to the West Coast when it happened.

It was an interesting story at the time—still is!!!!

R & L WELDING

Bunny's employer Welderon, was having financial struggles like many small businesses. She had been a book-keeper for them starting about 1971. While the business was in Hudson (Ma.), it became necessary to change the name to R & L Welding Inc. I don't know the particulars and probably would skip over them even if I did know.

So here we are, operating under a new name and at this point let's explain that the 'R' stood for Roger, one owner and 'L' stood for Larry, the second owner.

Before you get bored and flip the page or skip to the next topic————

Even though this topic is about a specialty welding com-pany—— let's follow it together and while it may not tickle every reader's fancy—this to me was an interesting place, not only for the products, but also for the companies R & L made connections with.

In addition to Roger and Larry, another employee was John and one more was Roger.

These four were all welders and I can imagine you immediately think of sparks—LOTS of spark flying—old cars or junk cars lying around and probably a guard dog in a pen in back of the building!?!

Naturally over a period of time, I slowly got acquainted with these guys and on the sidelines, watched them slug, watched them try to stay solvent!

What I did know was these four ALL knew how to weld tool steel—which was known nationally as an item TOTALLY IMPOSSIBLE TO BE WELDED!!!

I don't know how they did it and no one else did—they kept the process under guard.

Sometime around 1973, a building on West Main St. in Northboro owned by a friend of mine, Pat Zecco— had extra space available in a new pre-engineered steel building he had just had built———it was just the size that R&L could use—so they moved to Northboro. This was a benefit for Bunny being closer etc.

ROGER——— he and his wife were renting a house in Berlin (Ma.).He was happy go lucky, witty as they come—always laughing, very extrovertive and seldom without a joke or a reason for someone to either laugh or chuckle!

When their only daughter got married—after a time lapse at the reception, Roger got enough 'courage fluid' into him to stand at the front of the hall and sang "Daddy's Little Girl' with the band, did a super job and there wasn't a dry eye in the hall!!

Within the time span R & L was at Zecco's— Roger and his wife took a vacation to Las Vegas. When he came back, he had done well, and shared a healthy portion of that luck with the other employees.

About one year later——went again, BUT, this time he lost and heavily——SO HEAVILY— when he got back to Northboro, he signed ALL his ownership over to Larry and John. Then left the area —lock, stock and barrel—you fill in the pieces!!!!

By now, John had become one of the best welders and was probably taught by Roger—but he could even weld stainless steel—aluminum both very difficult to weld. He also possessed the qualities to talk with the customers —price quotes etc.

Then shortly, Bunny noticed a big black sedan in the parking lot with 2 or 3 men sitting in it ———and they sat there off and on for a week. This was a little scary—nothing you could do, they were legal, that is as long as they didn't see Roger!! They kept a close eye on Bunny and occasionally followed her to the Post Office etc,—but it scared her and also gave me some apprehension! We never did see Roger again ——but had an inkling. So we'll leave that topic right there!!

LARRY———he was totally different. He was poor with people. But, Larry was a heck of a worker——if he felt any job was falling behind or more production was needed, he would weld even if it was 6AM Sunday morning or 10PM Wednesday night!

So they kept plugging along. THE PROBLEM now was that Larry was NOT a Salesman (Roger was). Larry was impatient and unpolished!!

In talking to the customer he had to convince them R & L could do the impossible of welding tool steel —dies, molds, broaches, face mills, end mills, special manufacturing tools etc. no one else could repair.

He too often lost —he was a welder not a salesman! He was happiest sitting out in the 'shop' looking through a welder's helmet with a barrel of pieces yet for him to work on. And he was very apt to be doing it in a pair of shorts, a 'T' shirt even in the middle of March!!!!

Then in 1977 while I was associated with John Rogers Real Estate, I heard about another building not far from Zecco's, and again on West Main St. —that would be available shortly. It was another pre-engineered steel building with three stalls previously used for auto repair. There was a house also on the property, both buildings directly across the street from the only mini shopping center in Northboro. This contained a supermarket and 4 or 5 other stores. AN IDEAL location, a commercial building and a house to bring in rental income. I knew the owner and asked for a listing on the property —— which I got and with a reasonable market price.

Here, I made a big mistake — I should have bought it and leased it to R & L. Why didn't I? I just didn't dare to gamble!!!!

Regardless, the owner was very cooperative and after a few negotiations, R & L ended up by leasing it for a year and then the title transferred in the second year.

For a few moments—we'll leave this topic but I'll be back to it.

STANFIELD M. GOULD - 1978

Stan was one of my closest friends—he should have been, we became acquainted at my age of about 11 or 12 and were very close, ever since.

So on June 6, 1978 when I received word that he had passed away I was really shocked——after all, at age 49 is NOT anything you suspect or even think about.

A review of his obituary extracted from the Herald (of Randolph, Vt.), provides this background that he had worked for Scribner's Store, Ken Manning Con-

STANFIELD M. GOULD

struction, Winslow's Office Supplies, Randolph Sports and Valley Equipment Sales.

He was married in October 1951 to Joan Rye — they had one daughter, Andrea, better known as Andy, both of which presently reside in Randolph. He had founded Gould's Trailer Sales and later owned and operated Gould's Trailer Park.

He had spent four years as a Vocational Instructor in the building trades in Randolph Vocational School System, had supervised the building of a Vo-Con home on Mound Street in Randolph and was finishing the Superintendent's Office's on Central St.—he had taught driver education classes.

Also active in organizing the White River Valley Ambulance—served as an EMT, and had organized the construction of the ambulance garage.

He was a Randolph policeman, a former fireman, was a deputy sheriff in Orange County and a former deputy game warden.

In addition, was a former Selectman in Braintree, a Selectman in Randolph, A member of Phoenix Lodge #28 F&AM, Randolph, a member of Hartford Post 96 of the American Legion in White River Jct. and a member of the Green Mountain Post VFW, Randolph. We miss him.

RUSSELL A. DAY

Russ was my wife's brother and while I knew him and very well, he wasn't a friend who I kept in daily touch with. Most people called him Buster including his two sisters, however I called him Russ.

Russ was a class year ahead of me through the school years. He graduated from Randolph High School and at age 17 he enlisted in the Navy. This was the start of a 20 year stint as a career Navy man. Of course, this sent him to many geograhic points of the world including Morocco—the Philippines, Shang

Russell A. Day, Photo source and date unknown

Hai and places in between. He spent most of the years near the end of his career enlistment in California. Here, he specialized in electronics and was an electronics instructor. The particulars I do not know because most of this California time spent was classified.

He was married and had three daughters, Ellen of Florida, Maria also of Florida and Annette who made a career in the Air Force, retired as an Officer and now lives in Illinois.

Actually, I only saw him a couple of times after he enlisted either due to him traveling or making his home for years in California.

When he remarried and lived in Roanoke Rapids, North Carolina, Bunny and I did get to see him twice and unfortunately he died June 19, 1978 ———just two weeks after Stan Gould died on June 4. And, we'll miss him, also.

YAMAHA AND PIANO TUNING

As the 1970's progressed, my desires for a piano did also— that is —a good piano. I still had the player piano I bought in Randolph a few years ago. However, that was in the cellar and in all truthfulness—my cellar was NOT a great place. To start with, it was too low for me.

My next door neighbor, Carl tells of the time when the previous owner of 'our' house was changing it from a summer camp to a year round house. One of the chores he did, was to jack it up, put a foundation of cement blocks and poured concrete under it. During the process Carl said he suggested one more row of blocks would be appropriate. and heard the reply—" What for, it don't bother me!" Of course, he was only 5 feet tall, why would it bother him!!

Now, I'm paying the price for what he didn't do and naturally—it was our choice!

So, each time I go 'down cellar', at 6 feet, I pay a price by banging my head on the floor joists. I did toy with the idea to jack the whole house up at least one block of 8 inches, but finally tossed that idea for the work involved.

If I wanted to play the piano, I would go down cellar—— but bear in mind that the piano was a piece of junk to play manually, no matter how good it sounded with a piano roll being run through!

I think I was looking at a Shoppers News and saw an ad for a piano being sold in the next 'town'—Marlboro. Called the number and was invited to check it out and given an address.

This was a Yamaha studio model upright. This means it is a taller model than the typical spinet. Most of those were in the 40 to 44 inch height—a studio piano is taller and about 47-48 inches high. This translates into longer strings, which in turn give a healthier sound. Regardless of string length——I bought this black model Console for about half it's new price including a matching bench. And to top it off—it was only 2-3 years old. A Digital Engineer (Digital Equipment Co.), bought it to self teach and finally abandoned that idea.

NOW——I've got a great piano AND on the main floor.

By the mid 1980's—I saw an ad in Sheet Music Magazine for a course on how to tune pianos. This could be something I might do in the years to come. I could rebuild pianos and naturally, part of that rebuild would be tuning——or just tune pianos as a sole source of income. I did take that course—it wasn't only a few weeks—as slow or as fast as you want to progress.

I experimented on the piano in the cellar—I certainly didn't want to detriment my good Yamaha at least to start with. I made pretty good progress and finally got to the point where I did tune the Yamaha——and as I progressed, many sounds etc. became noticeable. Not only noticeable, but then I found as I played, my ear was getting critical. I would stop—get out the tuning wrench 'touch up a note' here or there.

Then it dawned on me——I'm hurting my enjoyment of playing a piano by becoming too critical ——far too critical of tones, relationships of tones, and THIS was something I knew would ultimately ruin my piano fun.

So I stopped with the tuning—put the tuning kit away and shortly sold it, with no regret since!!

I had also finished the electronic organ that I made from various kits—I brought that to Northboro and at some point in time, sold it—it sounded good, but not the truly jazzy voicings I wanted——more like a church organ. And that's understandable,—it was designed that way.

BUT, I did use 2 of the keyboards in the 'kit' organ and they worked good, both in physical size and with the multiple contacts under each note.

And with all the Hammond pieces I got from the Estey factory—I couldn't wire the Hammond main generator OR the chorus generator because I couldn't find a place to buy nichrome wire which is a special resistance wire to prevent overloading the generators. So, I used some of these parts, sold a few and retained the balance.

ADVANCE SALES WITH R & L

Near the end of 1978, I had made a lot of progress with Met Life and was fairly competent on what I was doing, but like most all jobs or professions, it can take quite a chunk of time to know what you can do and what you can't. I didn't like the long days and also the night work. BUT, the nights of Monday through Thursday is when you make the sales ——so the nights are important. And I couldn't get used to the free time during the day——to me, this is when I should be 'productive'.

While I wasn't looking for anything to change —even though I'm starting the fifties, I really hadn't made up my mind that this is what I'm going to finish out my working years. And by now, I had been here for four years.

Not only that—but I still wondered about the outcome of the motel plans—while by now, I wasn't counting on it as much as I previously was—it was chewing up too much time.

Before I really came to an answer with regard to either Met or the motel—one day when I went to R & L for some reason—Larry and John both cornered me and said if I had a couple minutes—they wanted to talk with me.

They unfolded a proposition. What they wanted was not someone, but me to come into R & L in a sales capacity. And in doing so, make contact with existing customers and contact prospective customers to expand the operating base. I offered some opposition saying I really didn't know enough about welding—tool steel—machining and whatever else would be needed to make a success. They both said that was the least of any hesitation—they both knew me—knew what my capabilities were and they knew I could not only learn what was necessary —but, I could do it quickly. This display of confidence sounded good and they fully believed anyone they hired for sales would have to be 'indoctrinated' at least as much or more than I would. Larry especially didn't like salespeople—he felt they lived in a different world totally from what he did!!

Then they suggested that, if I could get away for 3 or 4 days—Bunny and I should go to Chicago, (at R and L expense), and take in the annual International Tool Show which was a display of all Machines and Tooling. We talked about pay and benefits. If, after the trip if I had become interested it was a green light—if I didn't want to continue, we walk away.

Nothing ventured —nothing gained so after many arrangement were made——Bunny and I had a private compartment on a train (we had plenty of time and I don't like to fly), so we took the train.

Bunny at her desk working for R&L as a bookkeeper. The year was 1979. The furniture was obtained from Dasa Corp. in Andover (MA), as excess property. R&L was located at this time at 258 West Main St., Northboro, MA. Photo by C. Wells.

In leaving Worcester—it was late afternoon and soon became dark, so the scenery watching activity stopped but I moved around and talked to a couple of people.

Anyway, we finally pulled into Chicago—rented a car and before we headed for our Hotel about 20 miles south of Chicago, we went to the location of the McCormick Exposition Center on the shore of Lake Michigan. This way we could find our way back easier.

When we came back to McCormick Place the next day, we went into the Main Hall. There were 850 exhibits on the Main floor. I took all day to cover that floor and observe all the displays I felt were at all important.

I had brought a couple samples of tool steel welding with me, items called end mills and these were about an inch and a half in diameter. I stood outside the main entrance in front of about a dozen doors —held these end mills and stuffed them in front of people entering and leaving the building. They drew a lot of attention and, at times, maybe a dozen people were gathered around.

We spent three days in Chicago plus a day travel each way. And from this trip, I felt that even though I wasn't a manufacturing engineer or a tooling engineer I did have enough common sense and basic knowledge about rebuilding and repairing tooling, so I had little apprehension of acting in a sales capacity.

After talking this over with Bunny, and we had plenty of time to talk on the train ride coming back from Chicago, I decided this would be interesting, more appropriate hours, less auto expense, so I made arrangements to start work with R & L, which also included sufficient and proper notice to Met Life——basically Ted Anderson.

GETTING ORGANIZED AT R & L

After I came in as a full time employee, I could see a lot of places where there needed to be some organization. Sales forms and other paperwork that was essential was lacking. The worst part was no place for me to place my body—I needed a desk and a phone—didn't care what was on the walls or floor, but I certainly needed a desk. To fix that, we all got together and built a small second floor complete, of course with walls and a set of stairs. I then had room for the desk at the top of the stairs. No window—no heat—no A/C and soon I would feel the absence of these. Bunny had her own office with a window, an air conditioner and a door so she had reasonable quiet. Lack of a window where I was, made it really hot in the summer, a large fan helped some.

I started by making local sales calls and with each encounter I gained experience. Soon I gained enough confidence and as time went by, I found myself on the phone with manufacturing or industrial engineers with large and larger companies. An immediate and noticeable difference was the phone contacts. With insurance, I had to make 30 to 50 phone calls to get 8 appointments. Here, everyone I talked to wanted me to visit in person.

I was the only person in the whole country with this service or type of product available. However, I had no desire to travel the whole country——too expensive, too time consuming and too long in time per customer to cultivate a sale. I wanted many sales and in a short time.

In Westboro, a 'stamping house' had a contract to make pans——pans about 12 x 16 and 2 inches deep. They needed to have the four corners welded by uniting the existing material without adding any welding rod. The pans were made from stainless steel and the corners had to be free of anything to prevent the contents from being dumped out easily. Those pans started coming in from Westboro about 125 every other day —
—for weeks. Later, we found they were used in China or Korea to make paraffin blocks, but this was a good sale which brought in some steady money through steady work.

Fortunately, enough accounts sent work and created a money flow, so we weren't destitute——such as Sweetheart in Wilmington (Ma.), once a week would send the cutters for the styrofoam sandwich 'box' McDonalds used. And many manufacturers in Worcester sent a good variety of work —and these accounts I would call on personally in trying to acquire more work. Worcester was a very concentrated location for manufacturing of all types. Morgan Construction made machines that made paper—Heald Machine made machines that ground

Con showing a couple of "Paddle Broaches" which required repair due to broken teeth. These were very expensive to replace also in delivery time. Photo by C. Wells.

crankshafts for auto and truck engines etc.—Norton Corp. made all types and kinds of abrasives, also was experimenting with plastics and ceramics to be used in auto engines—Wyman Gordon, right in the city specializes in large castings for landing gears on all types of airplanes and then built a second plant in North Grafton (Ma.) and amongst others was Table Talk Pies right in Kelly Square!

In Hudson (Ma.), there was a company called LaPointe Machine Tool which made large and even huge machines for other manufacturers. These were so large I can't imagine how they were ever transported. I have seen some of these and maintenance people had to use stepladders to get 'up' to the 'business' mouth and then a man could stand right 'in the mouth' of the tool frame to install or adjust the broaches (cutting tools)!!

TANG REPAIR

Within a couple of months, John and Larry had setup a machine that gave R & L a new service and this was replacing drill tangs.

A tang is the top end of a drill bit——the operator inserts a drill into a chuck and the tapered surface actually drives the drill but occasionally, the operator doesn't get the drill fully seated and the top end, used to retrieve the bit, gets twisted off. This normally makes the bit worthless——but R & L can weld a new end (tang) and therefore restore the bit to the equivalent of new. This tang can be replaced on most any drill bit size—however, the bigger the drill bit, the more costly it is to replace. A drill bit 3 inches in diameter can cost hundreds of dollars to replace.

TANG REPAIR

BORING BAR AND TOOL HOLDER REPAIR

Another thing that happened, a machinist was hired and his main job was to repair tool holders and boring bars.

Both of these items could easily get broken or injured by a lathe operator allowing one of these items to strike the spinning chuck on a lathe. All of these items were very expensive to replace.

At R & L, the item could be welded and then be machined to a finished item comparable to brand new. And to finish off the tool holders and boring bars—— they were chemically treated to give a nice black appearance and then received a bright orange R & L Rebuilt Sticker. A new tool in that category could cost well over 100 dollars and in some cases could take weeks.

R & L could weld, machine, color and return in 2 weeks for just 20 dollars!!!

Before   *After*

ADVANCED SALES WITH R & L

If you have ever watched a good 'short order' cook work, it's surprising how each order along with the total order ever comes out and at the right time.

When I first started ——I made a 'ton of phone calls' and then which required a lot of notes—account cards to be made out etc—I felt like a short order cook at times!! It was such a change from phone sales calls for insurance, I couldn't believe people didn't hang up or tell me to get lost!! Instead, they were interested to hear what I had to say and why not? They were in tough position about steel tooling, and I tweaked their curiosity enough so they were interested.

During the 1970's ——the USA was importing one big item used in the manufacture of metal working tools. And this 'item' was cobalt. We had plenty of steel —or could get it— and it wasn't difficult to process it by heat treatment to strengthen it which then would end up as 'high speed steel'. This is a little confusing ——it has nothing to do with speed—it does have to do with strength. High speed steel is heat treated to give it more durability so—as example— a drill bit made of steel can drill a hole through a piece of steel—naturally the drill HAS to last longer and therefore be harder, or that hole isn't going to get drilled!

To increase the life of the drill bit—either cobalt or tungsten is added and this additive extends the life of the drill bit. Here's the problem —— tungsten is rather scarce and therefore expensive. Cobalt WAS cheaper —unfortunately the USA doesn't have any cobalt —ALL we used —was imported from Zaire in Africa. And in the 1970's, there was a political uprising in Zaire and the mines were flooded so the supply of cobalt slowed to a trickle for companies in the USA.

This action left this country with tooling made mostly if not only, from 'high speed steel'. All tool manufacturers were in a bind ——big time!! And here comes R&L Welding with the ability to take a tool and 'remake' it into an equivalent in 'wear qualities' to either cobalt or tungsten!?! At this point, I didn't know whether R&L had a special welding rod or they made their own. If they bought ready made rod—this would mean others could also buy it also and could compete with R&L. THAT didn't happen.

The word WAS getting out that R&L could do wonders with either worn or broken tooling.

As I started to work there, it was common to have UPS stop only once or twice a week. Later and not by much —it was common to have numerous deliveries per day by multiple carriers——mostly through phone calls and solicitations.

One man parked his car and came in to the building with a large 'broach' which probably weighed 40 pounds.(A broach is a metal cutting tool). It was big enough—heavy enough and precious enough so he bought a ticket,—and this 'broach occupied its own seat on the plane from Allentown PA. to Logan Airport, Boston. Then he rented a car to drive to Northboro. It belonged to Ingersoll Rand, had a couple broken teeth and was used in making steam turbine equipment.

A replacement was 48 months and the cost to replace—— 6000 dollars!! He left this to be repaired and flew back to Allentown—the piece was repaired in less than 2 weeks at a cost of 250 dollars!!

Soon work also started to increase with the drill 'tang' repairs and the toolholder repairs.One company was already sending 'work' and a lot of it when I started full time. This was an aero space industry in Connecticut, and by now were sending more than one shipment a week.

I had taken a trip to Geneva N Y to the American Can Co and we started a program of repairing all of the tooling of which many pieces were specially made and nearly impossible to replace. This was a large company and a good amount of work for R&L.

Then we landed a large helicopter manufacturer in Texas. They sent us end mills, 3 inches in diameter and over a foot long. An end mill is another metal cutting tool. After they had received a sample and tested it—it lasted nearly 3 times as long as their original new piece. This started a circle of shipments, a half dozen at a time. I later learned these were used to cut through the titanium block at the base of the huge blades and which contained the gears used for blade angling.

I rented a car and went to Detroit. Here, I visited GM headquarters and Ford headquarters. At Ford Tractor, I found out all the manufacturing was then done in Ireland. At the Chrysler engine plant in Trenton (Mi), I was ushered to the 'tool crib'in a section in this building, the total size of which was 10 acres under one roof. I would have bet the whole State of Michigan was under that roof. This was when it was being geared up for the production of the 'K'car——the name of one I remember is the Dodge Omni.

I spent evenings walking through the Renaissance Center building and also on the roof at a table looking out on Detroit as the whole room at the top did a full revolution once an hour—and it towered way over ALL the other buildings.

I spent a week on that one trip and was warmly greeted in many other manufacturing plants in places around Elkhart In., Cleveland Oh., and Geneva N. Y.

So we're well underway and now, I'm back at the desk on the second floor. And here, I might add —there wasn't any insulation in the walls of the area where my desk was and the floor was cantilevered over the area Larry spent most of his time. He was the type individual when things were going well——he would sing, yell or create a ruckus constantly (whether he was welding or not)——to the other guys there on the floor. That was OK, but it sure interrupted my phone calls.

FEDERAL ARSENAL

One trip I had to make at R & L—and I'm not even going to say it was by train, plane, bus or car because this was a federal arsenal and it involved armament, shells, cannons, and guns. I don't remember the man's name I contacted.

We spent some time on the two specific problems he wanted to resolve. One was for a group of 'hammers' on a machine that, when I saw it—it startled me. We climbed a set of stairs, a long set of stairs and ended up in a control room around 30 feet long with slanted out windows at the top. Here the controlling operator could walk back and forth with a 'box' containing many buttons and by watching these hammers working, he controlled the manufacture of a large gun barrel—— two stories down!!!!!!

By taking a large rectangular block of steel——heating it— and then pounding and pounding it——the block grew longer as a barrel took shape. I couldn't see it operate the day I was there—the machine had been laid carefully on its face so the back cover could be removed and a huge, ——repeat, huge gear inside could be replaced. A gear 30 feet in diameter had a worn tooth and its replacement was in the process. Interesting point—it was determined someone's finger print and the 'oil' on a specific tooth prevented proper lubrication while running and therefore that one tooth had worn excessively!?!

The main inquiry he had of R &L pertained to reinforcing the four hammers on this machine which were about 2 feet by 3 feet, to slow down the wear factor.

The other problem involved the process of machining 'riflings' on the inside of any gun barrel, done by a series of 'cutters' with multiple projections that actually cold cut these riflings. A cylindrical cutter with projections for the riflings was forced into the barrel—retrieved and then a slightly larger cutter was installed. Then IT was shoved the length of the barrel. It took 10 blades to cut the riflings to the correct depth. THE problem was that if one of the ten cutters had a projection break off——THAT cutter was now worthless, and—the manufacturer would not sell just one blade—a set of 10 had to

Barrels of 16 inch diameter guns used on many Battleships during World War 2. Barrels were manufactured on machines described in the text. Photo origin unknown.

be purchased!! They wanted to know IF R & L could restore just one tooth!

I asked what the material content of the cutter blades were—was given the answer and then replied, "Sure,—we can repair those cutters and the repair will be stronger than the original tooth"!!

During lunch with this 'man', he asked me if I could take time to see a machine, he would like to show me?

At this time in my life I easily replied , "I'll take time!!!" (Too many other times, I've said I would do it on the next trip —and then it never happened.)

When we got back to the 'working area', he took me into an unused building and here he showed me a lathe that was so huge —the bed on it was over 70 feet long!!!! It spanned the entire width of the building. Before I could close my mouth, he then asked if I knew what a chuck was on a lathe, and when I said I certainly did—he showed me the chuck on this humongous lathe——it was 13 feet in diameter!!!! A typical steel lathe might have a bed length of 4 to 6 feet —with a chuck about one foot in diameter!!!

There were 6 of these lathes right in a row—all packed in cozmalene ready to be degreased and put back into action if called upon. I was in awe for hours!!!

A TRIP OR TWO IN ASTONISHMENT

On another trip, I went to GE in Schenectady (NY), where I had 3 or 4 appointments with various people. This is where large steam turbines are made.

Inside one of the manufacturing buildings, I asked directions for a specific person and I was told to go down this 'street' and when I came to the railroad tracks(still inside), —turn left and his office was on the corner—that might give you an idea of the size of this building!!! On the way down the 'street', I looked up to see the largest crane hook I had ever seen—it had to be 5 feet across. Under it was a turbine generator being assembled. Inside the actual generator were two men installing field windings—the size of the windings made me cough, they were actually copper bars!! —and these men were inside where the armature would ultimately be installed!!

And to elaborate a little more——at the GE River Works Plant in Lynn,(MA.),—this is where MEDIUM steam turbines are made——there was a completed generator ready to be shipped. It was on a specially built trailer. This trailer alone had 106 wheels and the whole unit could 'kneel' hydraulically and actually rest on the ground if necessary for an over night stay!! Photos were not allowed inside the grounds.

A GREAT CAMERA—— AND ITS REWARDS

About 1979, my daughter Lisa and I decided we needed and wanted a good camera. I hadn't had a camera for years. I think it's fair to say neither of us could individually really afford to spend more than 400 dollars for a camera.

At the time, neither one of us knew beans about cameras, but we finally decided on an Olympus OM-1 which was a 35 mm SLR.

The main reason I'm bringing this topic up is that I had been going through life more or less with blinders on, looking straight ahead. I was always going to a specific place or to do a specific thing and never paid much attention to what I was passing by on the sidelines.

When we bought that camera, it taught me to look at life in a totally different fashion. When you look through the view finder I tried to compose the best picture I could see. This meant looking in the background—anything within the view finder that degrades the picture? —Is the focus correct?—Can I adjust the polarizing filter to improve the shading?— how about the distance? All these and more questions answered can make the difference between a fair shot and an excellent one!

Unknowingly, I started to apply this same viewing to everyday life——I started seeing 'things' as if I was looking through a view finder and that raised my enjoyment for life and 'things' within this life. I entered a whole new world of appreciation for what not only man can build or manufacture—

but a whole new world of appreciation for what Mother Nature provides!!!!

I now look out the window and many times say, 'What a great shot, that would make"! OR— "I wish I had my camera right now— THIS is worth remembering"!!!

Although I've had my eyes opened to some great 'shots' — I could easily say I wished I had done camera scene earlier— —BUT it is equally as satisfying to say, "I'm really glad I got this camera when I did and now I don't miss a lot of photographic opportunities, now that I recognize there are some!!!!"

As a matter of fact—the Worcester Telegram (daily newspaper) had a contest for the best fall foliage shot and for which I won first prize. It was a 'shot' sitting on the bed in our master bedroom looking through the bay window framed by the drapes and looking through all the small panes——across the water with the trees and foliage outlining Solomon Pond. It was one of those unusual photos!!

This prize was a meal for two at the Castle Restaurant in Leicester. THIS is known as one, if not the top restaurant in Central Massachusetts. Daughter Lisa wanted to go also, so she came along to enjoy an unusual meal. The parking lot wasn't filled with cars—one or two dozen cars per meal would be sufficient for the chef to really enjoy life!!

BUSINESS MEETINGS

While I was busy gaining new accounts, I was also having fun. Previously, I had experienced a company as it was sinking, such as Dasa (and others) and now, R & L was giving me exhilaration and a feeling of satisfaction as the efforts were paying off.

I liked the affiliation with manufacturing, I liked the machines, and now the machines were accomplishing more and through automated operation. I liked the people I met at various locations—even the people I talked with on the phone. I liked the idea of taking something existing —salvaging it and returning it to usage again, such as broken tooling.

I was pretty much my own boss—that is, I could schedule appointments when and where I wanted, but I also realized there was a balance between profit and loss.

Once a week, Larry, John, Bunny and I would have an after hours meeting and after sitting through two or three of those, I started to implement a schedule and a list of topics. In doing this, it was more business like, more productive and much less redundant of a previously discussed topics. Getting home at 8 or 9 PM made a long day after a meeting of 2 — 3 hours, or more.

One day, I looked out the front window to see a man approaching the building and once inside introduced himself as a brother to the man who was Mayor of the adjoining city, Marlborough (Ma.). He was a Vice President of a Broach Manufacturing Company in southern Florida and while here visiting his brother—had heard about R & L and wanted to check us out.

His company was in a real bind —— they could NOT get the material to manufacture new broaches, their customers were asking about repairing existing broaches with a broken tooth or more. And these customers were from all over the world. Would we accept tooling from them—repair it by welding and then ship it back? I said we would do it and when he left, I felt we had a new customer. Larry didn't feel as such, he said for me not to hold my breath waiting for this tooling to come in!!

While R & L wasn't equipped to do grinding or sharpening of any type—in this case, grinding would be done by them as that was part of their manufacturing process.

In about a week, UPS started dropping off parcels from this manufacturer and shortly we would receive 6 to 12 pieces a week once they received a few back to run tests on. These broaches would be from France, Germany and other companies from most everywhere around the globe—especially within this country

We also now had hired a receiving and shipping clerk which certainly was an asset and she would not allow Larry to open and start processing a part before it was documented on an incoming form. She brought the total employees to ten.

PUZZLING CIRCUMSTANCES

At this point in time, I had been there about two years and without even looking at the books, I could tell that business was on the increase. We had many new accounts. We had increased the volume from existing accounts and most important, we had more than one source of income. By that, I mean welding wasn't the only source of income as we had become somewhat diversified. That in itself pleased me and for one big reason.

I still didn't know how the welding rod supply situation was ——I just had a queasy feeling about that topic. IF and I repeat, IF there was a welding rod supply and it was running low——where is the replacement rod coming from? No easy answer is what was making me queasy. The tang repair along with the tool holder and boring bar repair could be accomplished without the special rod——and the paraffin pan welding wasn't a specialty welding item either. Those items along with other jobs was bringing money in. The specialty welding was the 'frosting on the cake'.

During one of 'those meetings', Larry made a couple remarks about sales not producing enough to keep everybody busy—he could see people standing around which he didn't like. This really surprised me so I suggested the meeting agenda was full —we can talk about that topic at the next meeting. That would give me time to collect some 'data' that should make him feel better.

At the next meeting, I came back to the sales topic and in remembering like it was yesterday—said sales were 46% ahead and we now had 110 new accounts over 12 months ago. And, I felt IF people were not 100% busy, it was due to the fact we now had a noticeable increase in the efficiency of the workers —which was good because it would allow still more work to come in without hiring more people which, naturally would require more expense!

Another topic at this meeting was that Bunny and I wanted 2 weeks off for vacation. It was time for us to make another trip to Florida as it had been about 6 years since we had a planned time off —not just a few days here and there.

Here, Larry said to Bunny that if she took the time off, her job wouldn't be here when she got back!?!?! No time like right now to clarify that statement. He repeated his statement. Let me say here that Bunny had been a bookkeeper there for nearly 10 years—had many weeks 4 or 5 years back when she didn't take a paycheck for a period of 4 to 6 weeks because money was tight! She had guided them through IRS audits, the books balanced right to the penny ——The 3 month outside audit had been adjusted to a yearly audit—she never missed work —a deadline—a tax payment!!

NOW, when a turn around was taking place her job isn't going to be there?????? WHAT THE HELL IS GOING ON????

THIS really irritated me—so I said "If her job isn't going to be here—MINE won't either——I QUIT.

So the time came, Bunny, the girls and I went to Florida. We took a train from Worcester (Ma.), to New York City— changed and another train to Miami. Rented a car in Miami and spent 2 weeks on the Gulf coast and had a lot of fun! The trip expense had been allocated and accruing.

(In talking about the R & L incident—we somewhat came to a conclusion that Larry and John were apprehensive that Bunny and I would probably try to take the business over. IF that could even be a possibility, and it wasn't for one big rea- son——I don't weld and I don't want to be a welder. AND I certainly wouldn't be any part of a business where I had to depend on someone other than myself to be the kingpin of any business I owned!!!!)

So when we returned from Florida——Bunny continued to work as a bookkeeper for Pierce Oil and Gas in Northboro as she had been a part timer for nearly ten years. I was with- out a paying job. I still felt the Motel on Dauphinais land would be a reality, so I would temporarily spin my wheels and also push to get that project going OR pull the plug on it totally.

THE CREW IN BLUE—1940's

I should put in a short topic to the friends in the Randolph Post Office—these were the people that through rain and sleet——you know the slogan!

In the late 1930's and into the 1940's the face of Jack Stehle, Hugh Seaver, Jehiel Williams, Bob Ford, Charles Holman were the people to buy your 3 CENT stamp or penny post card from, guided by a Miss Hayward or Olive Mayo the Post master(s) (not Postmistress in those days?). And I might say that the 3 cent postage stamp stayed at that price for years!!

Although Glen Bailey might have been there, I don't remember him —— but I do remember that Olive Mayo was followed by 'Cat' Richards as Postmaster.

Howard Smithers, Walter Wood and Horace 'Babe' Soule, Ed Pierce, Bob Ford, Glen Thomas, Homer Brown and John Moore were mostly outside carriers. In the mid fifties, Maynard 'Dingy' Wright subbed as a rural carrier. (In the years to come other locals would join the force such as Wendell Smithers, Jake Wright, Bill Carey, Bob Soule, Allen Wright and Wilbur 'Buster' Bowen and Clayton Butterfield).

AND, there was another member of the team whose name escapes me—but he delivered special delivery letters within the village.

He had a rather peculiar process for delivering. He always wore his blue postal carrier's uniform—visor cap included—but as he walked along the sidewalk or street, he was always looking down and if he saw a wood match (of which there were always many), he would stop, pick it up —shake it vigorously to ensure it wasn't lit and then throw it back down. As he walked along toward his destination, he would clutch that letter, hold it out in front of him, and if he felt someone was going to be in his way—he would say "Toot-Toot-U. S. Mail"! He used that phrase many times in a day!!

He also made sure any gopher matches were fully extinguished too! The fact that many people smoked, especially pipes, it took a lot of (mostly) wood matches to keep the tobacco smokin! It might take the forenoon for him to get to George Rye's Barber Shop!

And of course, the Post Office was on Merchants Row (with large windows on Pleasant Street) from sometime in the 1930's until about 1970— when Hugh Claflins house along with the house of Mary Carr Dadmun (the town Librarian for years as mentioned in Book 1), was torn down and the new Post Office was built at the corner of Salisbury and Summer Streets.

Ashley's Pub now occupies the former site of the Post Office.

THE MUSIC SHOP

When I left the area in 1955 to join the ranks of IBM, Dick Monroe was still at the Music Shop.

In October 1956, Elmer Ellis (Red), came in as a full time employee and in or around 1970 bought the business from Pete Scribner, when Pete retired.

Jumping way ahead, Red kept it going until he sold it to Jeff Jacques in June 1996.

During those years, the business of television and television servicing changed dramatically. TV sets became a 'throw away' item if they stopped working. It was cheaper just to throw the old set in the trash and start over with a new set. To fix an older one, in most cases, was not always the most satisfactory route to take for a couple of reasons. TV sets were rapidly becoming an item not easily repaired—the manufacturers didn't make them easy to repair—their components were complicated, the components were attached to a printed circuit board, and as time went on, these boards could be easier to get AND replace than any individual component. So, the customer bought a raft of parts on a 'board' with a fairly hefty repair bill, instead of getting a repair bill stating: 1-.001 capacitor—$.35 and labor $42.00!!!

ALL electronic equipment used in the consumer's home followed the same general trend——Made in China or Mexico or Korea— anywhere the labor was unbelievably cheap——— —THROW IT AWAY, and buy a NEW ONE.

And while Red Ellis, in his retirement years, to this day (after 2000), spends time still repairing TV and other electronic equipment with the present owner, Jeff Jacques—this is an exception—most of the business and the competition has long gone!

And I might add —gone to the same place the typical TV antenna has gone and that has been replaced with a dish antenna!

SCRIBNERS

Gordon Scribner in or around 1970, also decided it was a good time to retire. He had started in the late 1930's and I believe operated out of a building near the railroad tracks which later became Johnson Printing Co. Gordon bought the Hardware Store on Main Street from Walter Wilcox about 1939, as mentioned previously and kept the hardware etc. and added 'white goods', radios, and bottled gas, heating systems. domestic and commercial wiring and refrigerator service.

As he retired, another local man, Ralph Greene took over and continued the many services that Gordon had offered.

WATERBURY COMPANY

The Waterbury Company came to Randolph around 1960 —put up a brick building on the back road to Beanville.

This company was a plastic injection application where plastic pellets are heated and after it becomes liquefied, is forced into injection molds where various and many parts and objects are manufactured. Many sizes, shapes and colors made items from razor cases to watch cases, and quite a few Randolph people found employment here for a number of years. This would include Dick Monroe and 'KC' Warner. Dick left the Music Shop about 1962 and stayed until retiring and KC, after 12 years left the employment of Scribners about 1970, he also stayed until retirement.

RODCO

Rod Hughes was a local man, who being very capable in more than one business, came to be an Arctic Cat Snowmobile Distributor (not dealer—distributor) for New England in 1965. He employed many local people—one being Gus Sivret as the Vermont Sales Rep, Paul Howard and many more. Within a couple of years —this business 'took off' and grew like a weed! The building on Pleasant Street saw hundreds of snowmobiles pass through and then he progressed into Van Conversions, which also was to see rapid growth.

Unfortunately, somewhere around 1972, Rod entered into a sellout transaction with an 'out of state' RV manufacturer which turned out to be a fatal decision——the bubble burst and RODCO —the snowmobile and van conversion businesses made a disappearance similar to an inflated balloon with the neck band cut!!

URS——TEMPORARY FILL IN

Around September 1980, I drove to Stoneham (Ma.), to find a business called URS. This stands for Unit Record Service and this was a company owned by Tom McHugh. Tom worked for MAI, which I have mentioned before—— and which was another 'third party leasing' company. In this case, Tom had left MAI around 1968, took a gamble and succeeded. He had previously taken care of the IBM machines at GE River Works Plant in Lynn (Ma.).

GE had bought all the machines it used from IBM and up to this point in time, had them on an IBM Maintenance Agreement. I don't know if GE approached Tom or the reverse took place —but Tom agreed to service all the machines at that location for GE and I would presume offered a contract of less money, so GE agreed to the arrangement also. Around 1968, I can remember when Tom asked me if I would like to join him and the others as part of the team. I rejected the offer due to the fact I liked what I was doing and the company I worked for at that time, CTI Leasing. We were flying high at the time — had just acquired some 360 Systems and I was comfortable.

Presently, (1980)——I had the Motel plans I felt would materialize, but it was taking longer than I had predicted, So I called Tom and asked if he had need for my services, and he invited me to come and talk about it. I had no idea what, where, or how URS was presently. I also knew that Dasa had met its fate —at least the CTI part of Dasa was no longer around, just what the main part of Dasa was doing —I didn't know.

I came off Route 128 and headed south on I-93 and the sign for Montvale Ave quickly came in sight—so I exited, drove under I-93 and in moments found the building for URS.

I was much surprised when I entered—partly for the number of people in the office. I was directed up the stairs and found Tom, 2 or 3 other sales people and a sales secretary.

We talked for a half hour —he showed me the rebuild operation and a few more people connected with either rebuild or field service. Most of the rebuild was Keypunch machines as was field service. By now, much of the actual data at customer locations was completed by the use of 1401 Systems or large Mainframes.

At this point in time, IBM was succeeding in vacating the punch card business and was far more interested in promoting Sales and Service— on Terminals, Controllers and Printers. These were satellite units which were tied into Mainframes but were used as inputs and outputs. It wasn't wise for any 'third party' to even try to service the large Mainframes— —too expensive to train on and too many models to effectively have the manpower to even try. Nationally, other companies could try and maybe succeed, but not a regional company such as URS.

I really only wanted to fill in for about 3 maybe 4 months until the Motel solidified or didn't.

I left with a job offered to work on rebuild or field service as a contractor ——pay plus car expenses, but no benefits.

MOTEL CONCLUSION

After I started work for URS as a contractor—I still hadn't succeeded in gaining the ground I needed for the motel construction start and I also hadn't decided to pull the plug on it either. However, I now had a job and a good paycheck coming in each week. Even though I took this job as a temporary fill in——within a couple of months, URS was pushing me periodically to become an employee.

So apparently, I could stay or I could leave if the motel should materialize.

The timeframe on the motel by now had covered 4 or 5 years (too long!) and the fact I was in Stoneham most of the time, I thought this would be a good time to get some solid education on a specific subject.

So I signed up for a course of Hotel and Motel Management at Bunker Hill Community College, in Charlestown —— outside of Boston. It was like an adult education class and would be 3 nights a week from 6 to 9 PM. I've forgotten for how many weeks! I could come down I-93 from Stoneham and the building was right beside I-93. From there, when the evening was finished—I would head for the Mass. Turnpike and go west for about 40 miles and be home around 10 PM. Long day but I could handle it— and did. Now if the motel comes through I was qualified—I didn't cover chef—sous chef—bar tender or any other satellite subject———just management.

I should add that over the months—I had convinced myself I could stick with the IBM machines, just for the reason I like the work and URS is turning out to be a great company to work for. By now, I'm fully experienced, and can do it with ease—so why am I still playing the field?

Here's why—once I latch onto a problem—an endeavor—a topic, I'm part bulldog—I want to stick with it until I consider it's at the end!

We finally were in a position to get the motel article before the Marlboro (Ma.), City Council and with a public meeting. I was instructed by Armand to attend the meeting in the capacity as a representative of E L Dauphinais Corp. —to sell the councilors on the idea of a motel in that location, its size, type construction, height, number of rooms, building configuration, utilities and anything else pertaining to its presence.

The hearing progressed with various people speaking in favor and with city management asking for, and also giving,—information.

At this point in time, Marlboro could easily use another motel—this geographic location bordered by I-290 on the North, I-495 North and South on the eastern side, and with just a Holiday Inn at the intersection of Route 20 and I-495 nearby, was recognized as needing additional motel rooms. Addtionally, The Centrum, a Convention Center in Worcester (Ma.) was in various stages of construction. This was about 8 miles away and would create more demand for rooms even out here.

As we were getting closer to the end of the meeting—the last person to have an opinion was the Marlboro Fire Chief — —and he shot it down!!!!! Too far from the fire station—too long for fire engine travel time— lack of city water and that did it!!

With that, I pulled the article (without prejudice) before a vote was taken. I could easily see that rejection was a coffin call. Really didn't have any alternative right now, if I ever wanted to bring this before the Council again. (Withdrawing it would have closed the topic possibly forever, for us on THAT subject).

Later, considering all factors, I decided to pull the plug on the whole caper—I was a little too early, the timing wasn't wrong —it just wasn't totally right—that plus it kept my life in limbo and had done so, long enough.

AND just to make this topic a little more interesting—— — about 5 years later, a motel did get built on that parcel— probably by now it had city utilities, but there were 2 other hotels that came on the scene over on Route 20—one had 300 rooms, with convention facilities. Also at the next I-495 inter- section south in Westboro—2 other large hotels were built. With all of them—I would have been playing with the 'big boys' AND, probably over my head!!

Jumping ahead a few years——even though the concrete plant stayed, most of the land from the gravel operation was packaged with other parcels, some large and some small, so combined there was enough land that a large 2 story Shopping Mall was built— complete with J.C. Penny, Sears, Filene's and over a hundred of other retailers!

In retrospect, I should have concentrated on listing the land and forgot the Motel much earlier—but again, it was probably too early!

A typical example of my life——a day late (or early), and a dollar short!!

That doesn't bother me—long ago, I realized I could fix most anything with the one exception——my wallet! And I also realized now, fixing is the path I should follow!!

THE STEPPER MOTOR

When the first Personal Computers came about and let's say 1980— the printer available was called a dot matrix type. This means the characters it prints are made by a series of wire ends pressing against a ribbon and then the paper. This results in all the alphabetic and numeric characters printed as a presentation of various and many dots, and therefore the name——dot matrix.

The point here is the fact that each and every character and therefore each word of print, requires a series of starts and stops.

With a little background information here, up to about 1970—every electric motor ever made either runs continuously OR doesn't run at all. Every printing device I ever worked on in regard to IBM machines——(and the different types were numerous), there was the darndest collection of mechanical and electro mechanical gismos and widgets you ever could imagine, just to achieve selecting the right character and then the actual printing.

About 1980 —here comes the PC printer weighing about 10 or 15 pounds that prints and so fast, it was really remarkable.

Before I get to how this little box solves part of the printing —when I started working for URS, many of the keypunches were now a newer Model called a 129. This machine technologically, was way ahead of its predecessors and just one of its reasons was it contained a stepper motor. Actually, the first 129's around 1968 didn't have a stepper motor—an engineering change about 1969 added the stepper motor to the machine.

A stepper motor—is one of the most fantastic pieces of technology along with the desktop computer, and most people have never heard of it, and I really don't know who invented it.

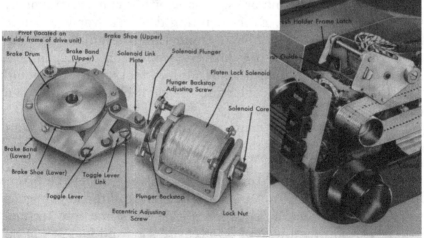

The mechanics necessary to print a line of information prior to the stepper motor in the early 1980's. Additionally was all the circuitry. These graphics may help to understand how the stepper motor simplified many items. Courtesy of IBM Corp.

Here's what it is —an electric motor, which in the example of PC printers, is about the size of a small aspirin bottle, which runs on a series of electronic pulses. Sticking with PC printer example—the stepper motor moves the print head across the paper by a series of starts and stops—and so fast it's a blur, doesn't even look like it does anything but moves very smoothly. At the end of printing a line—a second stepper motor moves the paper up (in a repetition of starts and stops), so the next line can be printed. OR the paper can even be ejected by a series of pulses which can be predetermined from a very few, up to thousands—all the pulses are counted and rationed by a computer!

All that's necessary is to have an electronic counter which sends a predetermined number of 'pulses' to either motor to accomplish the desired results—and of course, counting electronically is very easily accomplished!!!

This stepper motor is easy to make—cheap to make—takes little space and consumes very little electricity.

Also, using dots to make an alphabetic character really isn't new technology, dot matrix printing is from the early 1950's and when assembled together, were used on IBM 026 Keypunches, in that era.

URS—— OPERATION

For the first few weeks, I stayed in the rebuild area, and while there were always Keypunches to be either rebuilt or just reconditioned, I didn't get to work on them. Field Service people would come in from the field, and they were kept busy on the Keypunches.

I was assigned some of the other types such as an 088 Collator that was passing through——quite often a 557 Interpreter would need to be 'touched up', or a Reproducer.

Later ——we had a customer owned 557 come in for a complete rebuild. I was assigned the job. This one was a nonproof model, but I still spent 150 hours before it was finished. This would mean I completely dismantled it right down to the frame, where I spent enough time to thoroughly clean it up and then repainted the frame area. Every sub assembly came off — was completely torn down, cleaned up, degreased, inspected and any bushings or bearings were replaced. There were about 5 or 6 sub assemblies and it wasn't difficult to spend from 4 to 8 hours on each.

In the corner where I was working, was a degreasing 'sink' and another sink with cold and hot water. One of the owners cautioned me one day, about getting water in critical machine areas, especially the power supply——I didn't have the heart to tell him I generally put the power supply (from 557's), right in the sink to clean it up! (Naturally, I didn't soak it in water——I used discretion), and it sat around long enough to dry thoroughly before current went through it to do it any harm!!

Few, but still available, were 557's that had the proof feature——I did a rebuild on a couple of them that were customer owned—those required about 240 hours of time! Working a 40 hour week—it took around 6 weeks to rebuild just one. Most of these came in after I had been there a few months.

I should elaborate to say there is a difference between recondition and rebuild.

A recondition is mostly cosmetic—making sure the covers fit, the paint and appearance is acceptable (so the next customer is not disappointed). Internally, some fast wearing parts are replaced as necessary, the appearance inside is acceptable, and tests are made for operation.

A rebuild ——the machine worked on as described above and one BIG difference comes into play here. When reassembled—the machine isn't tinkered to get it running——the entire machine is now within design specifications and WILL run correctly in basic operation with only a couple 'tweaks' here or there on a special feature or special application.

Naturally, being in rebuild for weeks, I got to know the employees well, and I don't have the space to mention many names, especially all of them

One employee, Mike Mayers had been with URS by now around 12 years and was well known for his trait of being very critical and precise——believe me, nothing got by Mike. I didn't mind, and by keeping my mouth shut——I really sharpened my expertise on a 557 through his criticism. Mike had an astonishing ability to remember most everything pertaining to servicing

ANY of these machines. From my experience, I would easily bet Mike was one of very few top 557 experts in the country, and this would also be true of other machine types.

Here, I have to say that this 557 is a complex machine—but well engineered. If you get the machine within the engineering specs it will work and work well for quite a long time—however, you DO NOT change any adjustment 'to see what happens', or 'to see IF it fixes the problem' and especially without putting it back IF nothing is gained!! On this unit—you diagnose and then make a correction—there's too many interacting adjustments that can cascade and make your life miserable with future 'service calls' if you just try to 'shotgun' a corrective action!

Mike was a tech specialist —just about my age and also, Bob MacDonald was the 'Plant Manager'. Bob was in charge of rebuild schedules—parts— in house paperwork, weekly expense reports —also about my age!

Now, to go back to the days I was in Salem Ma. Office for IBM. I previously wrote about 3 Customer Engineers, all with many years of IBM service work—and the rest, (about 15) of the Customer Engineers were in their twenties—me included.

Now,—— at URS there are three Customer Engineers with years in service, (Mike, Bob and I) and the other 15 or 20 are young 'trainees'!! And let me add——they think and probably regard us three old bastards the same as we used to regard the 'old geezers' in IBM!!!!! The shoe is now on the other foot!!!!

While working in the rebuild area, it was necessary for me to go into the parts room and here I had a big surprise!! In looking through various parts drawers and vials within the drawers—I had to look twice—that looks like MY writing on most of the parts labels!!!——My God —it IS my writing and happened when I stocked the parts room at Cybertronics in Newton!!!

Come to find out——when Dasa in Andover stopped its operation—an auction was held and Tom McHugh bought all the parts——drawers, contents and shelving. Now I'm beginning to feel at home, and no wonder the writing looks familiar.

Another item——URS had another 'division' (under a separate name)—this was a scrap operation. The ironic part is— it was in a building in Andover (Ma.) and you guessed it —the

*Two URS employees, Kevin Clancy and Mark Waruszyla vent their
frustrations from working on Machine type 557. This could be a typical
feeling among many 557 Field Service Technicians! Photo C. Wells*

big building where Cybertronics rebuild took place, better
known as the J P Stevens building, AND part of the building
was where I had my office for Dasa when I 'vacated' my services!!

And to tally up what took place with Cybertronics (CTI)
after I left——Fred Adams, the Customer Engineer I hired for
the Springfield (MA.) area, was transferred to this same building in Andover and put in charge of CTI Rebuild—(one floor
down from URS Scrap). Fred stayed around until about 1975,
and when he left another CTI employee, Al Yellick was now
put in charge of CTI Rebuild—how ironic.

Unfortunately, Fred left to start his own service business
in the Buffalo NY area and had hardly started when he was
killed in an automobile accident near Buffalo.

Back to the present URS——one floor down from the scrap
area—and on the same floor previously used for rebuild—URS
now stores many excess machines and periodically, would be
visited when an urgent part needed to be cannibalized from a
scrap unit and needed either in the field, or for a recondition,

or rebuild where I'm now spending some time. How intertwined life can be at times!!!!

NEW PRODUCTS—COMPUTER PERIPHERIES

Presently URS (as when in Stoneham) had about 20 employees. A few months after I started there in 1980, it was announced URS would now enter the Terminal and Mainframe Peripheral Equipment in addition to the punch card sales and service. This meant a lot more sales and sales training for everyone, it also meant more service training. But, the service training did not include myself (yet), even though by now I was doing customer service calls. I later found out, it was felt I could be more valuable carrying more of the punch card load—and this made sense. But, I was happy to see other types of equipment being gained— I had been through that with Dasa, who was never successful in gaining other than the 'grey machines'.

This move would elevate URS to a more viable supplier for sales, (and service) on Printers, Controllers and Terminals —all attached to various IBM Mainframe Computers.

One account gained almost immediately was John Hancock Insurance. This account had the Mainframes in Boston within one or both of the tallest buildings in the city, and near Copley Square. (The only building taller was Prudential Insurance building).

While the equipment used at that time is now long superseded by later models—the well known and most common were 3278 and 3276 Terminals /Controllers, 3274 Controllers and 3287 Printers, all products of IBM.

There were also many John Hancock Branch Sales Offices throughout the state. In most cases—the forms and information sheets requested during the day were generated by the Mainframes and transmitted back during the evening to the Branch offices and, in many instances had Branch Office printers working on non urgent information and transactions throughout the night. When the office opened the next morning—yards and yards of paper had run through many 3287's!

Throughout the 1970's—IBM was succeeding in converting many punch card accounts to the use of 'Dumb Terminals'—these types mentioned.

This was the start of a radical change in the world of Data Processing, and is well known in the world of Data Processing NOW, but to repeat, was being accomplished by a person sitting at a desk —many feet or even miles away ——tapping into a Mainframe for various bits of information OR depositing bits of information. This was done by accessing this Mainframe through a 3278 Terminal. NOW—we didn't need to wait for the mail to bring the information 2 days later——didn't need to wait for someone to call back or even Fax——just turn to your 3278 (Terminal), key this in and your request leaves the terminal, passes through a controller—ends up regardless of distance in the Mainframe. Moments later, the process is reversed and is almost immediately displayed on the screen in front of you. IF, you want a hard copy (printed sheet)——give the command and again, momentarily its printed on the 3287 near you—a printer that is shared by others when you aren't using it. Before I leave this topic——while this was a gigantic step up in speed and efficiency, only large accounts had Mainframes, at this specific time it still left many many NON Mainframe users ill equipped.

URS at this time had grown and grown, so the name was recognized easily within southern New England (except Connecticut), and even to the extent that IBM was referring sales and service inquiries for punch card equipment to URS. Conversely, it worked out that IBM became a source for URS to find Terminals, Controllers and Printers, which had to be a plus for both companies.

For years I lulled myself into a belief that the 'card' would be around forever—how could business survive without a card. WELL—I found out, it didn't die quickly and it didn't die completely for years to come!

URS———EMPLOYEE

As a reasonable guess of 1983, Tom one of the owners, bought out the other two. 'Things were pretty tight' for a few months —which is understandable. That left Tom McHugh as 'sole owner' with Don Kilgallen as Controller/Gen. Mgr. and Bob Luck as chief cook in the Sales Dept. Also, Tony Del Signore was Service Manager.

But—we had a stroke of luck when Ralph Alfaro came in, about 1981. He had retired after 30 years with IBM and wasn't ready to just being a member of the Old Geezer Club!

In IBM, Ralph was a System 34 Specialist——also experienced on the System 36 and more importantly could very well handle the System 3—of which URS had a few and which were giving problems. Tony had to be called for assistance in too many cases and for a self trained 'service guy' did exceptionally well. And I might add, as a Service Manager without formal education in Business Administration or Management, he showed fine leadership and good control.

Ironically, Ralph spent a lot of his time at IBM within John Hancock and at the computer sections of the Hancock buildings in Boston.

Ralph really fit right in —not only for the 'fix', but helping to train others. I wasn't trained on any of the those units — really didn't want to be at this point in my life. Ralph also worked as a contractor and as a specialized tech— traveled especially on the east coast while doing contract work on the 34's and 36's, (customer or third party owned).

I was to get well acquainted with Ralph——always in a good frame of mind, also added a great amount of levity to the scene, plus his technical ability was a BIG plus to URS.

And about 1984, URS had to move from Montvale Avenue as the building had been sold and subsequently tied to adjacent ones, creating a mini mall with the multiple buildings now tied together. URS moved to larger floor space within an Industrial Park, in Wilmington. This would be one of a few moves.

Good thing—the computer peripherals were coming in (and out) by the truck loads, and Montvale location wouldn't have been able to handle the volume.

I had no idea the number of accounts URS had through mostly eastern Massachusetts and southern New Hampshire——many banks, more than one stock brokerages, insurance companies, town and city schools, town and city administrative departments, manufacturers, teaching schools for keypunch operators— and retailers. By now, URS was established as the Unit Record 'anchor' and other potential customers came to URS first and in many cases were now referred by IBM.

Both Filene's and Jordan Marsh were still in punch cards as well as using Mainframes. Filene's accounting department was right on Washington St, in downtown Boston and one of my first 'visits', I drove up to a Parking Garage— and after I got out, the attendant drove it into an elevator and when he got out——it was in a cubicle around the sixth floor delivered there by the elevator not only going up, but simultaneously sideways! But it wasn't handy for me if I needed a part or anything I might have in the car. Never realized Boston had a parking garage of that design! However, I did find another garage, this one with ramps and an elevator— easier access for me.

Jordan Marsh also had machines in a large warehouse in Waban—off Route 128, near Waltham.

As can be concluded, I was beginning to spend many hours in Boston——such places as Post Office Square, the Financial District, the 'old' Scollay Square, which is now known as Government Center. (Incidentally, Boston City Hall is right there also——that's the building when built—the contractor must have had the blueprint upside down———— the building sure looks like it came out, upside down!!)

By the end of 1984 and after nearly four years as a contractor, 'management' asked me more than once to become an employee. After considering that I'm now tickling age 57——I realize not many companies nowadays want to hire a person in the high fifties to become an employee. With many benefits as medical insurance for both Bunny and I, paid vacation(s), salary, and a company car with ITS many amenities— I did agree to join URS as an employee and I add, it was a smart move for more than one reason.

By mid 1980's, I seem to be averaging 800 to 1000 miles a week, a company car changes that topic a great amount, mostly to my benefit. With this amount of driving, I had Bunny do the weekend driving. This gave me a break —let me see some of the countryside, it gave her experience which built her confidence.

With over 20 years and the machine experience I now have, I can fix these machines with a low amount of stress and diagnostic time. I have also begun to notice that many of the machines are now off the 'front line.' They may even be in the back room—possibly a room with the lights out when I get there. Most interpreters and even many reproducers may now be in a warehouse or storeroom. Also, MOST accounts don't even have accounting machines (402 or 407's), maybe still a few, but no 602's—no 604's—no bankproofs!

In becoming an employee, I was told to go down to Stoneham Ford and pick out an Escort (1985) and if this probably generates a smile—— my own car that I had used, was a Toyota Corona, so I like a small car, and here's why——I developed a philosophy while driving in Boston, —if I see two inches of space, I 'gonna' take ONE of them, because if I don't, someone else will take them BOTH!!

I also found many other Boston drivers must drive with that same philosophy! And believe me—it's a lot easier to get into those tiny spaces with a small car, than a full sized one.

For months and months, I used to finish the day in Downtown Boston and when I headed home, it was always a scramble on the Southeast Expressway OR Storrow Drive and then to get on the Mass. Turnpike and head west—three lanes of traffic—bumper to bumper and many times right into the blinding sun!

Two other places I quite often finished the day was either Quincy or Lynn, take your choice—either fight your way right into the city, then the Pike, OR get on 128 for a LONG ride either way to the Pike. I generally averaged well over an hour getting to the house, and at times, it could be an hour and a half!

My Escort made a total of about 13 or 14 Escorts URS had —my first one was a 1985 a manual shift and I had to negotiate with Don to include A/C. More than once in the four years prior, it had taken me over an hour to go about 7 miles from Quincy into Boston and in the sun it would be VERY uncomfortable without A/C, and then to arrive at a customers account looking AND feeling like you had been dragged most of the way!

Soon, I was called on to teach a course or two starting with the Keypunch as Carla Bengston and Jimmie Flahive had been hired as Field Engineers.

Much later, I remember teaching Dennis Foley the Keypunch, only this time it was taught in the machine 'cemetery' building in Andover and during the 4 or 5 days—it much have been winter, the place was like a refrigerator, but we succeeded!

Later, Jamie Dennis and Vinny DelSignore were hired and they were taught on Keypunches also.

By now, Ralph Alfaro was also being used as an instructor of various machine types.

As time passed, I taught a couple other machine types and occasionally, offering a little guidance with customer relations and common sense. After all,——I am getting quite experienced—even if I am becoming an old geezer!!

BECOMING GRANDPARENTS

On April 19, 1983 our older daughter gave birth to our first Grand child in Framingham, Ma. He was so small (and premature), he was immediately moved to New England Medical Center in Boston. I was late getting to the Framingham Hospital—then Bunny and I also went into Boston. He was making good progress and was in good hands.

Bunny and I came back to pick up her car in the hospital parking and as we drove in——some yoyo had driven off the road across the sidewalk and slammed into the front end of Bunny's car. It was damaged enough so it had to be towed to a body shop in Westboro. It was repaired and with a job done so well, you would never know it had been clobbered. This car was a 74 Cadillac Bunny had bought from Regina Pierce who she worked for. Man—what a car, two door white hard top. As a matter of fact, Regina had gone to one Caddy dealer to look and typically her——didn't change clothes etc. and was dressed so to be able to pump gas or whatever—looked like a 'bag lady' and the salesman wouldn't give her the time of day let alone show any interest as a salesman!

So she went to another Caddy dealer—found what she wanted and wrote a check for it! Never judge a book by the cover. (This woman was a sharp business woman —owned a lot of property and—,a few bank books also)!!

Here, I could insert a joke, but in the interest of good taste ——I won't!!

The Framingham Police had found who did the damage—— he didn't have enough money to cover the damages—but our insurance company covered it. In the meantime a court date was set——some insurance agent from Greenfield was supposed to represent the insurance company in court,—but didn't show up. But, Bunny went as planned and explained to the judge what happened The defendant had 200 dollars—and was directed to give it to Bunny. Later, the missing insurance rep called us at home and stated that 200 was supposed to be his fee. I told him he didn't earn it by not showing up in court, so we're going to keep it to cover the deductible. This must have irritated him and he made some sort of 'legal' procedure remark. By now, he had irritated me and I told him to get lost!! (Must be he did— —never heard from him again)!

BUNNY'S HEALTH EXPERIENCE

1983 was also the year Bunny was experiencing pain and in being shuttled to a specialist in Boston—was told she needed to have a hip replaced. This came about from a serious asthma condition which could take quite a detailed explanation——the details which I'll pass over but regardless, she went to Boston Medical Center and had the hip replaced. It was deduced that the steroids given her for a short period of time, had shut off the blood flow to her hip. Before she left the hospital, she had the other hip Cat Scanned and which looked normal.

However about 18 months later, the second one gave problems and was replaced also. She has fully recovered and without any apparent side effects, but still does have to treat her asthma medically and with respect! But this does give her reason to want to leave Vermont or New England during the winter months, so we head south to Florida.

The author and his wife, Bunny, approximately 1983. Location and origin of photo is uknown. Apparently sideburns were still common – at least to me!!

COMPANY CAR

It was in 1985 when one day I was in the URS building, Tom said for me to give my Escort to—well I don't remember, but one of the Customer Engineers. I should have the 1985 Mercury (Marquis) 4door sedan. This was quite an improvement—this had automatic—A/C and many other accessories. This was during the time most manufacturers were down sizing their cars—this one was a smaller sedan

In 1987, I again went to Stoneham Ford and picked up a new Escort as the Merc now had enough mileage so it was requiring a lot of attention. And I really didn't mind going back to an Escort—they were dependable and covered the ground well.

LISA IS MARRIED

On December 7, 1985, Lisa and Kenneth Wall (better known as Kenny), were married in Leicester, Massachusetts. A fairly large Catholic Church provided the place for the marriage. The reception was held at the Spencer Country Inn in Spencer Ma.—a few miles west of the church and on Route 9.

This was decorated as a Christmas type theme, being the wedding was in December. As this is being written—that date was 21 year ago—how time flies!

THE MISERY PREVENTATIVE

I really don't know when I initially thought about this topic ——but let's take an educated guess and say————1985.

The hairs in everyone's nose is put there by Mother Nature and it's there to filter the air you breathe. There to filter out any and all foreign material so the air that goes down into your lungs is CLEAN.

Now —before you bend over in laughter and start slapping your knees——stop and let me tell you what I've been doing for about 15 to 20 years and during that time ——I haven't had a cold, that I can remember! Once—maybe twice I had a couple of sniffles, but that's all. SO —WHAT'S the answer?

Each day, in the shower, I cup my hands —fill them with water and then bring my hands up and toss the water in my nose!! I don't breathe in and I don't breathe out—I just toss this water into my nostrils and let it fall out——at least three times each shower.

It is my sincere and honest belief this washes the hairs and cleans them to the extent any germ picked up and then filtered out by the nose hairs prevents most —if not all- germs in the air that causes colds, or a condition that can lead to a cold.

After all, how many germs can adhere to these hairs each day without THE ONE that passes through and then causes a cold?

For me, flooding the nostrils, each day, cleans sufficiently to certainly minimize the chance of having one pass through, and while I can't guarantee this works for everyone—try it—it just may work for others! And naturally, watch your vitamin C intake.

HOUSE————GETTING HELP

Some topics back——I explained how the old house we owned had progressed through various stages of remodeling. This included the upstairs bedrooms, the upstairs bath—the kitchen, adding a half bath near the kitchen entry door (which is now finished and useable), and the living room where the pond side closed porch used to be.

Outside, I had succeeded in removing the old shingles (of multiple colors) and in their place installed Insulite siding, which really was Masonite. To do this job on a two story house required staging to be built —then disassembled and again built in the new location in addition to actually applying the siding. This was done on three sides of the house and I purposely left the garage side undone because of the work left, in regard to the garage.

Through the months of getting acquainted with the 'guys' at URS I had mentioned that I was going to tear the old garage down ——so Tony DelSignore, Mike Alloso, Jamie Dennis, Vinny DelSignore, Kevin Clancy, Jimmie Flahive and a couple more volunteered to come to Northboro one Saturday and make it a project. They arrived in mid morning and by late afternoon, the old garage and attached tool shed were on the ground in a heap. (I would still be working on it if they all hadn't pitched in)!

I would imagine there might have been a beer or two— they were all of age—but when the work was finished Bunny had a full course meal which quickly disappeared, and a couple hours later—they had left.

I was really thrilled to see all the scrap go to the dump— which then was just beginning to be a problem and while the garage was gone —this is the time to have the OLD big tree removed that used to be between the garage and the pond—it had about three trunks, was in poor shape and would have been much more difficult to remove with any garage there, old or new.

Naturally, I had been working on a floor plan to the new garage, which will now tie on to the house and also will allow us to go from the garage into the house WITHOUT going outdoors. This will really help Bunny after backing the car in the garage and bringing in groceries if I'm not there. Eliminate one more chance of her falling on ice or getting wet in the rain. It WAS necessary for her to back in ——with any snow or ice— she needed that 20 feet of start to make it UP the drive, being rear wheel drive, it could easily get stuck on a horse bun! (My car stayed outdoors, and I never ceased to be amazed how that front wheel drive dug right through snow and without snow tires)!

In the meantime —I now have to plan the construction and get the permit to continue with this project.

HOUSE——SLOW PROGRESS

The house was on the edge of a pond, but the ground was just high enough to require a retaining wall. There was a wall there made of cement blocks—but through the years, age had taken its toll and now—now something had to be done. Over time I had wrestled with a solution to this and for a time, I felt I would hire a front end loader to cart a couple of 'jersey barriers' just by the house —my side 'lawn' to the north had about 8 feet (plus) to the property line. Then, I was afraid this would cave the block foundation in due to the weight and being too close to the house.

I knew any type of wood was out—fear of pollution to the pond—couldn't easily pour concrete—it would have to be hand carted, which could be done—but here again, pollution—forms in the pond etc? As you can imagine—the house takes all but about 8 feet in width of the whole lot! And by now in 1986, the town conservation committee has become very strict and very restrictive —as are all the other building restrictions. I finally hit on field stone and found the man that would remove the block wall and then build a field stone wall —my neighbor, Art Chaulk wanted his done also.

We had to have a conservation committee meeting—advertise in the paper of the meeting and fortunately he went to the meeting with Art and I, and answered a few questions—— it was a hassle and by now, it was November.

We got the approval, it was done and really looked great!

The house outside has progressed from the pond side around the blind side to a point where clapboards and painting are in process at the top. Still to be done is the porch extension, porch roof across the front — new clapboards, paint and shutters.

FRONT PORCH

In the meantime, I had torn down and built a new porch on the road side, which included the finishing touches to the entry around the front door, finished the house with clapboards —painted grayish/blue and added shutters—and also had gained the permit for the garage. THIS wasn't easy!

GARAGE PLANS

I had drawn plans for the garage addition and in doing so, had moved the garage wall closer to the house by 2 feet or slightly more. The wall was presently right on the property line and I wanted to stand on my own ground to paint in the future. Also, future owners may NOT get along with the neighbor as well.

The building inspector shot this down————can't move walls and design this, the way I wanted————side line clearances come into play here. ALSO, if I tear the whole garage down, it can't be rebuilt —violates existing building code. BUT—I can remodel the garage by removing all BUT one wall and then rebuild—called remodeling, providing I didn't exceed floor area by more than 50 % from existing.

I redrew the plans using these guidelines, and I varied the tiny alley between the house and the garage, (where the wall would remain standing) and also moved the face of the garage back and forth on paper to the spot where I increased the floor area, BUT DIDN'T exceed the maximum allowed—actually I left a couple of square feet for insurance.

The permit was issued—now to proceed.

JOE PULSIFER AND PIANO LESSONS

About 1986, someone asked me if I had ever heard 'the guy at Tom Foolery's play the piano?' As I hadn't heard of him, I also hadn't heard him play the piano. Tom Foolery's was a unique and classy restaurant on Route 9 in Westboro, less than a mile west of I-495.

So after being told he was there 5 nights a week in the lounge—I wound my way over there one evening in the middle of the week.

I easily found my way into the lounge and, although this place had been there for a year or two, I had never been in it. The lounge was done in a Victorian Style, —you know with the old style chairs and love seats—the walls were all bookcases and an abundance of books on the shelves, actually thousands of them. In one corner was a large grand piano with Joe seated so he could look out into the room. It was a piano bar—high seats around it and a top over the piano where the women deposit their handbags.

I took a seat at the side where I could look right at the keys —at the time, there was only one or two other people. As Joe played, I knew this was someone who could really entice me to work and try to develop a style. He played songs from the 1930's 1940's and a few from the years following, what is known as Main Street Jazz. Joe was a professional musician and had worked the Boston area all of his life.

After he had played songs I knew and liked, he announced he would take a 10 minute break. So before he headed for the bar——I asked him if he gave lessons. He said he did and whipped out a business card——and added for me to give him a call to set up an appointment. His studio was in Newton (Boston suburb). Later, I gave him a call and we arrived at a time on Saturday at 11 AM.

The day of the appointment, I was on the Massachusetts Turnpike headed east when it dawned on me, "What am I nuts——nearly sixty years old and going for a piano lesson?"

However, I had made the commitment so I didn't turn around and cancel out as I had an impulse to do!

After the initial 'lesson' or two, my interest greatly increased and this was for a couple of reasons. First—there was his style and type of music, which was just exactly what I was after—and secondly after a few 'sessions', he started to 'take apart' a few of the displays I had 'kind of slid into'. In place he showed me numerous ideas which were really interesting. This also gave me more insight to his capabilities.

Joe Pulsifer — the King at Tom Foolery's

Over a period of time, I had progressed enough so Saturday mornings became an important AND interesting part of the week.

Here, I should say that I had numerous prerequisites that are helpful in becoming a piano player. Some fundamentals were inherent or perhaps occurred just hearing my Mother play the piano, these fundamentals became somewhat natural through the repetition of hearing her——— some fundamentals were taught to me by her and the con-

and Con—as second banana!!

stant drilling and again repetition whether I realized it or not, at the time were embedded in my mind—playing trumpet for years gave me a good insight to song construction——listening to the music styles I liked provided sounds I wanted to duplicate——working with hand tools for years certainly helped me to develop dexterity or a 'touch'———my memory I was blessed with contributed a lot and also made the piano a lot easier and now—Joe showed me the 'ropes' and did it in a style that made the whole damn effort fun!!! If I hadn't met him, I probably would not have progressed enough to make the effort pay off,— and just for my own satisfaction and enjoyment!!

One evening after I had been taking the Saturday morning lessons for about 2——3 months, I was sitting at the end of the piano listening to his presentations. After 30 or so minutes of playing AND entertaining, Joe stood up and announced he was going to take a break and during that time——Con sitting 'here' will fill in for a few minutes. Little did I know that was coming——and my initial impulse was to back away!! However, the place wasn't packed, although there was probably 20-25 people around but the seats around the piano were all filled! So I took my position on the piano bench and started producing a few tunes I knew quite well and thought the listeners would appreciate. I know I was up tight——even though I had played at gatherings before—playing for people who were paying to be entertained was a whole lot different than yakking with friends!

To be honest——Joe did the right thing by just announcing I was going to do this—I didn't have time to get up tight, let alone back out at the last minute!!

And since that time, my courage to perform has greatly strengthened.

Here, I should say playing in public or as a presentation isn't as difficult as it was——and I'm just now getting to a point where I can look around some and NOT be so darned uptight.

I will come back to this topic.

HOUSE—LONG TIME PROBLEM

In 1986, I felt the time had come to do something about a long time problem and this dealt with town sewage. None of the houses on the eastern edge of Solomon Pond had anything but septic systems —appropriately called 'on site sewage' vs. town/municipal sewage.

I know this is a poor subject, but you may someday want to get **your** sewage treated(!!)——and it does have information that could be of value to a reader somewhere—it may be worth it. It will also exemplify how complicated this world can be and unknowingly at the time—something to throw money at!!

Solomon Pond, where we lived was clean water without any pollution—however, that is becoming a rarity and probably if the truth were known—it WAS becoming more polluted than anyone realized, in spite of testing every three years.

Town sewage had been installed in the Industrial Park across the pond —voted by the town in roughly 1968 and the line came down the main street within the Park, and then through the 'woods' to a treatment plant about a quarter mile east from our house on Boundary Street.

Later, in 1984—the town of Northboro installed another 'line' in Solomon Pond Road right past our driveway on its way from the existing line in the previous paragraph toward the town center. The pipe as it passed our driveway was buried deep——actually it was 28 feet below the surface.The installing contractor had major problems getting it so deep. During the process, a survey was done to see if the houses 'down' on the Pond (ours and at least 6 more)—could 'tie in' using the gravity method——no one ever heard and I wasn't that anxious to spend money I didn't have.

Now comes a complication. The State had passed a law years prior, but had not enforced it——Title 5—a law, part of which, that requires septic inspections prior to any property sold, for compliance (to Title 5). ANY cesspool is now illegal—full fledged septic systems are now required by law to have a tank and with adequate leach fields. Any property found illegal during an inspection must be brought up to level of the present law——even if the seller decides to pull the property from the market!!(Later, that was reduced).

One house, near my daughter Lisa's house in Leicester, was put on the market for 80,000 dollars and the owner had to spend 20,000 dollars to bring the septic system in compliance!

OUR house had 2 cesspools and NO WHERE NEAR enough land to install a legal system.

THIS MEANS WE NOW OWN A HOUSE THAT CAN'T BE SOLD!!!

Our only alternative is 'tie in' to a municipal system. Even though, right now, I don't really want to sell——but there will come a day when we will.

So in 1987, I went to the six other people near us, to sample their feelings. I was the ONLY property owner with access to the street—all the others used a varying portion of our driveway for access to the street. This means any pipe to go UP to the street would also use our drive. And now the open lot bordering our drive and at the corner of the street was sold —a new house was going up and the new owner(s) might not want to allow a backhoe or excavator to wander over the 'lawn' digging a trench for us.

Everyone agreed NOW is the time to advance this project. We asked the contractor, who was also an engineer, and who was building the two houses to quote an estimate for the pipe installation down to a certain point. Also, this would help bring him —hopefully —to allow the pipe to be installed.

He and two other excavating contractors estimated a cost of 35 to 40 thousand dollars, which divided 6 ways would be 5 to 6 thousand apiece. Could be done, BUT ALL excavator contractors wanted plans drawn to be more specific and then an accurate estimate would be given.

Next, a local Engineering company in business for at least a dozen years was brought in——did the surveying—drew the plans with side elevations, topographical etc——but for a cost of 11,000 dollars!! This was paid for by the 6 parties and now we went after an accurate estimate. Guess what —this now came in —all about the same with an **installing cost above**——130,000 dollars!! Guess you know that drove a nail in the pine box containing that whole idea!

TO REPEAT—WE STILL OWN A HOUSE THAT CAN'T BE SOLD!

So for the moment, this project stopped and we all went about our normal lives—I did most if not all the leg work and IT required a lot of time, telephone work and effort to keep this pushed along. Now I'm putting it on the back burner.

This did bring about many questions about my property and its boundaries, and which I also wanted answers to—especially the property boundaries 'up the drive' to the street where other people had access to, and usage of.

The driveway also had a gas line and a water line, both buried that was 'common' down to a split point, in the driveway.

So, I had our property resurveyed to accurately define the property and this plan was mailed to me with a bill for 500 dollars. THEN —the engineering company closed its doors and disappeared!! No explanation of the plot plan and no additional info could be had——been in town for 15 years and now——they're gone!!

At least, now I had an up to date plot plan——when we bought the house—there was no plot plan—most houses in the 1960's didn't have plot plans.

The boundaries to our house, were pointed out by the Real Estate Broker, before we bought and collaborated by the Carl Daoust, my next door neighbor and who had been associated with his property and surrounding ones for decades.

So my attorney now took the plan and had it registered at the Worcester County Registry of Deeds. (At the time, it seemed like the right thing to do).

URS——TIME FLIES

After URS had moved more than once, around 1986, Tom McHugh bought a piece of land just south of Route 128 and east of Route 28 right at the intersections of Stoneham, Wakefield and possibly Woburn. Tom liked the location, it was near the golf course he was a member of!

Here, he had a building put up, (a top notch well engineered office type building), at the end of a dead end street with city utilities. URS occupied the upper level and a tenant leased the lower level, as it was built on an incline. This was Corporate Headquarters, and Sales offices——URS Service was separate. I don't recall just where we were at that specific time— but I suspect it was in a separate building in a Wilmington Industrial Park. The ground floor of Tom's building wasn't large enough at this time for the entire company, due to the number of Mainframe Peripherals coming in and going out. In addition, Punch Card equipment was still moving also. It was easy to see the 'old gray stuff 'was diminishing and equally easy to see that by now, URS was heavily into Personal Computers. PC's are operating under the DOS system and will be for some time yet. I didn't get into PC's, however by now, I did spend time on the 3287—3278 and 3274 units mainframe peripherals, which are a lot different than Punch Card machines.

One account in Worcester had over 300 terminals in one room which is a lot of units—I can remember if you dialed 1-800 FLOWERS, this is where the phone order was received——you can imagine what it must have been like prior to Mothers Day!!

Once again, I was told to relinquish my 87 Escort and pick up a new 1989—this one was factory equipped with A/C and one I'll get to know very thoroughly.

URS had gained Pratt and Whitney Aircraft in Hartford, Ct. for an account with about 18 to 20 keypunches. A service call, when dispatched in the manufacturing plant that was so large— URS dispatch was to obtain a building post number so the machine could be found!

At another Pratt and Whitney location and in the major rebuild area for customer owned engines —I walked around with my mouth open in awe while viewing some of these engines up close—just imagine an intake fan on a jet engine nearly 8 feet in diameter!!

This also brought about the Electric Boat division of General Dynamics in Groton for Punch Card machines they owned, and needed service. I couldn't help but think each time I went there ————here is the leading technology in submarine construction——atomic power, latest armament, radar etc.—and being accomplished by IBM Punch Card machines, most from the 1950 vintage, if not all!! An 082 sorter there was a 1953 model and finally was replaced by a 1960 083 Sorter——however, the machines did the job and there was nothing newer, so the age of the machines was incidental!

This location was not the easiest place——once through the gate, you had to be constantly escorted—even to the men's room and all the people in the department were women. It could be a little embarrassing having a woman wait for you in the hallway outside the Men's Room, while you spend a few moments inside probably looking at the ceiling!!

I never did get to see a sub under construction—totally off limits and well it was!

URS—GOES PERSONAL COMPUTER

At the beginning of the 1990's, URS bought Data Spectrum, located in Wilmington (Ma.). This company was heavily into Personal Computers, both sales and service. URS gained many good people with this acquisition and, of course many new accounts—even in Connecticut where there was a sub office.

The operation was soon moved from Wilmington to, — and incorporated into the URS building, also in Wilmington (Ma.). Naturally, as time went on, some newer employees drifted away and the total workforce from the acquisition was reduced. But those that remained like Lynne Duncan, Linda Gangestad, Ralph Martucci, Marilyn King, Steve Rossi, Greg Rasso and his wife Kerrie joined some of the existing URS people like Mike Allosso, Kevin Clancy, Bob Jarvis, Walt and Kevin Duffy, Eddie Mark, Doug Hardy, Ritchie Racine to name a few helped URS (plus management named previously) to become a bigger sales 'house'. Also, a stronger supplier of service on Personal Computers, computer related equipment plus new and 'older' peripheral equipment. Greg Rasso and others made huge strides in the service depot on peripheral repairs especially monitors.

Tony's wife, Barbara was also an employee in the administrative department of the office.

I have never been against nepotism——and here are people—related to Tom McHugh Sr.—Neil Harrington, Kevin and Walter Duffy and Anne Colleran which are fine examples of relatives working———very reliable and dedicated to their jobs, related to the Boss or not!!

Two of the 'old timers' Bob MacDonald and Mike Mayers retired in the early 1990's

The Corporate name was changed to:

URS INFORMATION SYSTEMS INC.

This was for the fact that Unit Record Service was now no longer servicing Unit Record Equipment as its main source of income, even though the equipment was still available as was the service. The Personal Computers and Mainframe Equipment now provided the main source of income and it also conveyed to the public that URS was a viable supplier of the current and 'in demand type' of IBM Data Processing Equipment.

Another account was Hamilton Standard in Windsor Locks, Ct.,—also Southern Connecticut Gas in Bridgeport/New Haven and a couple of hospitals. Those paved the way to open an office in Glastonbury, east of Hartford. Gary in sales and I worked out of this office for over 3 years. I commuted to and from Northboro (Ma.),—about 85 miles each way. I used to bring dozens of monitors back from Connecticut for the depot to repair and later, deliver them back to the customers.

Opening this office brought another employee into URS—his name was Patrick Hayden. Patrick lived in Connecticut and had many fine qualities especially in the field of Personal and Business computers. Patrick was fully knowledged and very fast in solving any type of problem—many times right over the telephone and saving a trip plus his time and machine downtime!

And with Gary working to bring in sales—he soon landed Northeast Utilities, a power generation and distribution company which served the whole state.

Northeast Utilities had so many computers and equipment in total, we interviewed many additional service oriented candidates and from those hired Peter Donat. He and Patrick became not only good employees, but good friends.

URS is going to change the automobile arrangement —— so about 6 months into the 89 Escort, the operators of all autos were given the opportunity to buy the car they're using. The change was primarily due to the high numbers of accidents and naturally the insurance costs went through the roof!!

URS will allow monthly payments on the cars sold, with no interest and an excellent deal on the price—so I bought mine.

Here, I started a separate automobile account, so every check went into the account. By the same token, every expense came out of that account. The mileage reimbursement allowed the account to build —— I took very good care of the vehicle, it was part of my income. In the years ahead, I put way over 200 thousand miles on it with minimal problems! Here, let me say that over the years cars are way better than we used to own. In general, the cars last longer, are way more dependable with far less breakdown.

In the meantime, I did a good part of the Unit Record servicing, whether it was in Connecticut, Rhode Island or Massachusetts. And——by now, this arrangement really piled the mileage on——it was not uncommon to hit a 1000 miles a week minimum and as high as 1300.

We had other Field Engineers that did cover Punch Card service calls, especially if I was a great distance away. One was Carla Bengston and another was Bill Smeltzer along with Bob Jarvis, Bob Gill, Mark Waruszyla, John Malinowski and Dennis Foley—all VERY competent on 029 and 129 keypunches and many with strong abilities on the 'bigger' Unit Record Equipment.

This activity carried way through the 1980's —into the 1990's up to about 1994.

HOUSE ——BUILDING CONTINUES

As, I moved this problem with sewage to the back burner— I certainly didn't forget it ——just shoved it from near the top of the priority list, down a few steps and then came back to the garage.

The garage was down —the scrap and debris had been hauled to a dump and the large tree between the garage and the pond had been cut down and also disposed of.

What I had now was the remains of a very poor concrete floor and a very forlorn looking wall of about 10 linear feet and single story height.

I hired a man and his son with a backhoe to come in—dig the hole—install the necessary concrete blocks and do the ground' work in preparation for the garage.

Very shortly,—it was done, now it's my turn. Within a few days, I had put up the walls not only for the garage, but the hallway between the garage and the house. Within this hall-way there would be an entry closet and another closet for clothes or misc, an entry door to an added room in back of the garage, a set of stairs up to the room in back of the garage, a door to the garage, a new front entry door, an entry way to the main house and another closet hiding a washer and dryer— the only place it could go— will get these units up and out of the cellar.

My neighbor, Art Chaulk gave me a lot of help—good help. He was very experienced in house construction and also worked for a door manufacturer about 5 minutes away. This, and his help were good reasons to buy doors and an overhead garage door and opener from where he worked at Banner Door.

So, we're really adding a one car garage, 2 rooms (1 up-1 down),couple closets, a front entry way and another entry door out the pond side of the house.

I added the plywood to the walls——placing it vertically as I had allowed for 8 foot walls with no cutting needed. Now, I'm ready for the roof to the garage part (only)—the 2 rooms in back of the garage are not on the schedule to be done yet. I called Rich—the backhoe guy and his 3 men came and added the roof. THIS was a project I couldn't do AND didn't want to do. Too many hips—crickets, and soffits to contend with—I couldn't handle it. They did this and roofed it within 3 days—the room to be added was sealed on a temporary basis. (If I had done the job—would have taken months!!)

The second day—they told me the building inspector had been there and instructed them the vertical sheathing had to be removed and placed on the studs horizontally!! Of course, by now the rafters had been installed and the 'bird mouths' came down over the sheathing. Before I had a chance to question the inspector—they cut the sheathing —removed it and reinstalled it horizontally. When I talked to him—he told me it was stronger horizontally and that's the way he wanted it. Right here——you do what HE wants—he has the power to stop the job —so, you don't argue. I didn't agree with him—he wasn't totally right but— don't win the battle to lose the war!!

It was now my job to get the clapboards and the trim boards on and to paint—if I didn't get all the outside done—no matter, it will keep till spring and the day after they left—we had snow!!

It took me a couple of weeks to rough wire the garage and entry way—to install a new large entrance panel—to install the over head door—some of these with help from Art——and then winter set in. Bear in mind, all the work done on the house was done nights and weekends——I had a full time job!

We lucked out on time, just right—Bunny could use the garage during the winter, but still had to go outside —I didn't get the hallway opened into the house yet.

Through the winter, I continued to work inside the garage—even though I had most of the rough wiring done—I still had the heat and sheetrock to contend with.

Here's the problem——I'm not sure the existing boiler will handle the extra demand, if not only for the garage—the other two rooms could be too much demand.

In addition—getting the feed and return pipes are a problem, but the biggest is that I want the 2 rooms (when finished), to be independent about heat. This means more pipes for the added zones—I certainly don't want to heat the garage if I want heat in only one room.

I should add, the room downstairs is going to be mostly a music room—piano, music, hobbies, memorabilia and more or less mine—the room upstairs will be mostly for Bunny and her 'work' area on one side and a hot tub on the other side—— when everything is completed.

The answer to the heat came easy enough—I'll put in electric heat—easier to install—cheaper to install, probably more expensive to operate, but this won't be full-time, every day.

By now, my relatively new next door neighbor—Larry McLeod, has been doing a few changes and had multiple electric baseboard elements that were going to be trashed. That solved most of the heat element 'shortages'!

Installing electric heat is pretty much duck soup—just run the Romex before the sheetrock is put on.

Everything was going great, until the building inspector made a routine visit. AND THEN gave me a surprise by stating the stringers (from rafter to rafter) were under size!! These were 2X6 and he said they should be 2X8 for that size span. I explained the lumber salesman determined what they were to be and had ordered them. The inspector wanted a certain three to be doubled, which wouldn't be easy, but I agreed to do it. And with that—he was satisfied——I kept my mouth shut after we agreed, and it wasn't easy putting the three doubling stringers in!

So after the wiring was run——sheetrock came next—and so this is how the work was done until spring. Big difference to have a garage even if the thermostat is set to 40 degrees most of the time—this prevented the paint etc. out there from freezing and also let the Bunny's car just start and go. What a big difference in having a car in a garage in the winter at 40 degrees as opposed to outdoors at 20 degrees OR lower!

We used the garage to keep most items that normally would be in the cellar—at least my 'things'——house, car and yard items.

SOLOMON POND AREA—NORTHBORO

Solomon Pond is located in the northeast part of Northboro (Ma.). After leaving Hudson Street, and then continuing on Solomon Pond Road toward the north, there is only one house on the left hand side of the road. Continuing, you will soon come to where Interstate 290 is being constructed—with an interchange at Solomon Pond Road. This will be one of two interchanges, the other being at Church Street—farther west by about 3 miles.

From the interchange at Solomon Pond Road and going east, after about 2 miles, there is another interchange with I-495.

Postcard showing Solomon Pond swimming at the future site of the Grill Restaurant. it appears that the red roof would be the roller skating building. Postcard origin can't be read. date about 1940's.

Closer to 'our' location, there are about 8 or 9 houses on the right—all single family houses and after the single house on the left, shortly will pop up the Grille Restaurant. This is right at the edge of the Pond, and started out in 1939 as a hot dog stand for the swimmers at the beach. Soon he had sold enough hot dogs so he put up a small building——just what size or dimensions, I don't know—I never saw an early picture.

Also, sometime near this—a large building was built right at the edge of the pond and was used for roller skating. Not a very fancy building—but why should it be, the only good requirement for roller skating is a smooth floor—the bigger the better.

Through the years, the roller skating interest dropped off and when we moved to the neighborhood in 1967——the building was being used as a furniture warehouse by a Northboro furniture store—R & T Furniture.

In the meantime, the Grille had increased its size in increments, so by now it was fairly large with a nice dining area overlooking the pond to the west. It also contained a Cocktail Lounge, naturally a bar and business was on the increase. By the mid 1980's the bathing beach had been shut down for liability reasons.

This establishment was owned by a (single) man by the name of Raymond LeMay. Ray lived in a small apartment upstair——served good food and at a reasonable price—so he continued with the expansion and by late 1970's, did a large remodel by adding a banquet room on the 'roadside' and also moved more tables toward the pond with a lot of glass on the west. By now, it had a large 'footprint'.

Being close to 'our' house, quite often Friday night, or sometimes Saturday nights——Bunny and I would join our neighbors and good friends—Carl and Rita (Daoust)—we could walk past 2 houses, the warehouse and next building was the Grille. Over a period of time, the wait time stretched further and further until the wait could be well over an hour to get table, even with its increased size.

I want to describe the Restaurant and the land around it for a couple of reasons—first, Ray had a private septic system and utilized the entire field beyond the building for a leach field——he had to, the number of people patronizing the business required it.

Secondly, during the spring, the sump pump in my cellar worked almost continually for about 4 weeks. The pond water would go under the house, get pumped out into the pond, under the house etc.——we had a circle there and the electric company was the only gainer from this action!

I knew Ray had built a "sluice'" from the pond across the (leach) field in the years prior and during the spring would control the height of the pond——holding it back with this "sluice" which he could add or subtract (height) pieces——all in the name of controlling the water so it minimized the effect on his leaching process. Carl knew about it and between the two of us we were pumping like fury! So, I went to the Grille, found Ray and asked him DISCREETLY if he would lower the pond so the water table would be lower. Ray didn't like that idea and was quite indignant I would even ask!! I accepted his decision and at that time put that solution in back of me —— so did Carl. The other 10 months —it was all right, and our electric bill reduced to an acceptable amount. (Kind of keep this topic in mind ——I'll touch on it again!!)

The only time either Bunny or I had steak was when we went to the Grille and she ordered steak ——the problem was she liked it RARE—very rare!!! Numerous times we sent it back as over cooked————Rita ordered her steak any way it came AND most of the time it was grilled less than Bunny's. It became harder and harder for the waitress to convince the chef to drop the steak on the grille —scoop it up, flip it and then scoop it off the grill and serve it!! "Pass it around a light bulb"!!! What could be easier?

And then——one evening Ray came to the table and informed us it would be impossible to satisfy her with a steak!

I said, "That's it?" And he nodded.

With that, we all got up and walked out!!

I doubt if we went to the grille twice in the next 2 years!!

It wasn't many months after that —Ray's health failed enough so his Manager, John C. took over the daily operation of the restaurant.

As a guess, I would say Ray died in the late eighties——John bought the business from the Estate including the land around the restaurant.

When Town sewers came down the street in 1984—the restaurant tied in and this freed up the field previously a leach field——the land was sold and condos were built there.

The 'warehouse' was converted to 2 apartments and was tied into Town sewer——but neither Ray or John would allow any of the neighbors to use the 'line', or 'encroach on their property', which would have been so easy AND so simple!

There were 2 lots between my neighbor, me and Solomon Pond Rd, which John sold and 2 houses were built there about 1988.

This land had about 4 construction trailers parked there in the late 1960's into early 1970's——used by the State and contractors while I-290 was being built. There were enough trees and growth so we had some privacy.

THE COWDREYS OF RANDOLPH

Fay Cowdrey and his wife Rose, lived on Maple Street for years. Over the period of time they had 4 children —Coleen, Rainey, Phyllis and Jack. The family was very religious oriented and faithfully attended the Randolph United Church.

The family was well known, well liked and well respected throughout the community.

At the residence on Maple street—Fay had a few of the old style soda/acid type fire extinguishers stored in one of the small buildings on the property. Inside the tank—was a 'rack' near the threaded top that contained an open bottle of sulfuric acid with the body full of water plus bicarbonate of soda. When the tank was turned upside down the acid mixed with the soda water and through the chemical action—pressure was built up forcing the water out the small hose held by an operator.

One of Fay's grandchildren took a liking to one of these fire extinguishers which on the outside probably was chrome plated. Fay asked the youngster if he liked it —and then told him, "When Grampa dies, you tell Uncle Jack that I said you could have THIS extinguisher."

On April 18, 1988, Fay passed on—so at some point, the grandson and Jack went to the extinguisher and as Jack tried to pick it up——he could hardly move it. So Jack unscrewed the top and it was full of Susan Anthony quarters——many pounds of weight AND MANY dollars worth!!!

Fay had a knack for doing things like this and in this case, I'll bet the Grandson will remember that instance for years to come!

JEAN B. MONTGOMERY—1988

There have been a couple of topics in one of the three previous publications of 'A VERMONT SON', that have mentioned Jean Brigham, later becoming Jean Montgomery.

Occasionally, Jean and Dick would be present at a birthday party, or a celebration where many other friends would be present. AND, once in a while, a piano would be there also. Sooner or later, Jean would be induced to sit at the piano and give a few POP TUNES of the times.

I can attest to the ability of Jean, as I had the pleasure of 'working' the upper keyboard while she 'worked' the lower half on a couple of instances. I never ceased to be amazed at what came out of those lower keys AND oc-

Courtesy of The Herald

casionally the upper half as she did a sweep in the middle of some tune!

I was so overwhelmed at times, I toyed with the idea of walking away from any and all keys or keyboards, realizing I would never be able to 'cut the mustard' as she could! I finally realized if I screwed my head on backwards and used her abilities as a goal for my own achievements, I could turn a negative feeling into a positive answer! It worked to some extent—— only she was taken from everybody way too soon. We ALL miss her!!

GRAND PARENTS AGAIN

In April 1989, our younger daughter, Lisa gave birth to her first child—a daughter, Sarah. About 15 months later, she gave birth to Katie, gave birth to Mike, and gave birth to Chris. YEP—triplets but actually she really was playing Mother to four!!

Believe me—this is something—something not only for her or the children—something for Everyone!!

"We're One!"

THE WALL CHILDREN

Hi! Our names are Christopher Patrick, Michael Kenneth, and Katherine Anne Wall. We celebrated our first birthday on Aug. 14, 1991. We live in Leicester, Mass. with our parents, Kenneth and Lisa Wall, and our "big" sister, Sarah Elizabeth, who is 28 months old.

Our grandparents are Conrad and Bunny Wells of Northboro, Mass., Bill and Joan Wall of Leicester, ████████, Mass. Our great-grandparents include Mrs. Mary Wall and Mrs. Helen Adams of Worcester, Mass., and the late Albert Day, Ola Day, Alfred Wells, and Gladys Wells, all of Randolph.

We'd like to send a special hello to our great aunt and uncle, Lindy and Barbara Lindquist, and to all our other friends and relatives in Randolph.

Reprint courtesy of Herald of Randolph

RANDOLPH HIGH AND GRADED SCHOOL

Under the eye and guidance of Ed Sault, a local resident and contractor, the building for Randolph High and Graded School made its debut in 1911. Located on Main Street at the corner of School Street, the two story building (plus a full basement), slowly came to being and started an obligation of turning out students for many decades.

Over the years, many students came out of this building much better equipped to face the future with a rounded education. I was one of those students——starting in 1934 and staying until 1943, at which time I would transfer to Lyndon Institute in Lyndon Center, Vt. for my Junior and Senior years, ending in 1946.

Over the years, the building slowly showed its usage and evolved to become a difficult building to contend with——difficult to bring up to much later standards—equally difficult to

modify considering that construction principles and methods were considerably simpler and not likely to be as acceptable in the later years.

It was torn down in 2003 and replaced with a new building which was confined to nearly the same size footprint due to lot size. The new building is being used by Dubois and King—a local engineering concern, which had grown rapidly and outgrew its space on Route 66 —the road to Randolph Center.

UPDATE ON SISTER—NATHALIE

The last information I gave about my sister was that she had a job with an architectural company in Boston. This was about 1960. She and a room mate 'Tina" lived in an apartment on St Paul St. in Brookline—a Boston suburb. This is where I stayed when I first started to work for Cybertronics——in 1967.

My sister's company —Markus and Noka, had by this time, finally oriented themselves mostly toward hospital design — —either additional construction—add ons or the complete design from the ground up.

One job they designed and which consumed an unbelievable amount of time —was in Pakistan! I'm quite sure they worked on this hospital for 7 years!! Another job was in the Philippines—but most were closer to home and in the New England area. As a guess I would say the total employees now was around 25.

Tina was a secretary and administrative assistant to the chief surgeon of the Massachusetts Eye and Ear Infirmary in Boston and spent most of her working years at that location. The building is near Storrow Drive and close to Leveritt Circle. A very distinguishable building——the new addition added actually encircled the original building on three sides and was even built OVER the original building. In doing this —the medical operation was not stopped for the demolition during construction, and the result was a very unique building presentation!

The two of them used to take a vacation in Harwichport on Cape Cod. They both liked it well enough so about 1985 Nan bought a lot right in Harwichport, very close to the Wychmere Harbor Club and other associated buildings.

As time went on, she then designed a house and shortly after, had this house built. In doing so, they would spend the week in Boston and on Friday's, would journey to Harwichport for the weekend. This went on until Tina retired and she then spent her full time at the house and Nan continued to spend week days in Boston. This would bring us up to about 1990.

By this time, I'm quite sure the total employees would be over 100, the name had been changed to Payette Associates, the location had changed (more than once) and the architectural jobs now were many——large and complicated!

Also, the records and plans of previous work had been 'filed'— as in mess! So she volunteered to take ALL the plans, spec sheets, correspondence, develop a system of filing and originate an archival section where all documents would be in order and a great degree of organization was established—— which would be right in fashion for her life style!!

I didn't see much of her. During the week—she was quite apt to work overtime at the company. She would travel up to Boston Monday mornings and return to the Cape on Friday afternoon.

HOUSE——OTHER ITEMS

I had Mike Yellick come and re-roof the part over one bedroom —a roof that had given trouble off and on for years. So now we can get rid of the underlying cause. In doing so Mike wanted to buy our trailer which had been sitting in the yard with little use in the last couple of years. It was good to see that go as we had decided we probably wouldn't use that one anymore OR, until we reached retirement.

My next project would be the upstairs hall. Here again, Tony Delsignore, Patrick Hayden, Kevin Clancy and a couple others came one Saturday and we ripped that apart and this time I had my table saw and jointer moved right up and set it up in the hall—a lot of molding work coming up, so this would make the job easier.

I also finished the downstairs hall ——doors hung on closets, sheetrock finished, paint and stain work done, closet clothes poles installed etc.

It's now about 1990, and normal retirement date for me is 1993—— however, I plan to work beyond that for as long as the work holds out and also as long as I 'hold out'. I really never planned to retire—I like to work—BUT, the mind can dream —the body can't keep up with the mind, so now I'm thinking differently!

I'm running into a problem here—I want to finish this house in all aspects and do it without a debt.

The mortgage has been paid off and if I retire or rather when I retire —I don't want any thousands left as a debt!!

So I'm now done with most everything connected with house except the back two rooms tied to the garage.

Porch on west (Pond) side, off the kitchen as described in text. Photo by C. Wells

HOUSE—PORCH

A few Saturdays, and I had finished building a porch on the pond side. I liked this as either Bunny or I could come out of the kitchen and sit for a few moments or take a rest. This had a roof which kept it reasonably dry.

I had to put a railing on, but I kept it low so I could sit on the porch and see the water or who was fishing as I sat, and without staring at a railing!

HOUSE ——DECK FINISHED

By 1990, there were many other unfinished projects still to be done. One of those was the deck on the pond side.

It was my original intent to continue the deck on the main house and bridge it over to the next room which actually was my music room (with a Bow window).

I had placed a door for that purpose (it was also required by the building inspector). However I never went that far —— I might have, had I stayed there for a longer period of time.

Part of the view from the porch and the deck. Photo by C. Wells - about 1990.

A Progression from a camp, to a house. Photo by C. Wells - 1967

Deck on the Pond (west) side. It appears like 2 seperate buildings –and it is. Between a complicated roof and the building code restrictions, there is a partial alley between the two buildings. I didn't like that – but was powerless to change anything! Photo by C. Wells about 1990.

9 Howe Lane - Before

9 Howe Lane - As in 1968

Pond side of the house after 30 years of remodeling and modifications in 1998.

RANDOLPH DISASTROUS FIRE

In December 1991——the fire alarm sounded. The trucks and firemen didn't have far to go. The fire was in 'downtown' at the corner of Main Street and Merchants Row——actually the Sowles Block was in its last few hours of remaining at that location, as a usable building.

This was a large building and about 4 stories tall—difficult to say exactly due to the fact the hall occupied the upper stories. All the stores in the building would be destroyed as would the 2 store fronts at the top of the well known concrete steps facing Depot Square. Up the long flight of stairs to the hall were a couple of separate rooms. I don't have the slightest idea if they were in use.

I don't have the particulars of the fire——I wasn't living in Randolph at the time and all the information I have was from the article(s) in the Herald.

Again, the date was December 1991 and this could be labeled disastrous fire #1.

Regardless, it was a tragedy at the time and the building replacing it is an improvement.

Sowles Block after December 1991 - Photo by Barbara Lindquist

FIRE STRIKES AGAIN

In January 1992, fire again hit the village of Randolph—and again on Main Street—this time at the intersection of Main Street and Pleasant Street.

This was a building that had been there for many years—a wooden structure built (due to the street configuration), in the shape of a triangle.

For years, there was a gas station on Pleasant Street, — only 2 pumps with a tiny office down a few steps into the cellar. I can easily remember Harry Hudson operated this gas station—and I would estimate,1939 to about 1942. I can also remember George Manning as an operator. And again, estimating—1942 to about 1946.

At the street level and on Main Street, the stores I remember back in the 1940's was a clothing store operated by Charlie Stockwell —this was on the south end of the building next to the Christian Science building.

Next to it was George Rye's Barber Shop starting in 1924 and continuing until 1978—54 years in this location!! And during those years, others worked scissors with him such as Harold Sault. George died in 1983—but, in June 1953, in addition to many haircuts over the years,—he gave me a haircut and one of those professional Barber Shop shaves, 2 hours before my wedding!

One store farther north was Jerd's Market and after he moved to Merchant's Row (about 1939), part of the store was occupied by Lewis MacLean and his wife as a dry cleaning business.

At the end, in a separate building, was a diner—a very small diner and the FIRST operator of that was Spud Coffin. While he was the operator there, an early morning fire (about 1938), really gutted the inside to the point, it almost didn't survive. After rebuild, he vacated that to buy a house in Beanville and became a Fridgidaire dealer. He and John James, his salesman, sold a LOT of Fridgidaire appliances!

He was replaced by Percy Abare. This had to be about 1939. After a few months, Percy went to the Atlantic Diner (near the intersection of Route 14 and 107) in Royalton. Merritt Follette also put in a few months then this became Hayward's Diner operated by Chikey Hayward. I'm quite sure Leonard Porter was going to remodel it——then found out it was too far gone and the remodel became a tear down!

This Diner was two of three——the other one was operated by 'Pud'Abare in the Dustin Block, beside the Theatre ——and about 1950, John Bohnsen took over the restaurant on the corner of Main St. and Merchant's Row. He operated at this location until about 1985.

Now, not only is the Hayward Diner long gone——but the Stockwell Block as I knew it, is now gone. Actually, I knew this block as under a different name ——so I checked the reliable source——Wes and Mim Herwig's Randolph Book of 1986. The building was the Austin Smith Block and this fire wasn't the first one—a fire in 1893 burned the roof off.

Unfortunately— I do not have a photo of the Austin Smith— Charlie Stockwell Block engulfed in fire, and on its way to oblivion.

FIRE NUMBER THREE – BEN FRANKLIN STORE

In July 1992, the third fire struck the village of Randolph right in the heart of the business district. The Thomas Store, was in the middle of the long block on Main Street.

But first,——let's back way up and create some groundwork for the benefit of some local people that may be interested or have some questions a few years from now.

Belmain's had originally started on the corner of Main St. and Merchant's Row——that is, after the Post Office moved to the opposite side of Merchant's Row at the eastern end, —the year must have been around 1935. Let's assume Belmain's stayed there until about 1940. At the corner, this became a restaurant under the direction of a Mr. Brillante until 1946-1947. Then it was managed by a man and wife by the name of Gildemeister until about 1950— when John Bohnsen acquired it and continued it as John's Restaurant, until about 1985.

Back to Belmain's—after moving to the former First National Store—he expanded into the Eddie Morse Store and later, took over the former Grand Union Store. This gave him

three storefronts starting at the W.E. Lamson store and as designated by the white storefront right over the pickup truck in the photo above.

Sometime in the future—Leonards Drug store became the Randolph Savings and Loan. When that closed, Belmain's took that storefront over.

When George Belmain retired in later years—the store was run under the ownership of his right hand man—Norman Ouimette.

The Thomas store passed from Ruth and Pete Cooper to one or two other operators.

Main Street – Photos by Barbara Lindquist - July 1992

WINSLOW'S MAKE AN ENTRANCE

In October 1979, Peter Winslow bought the 'block' which contained the enlarged Belmain's Store and now would come under the jurisdiction of his wife, Joyce with considerable help from Janet Kirby —'and many others'.

This arrangement continued with the typical ups and few downs of most businesses, into the 1990's—and one of those 'ups' was— Winslow's became franchised with the Ben Franklin name.

Again, in July of 1992, the Randolph fire alarm called attention to the people of Randolph ——that FIRE- NUMBER 3 was underway and centered around the Ben Franklin Store— —Winslow's Ben Franklin Store and the adjacent well known Thomas Store——a store for basically women's clothing, shoes and accessories.

Before it was over, the Winslow block and the Thomas Store block was a total loss AND a total mess. After the debris was cleared away—all that was left was one large cellar hole from the combined two business blocks. Many employees from both stores were now out of work. After the fire, Winslows also took over the space the Thomas Store had.

'THE TENT'—— BETTER KNOWN AS THE 'AG BAG'

Between July 1992 and Christmas of the same year——— —dozens of people, local and distant scratched around —located a humongous plastic 'tent'—— one of 8000 square feet— —poured a foundation at the intersection of Main and Pleasant streets, erected this 'tent' and had a going business by December!!!

This included getting permits—sufficient money, utilities, electric power and stock!!! Amazing what can be accomplished when motivated people roll their sleeves up and head toward a nearly impossible goal!!!

Over time, the continuing effort of some of those same people slowly but surely came up with the plans, the stamina, the will — the finances—some at the State Level, ——so that hole in the ground became a real building again——a living,

"Ag Bag" temporary location for the Windslows
Photo by Barbara Lindquist, August 1992

shining example of the Winslows, other people and town offi-
cials!!

With that—— the stock was moved back to the new store,
and the tent, or the AG BAG was removed——Only NOW——
the Thomas Store location became part of Winslow's Ben
Franklin Store! The year is now 1995.

PETER DONAT

Peter was hired to work the Connecticut area and was
based in Glastonbury, for URS.

By the time he was hired, one account, Northeast Utilities
could easily keep one man busy as this account was spread
over most of the state and was loaded with PC's, but also had
terminals—printers. Peter handled himself well with PC's and
what he lacked in this area, he made up through his personality. If he got stuck, he could always call Patrick for assistance
on PC's, either over the phone or, if necessary in person.

Peter lived in East Haddam, which in geographics was
about in the south middle of the state. This was good due to
the fact that Northeast Utilities had 2 atomic generating plants
along the southern shore—town names I have forgotten.

240

Peter had a good sense of humor and was fun to be around. One day, he and I went to Hamilton Standard and to get by the receptionist always took a few moments. In this case he stated he had to see "Frank in Data Processing' , she picked up the directory —looked up and asked if he had a last name—which for some reason he didn't, so he quickly added, "Furter, maybe"! And to which I blurted out a hefty snicker—which turned into a healthy laugh by both of us——she never realized the connection, just called and someone was sent out to escort us!

Peter fell off a ladder while he was working on his barn— fell maybe 6-8 feet, but high enough to break a leg in such a way which kept him off his feet for weeks——some thing odd about the break and shortly after this happened, I retired so I didn't see him again.

A few months later developed a serious medical problem of some type and died—must have been in his mid thirties. I couldn't attend the funeral for some confliction——but, I miss the guy and—— still do!

HOUSE——TWO ROOMS FINISHED

The last large construction job was to finish the 2 rooms in back of the garage.

I had a contractor friend come and he, with his 2 men, built the frame for these two rooms. These guys were fast and did good work—but even with that the work they did, it took over a week!

I did the finish work on the inside —both up and down.

Upstairs, there were no windows on either side and on the only outside wall left, we used an 8 foot high grade double glass double door, on

The room upstairs behind the garage. Bunny's work area where various and many crafts were accomplished. Stairs are behind the TV. Photo by C. Wells 1996

the pond side. A small balcony was outside that you could stand on.

During the winter, the wind whistled across that pond coming from the west (and north) and a cheap door would be a disaster. I found that out when I put in double glass doors (totaling 16 feet) in the living room, but the doors were a low grade and made the room very chilly all winter long with the cold air leakage!

UPSTAIRS

This room upstairs was to serve two purposes——one for Bunny's crafts and other goodies she needed—also a door to the storage area over the garage, but the most important was a space for a hot tub. THAT was really enjoyable —sitting in that hot tub in the winter, getting warmed up and watching the snow blow outside with the flood light on with the temperature at 15 above or colder!!

Downstairs—again no windows on either sidewall, but a nice 8 foot wide Bow Window right in the middle of the wall looking out on the pond. At one end, were stairs going up, but in my room, I had storage for a couple of file cabinets under the stairs.

The room upstairs – the other half from the craft area. The Hot Tub was a certain delight on a cold winter night, especially when it was snowing. Photo C. Wells - 1996.

The main floor was taken up by my studio piano and by now I had acquired a Hammond A-100 organ. The walls became a display area for various and many memorabilia—wall hung photos—documents and certificates. Over the Bow Window, I installed a shelf so I could display about 15 to 20 models I had assembled from kits.

Through some referral, I made the acquaintance of George Smith and Associates, an Engineering Corp. in Worcester, Ma. —— with one of the associates being his son, George Jr. George Sr., was a retired Chief Engineer, Dept. of Public Works for the City of Worcester. In talking with him about our 'sewer tie-in' dilemma — he immediately suggested using individual pumps, one at each residence with all four pumps tying into a single 2 inch pipe running up the driveway and then dumping into the municipal sewer line in the street. This method eliminated a couple of complication factors we previously had been living with — one of which was burying the pipe in the driveway as deep as 28 feet! NOW, we only had to bury this 2 inch pipe 4 feet. He guaranteed this would work and it made the

Note the hammond A-100, also the models over the window and, in the upper right corner is a Red Comet fire extinguisher I found at a flee market and described in book – 1! The large framed picture between the window and the door is A.C. Wells and his dog, in a special type photographic finish ——circa 1888. Note pond through the window.

The south wall in the downstairs music room contains a couple of
items of posible interest. In the left photo at the top is a clock I made
when I worked at Raytheon –all reject parts of magnetrons–beside it,
my Mothers camera, and a Kodak bellows type camera (1930's). My
Mothers small hand type ice cream freezer–a steam shovel and a red
truck, mine at age 6 (behind the red shade). In the right photo–an A. C.
Gilbert chemistry set (mine at age 9)–4 IBM control panels attached to
the wall. At the very top, My Mother's cake carrier and sprinkled
throughout, various antique model cars of the 1930's. Below–my prized
Yamaha console piano!

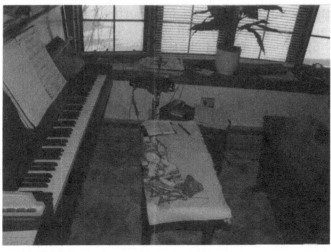

job much simpler and much cheaper! So, we arranged for him to continue for us and which brought this project off the back burner, and on to the front again.

URS——WORK THINS OUT

By 1994, work had noticeably thinned out, that is in the punch card equipment. Although there still were accounts left—a lot had gone.

I still made trips to Western Electric, (now Lucent) in Haverhill (Ma.), Electric Boat in Groton (Ct.), Hamilton Standard in Windsor Locks (Ct.), Kaman Aircraft in Bloomfield, (Ct.),—this was an interesting place, the machines were upstairs over a hangar at an airport where Helicopters were worked on and then test flown, Woburn High School (Woburn,Ma.), Brockton High School,—this is the largest High School building in the country—I guess other cities have multiple buildings, but here, get the hell out of the way when classes change or you will get ground right into the floor——it was similar to a cattle drive!

GE River Works in Lynn still has a few machines including a 108 and all the service calls in 10 years have been only feed problems on this machine —not one on any electronic problems. One day while here—through the door on the east wall— I used to spend many hours and the place was a real beehive of activity with dozens of people—so I opened the door to see what's happening now. This was eerie—not a soul in there, lights were turned dim and all you could hear was a noticeable hum——place was full of disk drives—I mean FULL and to satisfy my curiosity, I counted them —twice. There were 188 disk drives —all tied to a Mainframe somewhere, but not one person in here now!!

How times change!

I also spent a lot of time at Simmonds Saw in Fitchburg—interesting place and GE Fitchburg—Turbine manufacturing and here, for one item, I chased a problem the operator said had been on the 519 for years—no one fixed it, but a few had tried. This, naturally lit my fire and nudged my curiosity—so I had the time, spent 2 hours and found the problem in the print unit—never had that cause before. Sort of made my day!

URS had acquired Starrett Tools in Athol as an account a few months prior, and this place at the front entrance took me back to the 1950's with the woodwork —I hope they never change it, but the account took a lot of time—the machines were in questionable condition and the 088 really scared me—in the bottom of the machine were dozens of relay dust covers—whoever worked on it —would look at a high speed relay and throw the dust cover WITHOUT returning it to the relay! Wasn't many weeks I found out how bad that situation was and about the tenth time I had a relay problem——I went through all the permissive make type relays, must have been 200 total—I cleaned, checked armature motion, clearance and then placed a dust cap on each relay, which made problems **go way down**.

At Bay Banks in Waltham——there was one Keypunch in the Computer Room way down back—probably used to remake damaged cards. However to get there, I had to pass a couple of 'walls ' of monitors in subdued lighting—must have been 70 to 80—looked like a different world!!

At Raytheon in Andover (Ma.), —as you pass the receptionists desk and go down stairs——I think you must have been able to see Government Center in Boston, it was that far to the end of the corridor!

At another Raytheon site ——I was asked to check the keypunches tied into large special machines —these machines were about 8 feet square(at least), must have weighed in the tons!—I don't even dare to guess! These did a process called wire wrap. This topic was touched on many many topics back with reference I would touch on it again.

Ironically, these were in a building which displayed the FIRST Microwave oven—invented here in the late 1940's..

They were using Keypunches to feed and read cards that gave commands to the wire wrap machine— how to and where to 'make connections' while working on a special connection board about 2 feet by 3 feet. These were used in a military operation which I prefer not to elaborate on.

The keypunches were the old style 026 and this department was getting concerned about parts availability. I had an idea and told them I would be in contact if I could prove my idea was a possibility.

This had taken place before Mike Mayers had retired and I felt the 026 types could be replaced by the newer 029 Keypunches, of which we had an abundance. Parts were easily available and the 029's were advanced in many ways over the 026, therefore much more reliable.

I talked with Mike about the possible switcheroo and he worked on the project— this was right up his alley. The biggest problem he found was the 026 was opposite polarity to the 029. So I suggested why not reverse the 029 power supply polarity so it could tie into the Raytheon relay analyzer?

To make this shorter—he did, we shipped an 029 and after a few minor changes—it worked. They gained a newer type,

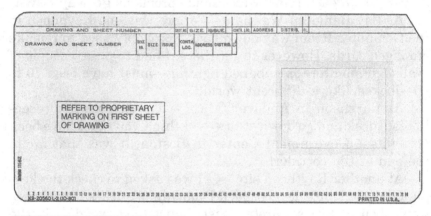

Two IBM Microfilm cards as an example described in topic.

we sold a machine and everyone was happy. Raytheon shortly bought three of these 029's.

In the future, I would make a service call here once in a while—I think they got about ten years more out of that project.

Another Raytheon location was in Portsmouth R.I.–where Naval vessels were serviced—and to which I still made service calls!

And not to forget Micro Image in Waltham who still had numerous machines. This account and most of the remainder straggler accounts used a microfiche application where a microfilm is inserted in an IBM card, as shown on the previous page, and therefore can be sorted or selected by machine for faster locating a specific engineering drawing.

GRAM SCRIBNER

During most of the 1990's, Bunny and I would travel north in order to be in Randolph for July 4th weekend, Randolph High School Alumni Banquet etc.

We stayed for a total of about 2 weeks——and in doing so, we or I could get caught up on visiting mostly friends, maybe a couple of relatives.

One trip, I was at Bunny's sister's and Lindy's house when the phone rang and the caller asked for me. It happened to be Gram Scribner. She lived in Randolph House across from the 'old' High School on Main Street .And she wanted to know if I would come over and play her piano for a short while.

I've known Gram Scribner all my life——she was also the mother to Gordon and Pete Scribner—both of whom I have worked for and described in previous issues of 'A Vermont Son'.

We agreed on a time and day and as I arrived at her apartment—she lived alone, did all of her own housework and meal preparation. She asked if I minded if she had a few of her neighbors in to listen. Fine by me!

As I played the piano, and had for a few numbers——I was looking in the kitchenette where Gram was busy. In the living room were about 20 neighbors of various ages—but all certainly over 70 and up into the 80's for a few of them. Gram was in the kitchenette fixing some punch and cookies for the guests, which

Eleda 'Gram' Scriber
Reprint courtesy of The Herald and Robert Eddy

she brought in shortly. Now, there's nothing wrong with this scene, except, at the time Gram was 100 years old!!!!

Great shape——took care of herself etc., and she's waiting on her guests!! Gram had told me in the past——she never has had a headache and I believe she also had said she was never in a hospital—quite an achievement. She was one of those rare individuals who was ALWAYS soft spoken, gentle, kind, considerate and just a real joy to make her acquaintance!

She died October 1995——we miss her!!!

MINERAL DEFICIENCY

This may be a rather peculiar topic to be in this book—however, it is part of my life and I feel it is important enough to include it. And even with that, my wife, 2 daughters and sister will have a fit—I'm always talking about my potassium level!

By age 65, I was still working full time and in doing so, I was still burning a fair amount of calories and on that basis, I was consuming an equal amount of calories.

As the years passed by, one of the prescribed medications my doctor had me consume, was hydrochlorothiazide—a diuretic whose sole purpose is to flush sodium out of the system as a way to help control blood pressure (hypertension). Unfortunately, flushing out the sodium, can also mean flushing out the potassium as SOME diuretics do AND, the doctor didn't tell me it might flush the potassium out in the process. It was here that I noticed some and/or all the symptoms listed below. (There is at least one, that is NOT supposed to reduce the potassium, and one which I now use.

Now before anyone will conclude that I am going to act as a doctor and get into prescriptions, drugs and diagnostics—I'm not. But, I will talk about what has happened to me and more than once, with regard to this topic. And I MIGHT ADD—apparently I'm more susceptible to a lack of potassium than 'others'.

Anyone approaching senior citizen age, naturally needs to reduce calorie intake, because all those calories are not going to get burned and the net result is a weight gain. It stands to reason that with less calories, there is also a reduction in the intake of vitamins and minerals.

This is where the problem(s) start—your body needs a certain minimum amount of these items and the answer may be to take a daily multivitamin. That may help in meeting the minimum of vitamins and minerals, PROVIDING the correct ones, in the correct amounts and ALL taken are properly absorbed.

It isn't the point of this topic to get into a discussion of vitamins and minerals—it IS very important, providing the intake is digested and distributed throughout the body for one good reason. Your body is one big chemical tree and needs to continue receiving these vitamins and minerals in order to provide all of the various organs with the necessary fuel to function correctly.

ONE of those really important fuels is potassium, and this element may not be in sufficient strength in some multivitamins. It can be taken as a supplement—but I don't take potassium pills and I wouldn't feel comfortable in taking them —— I feel too much potassium may be as detrimental as too little!

I get my potassium through regular food intake—it's easy— it's cheaper—it's easier to keep track of. Everything that I have read in relation to amount states around 3500 mg as a daily intake. From a personal exposure, I need to intake a minimum of 3000 mg (or more) a day, which will prevent weird effects if I don't consume nearly that amount.

Quite often, I either get distracted or diverted and over a period of a few days, potassium will start to run low. Here's what I feel when I start to get potassium deficient. I feel weak— a definite lack of strength or drive—I get unstable, my balance is touchy to start with,—low potassium amplifies this imbalance. I experience a peculiar 'presence' which is hard to explain. All this starts very slowly and soon I feel like I'm coming 'unglued'.

To think about low potassium often escapes me—even as many times as I have experienced it, until it finally dawns on me! It's a very peculiar feeling but there is a very easy way to feel better and quickly!

Here's what I do——drink 3 — 8 oz. of low sodium V-8, (8oz is about 700 mg of potassium!), eat a banana or two (about 400 mg each), and with that, I'm nearly at the 3000mg. It takes about 20 to 30 minutes and slowly, a change to 'normal' feeling will come about. The third 8 oz. should be at bedtime.

Other items are a can of carrot juice (1 can is about 800 mg— I can easily drink 8 oz.—but you may have to acquire a taste), have a baked potato (about 800mg for a medium to large potato), drink 8oz. of milk, drink 8 oz. of orange juice or eat 4-6 ounces of raisins and repeat in a few hours. I like Dole raisins —their sweet, soft, tasty and work quickly, but watch the calories!

Here's another item I've found————when I get low in potassium, my blood pressure goes up—soon as I get a day or two of potassium working—my BP ultimately goes down.

Back in the middle 1980's, I brown bagged lunches, so I experimented with various foods and it was here I found raisins would really help to lower MY blood pressure. My doctor didn't believe it—said there hadn't been any studies done to conclude that. About 10 years later, it WAS concluded raisins or the potassium in them WAS beneficial!

This MAY be unique to me, but I doubt if I'm THAT much different!

PROGRESS ON HOWE LANE

All the pieces have now dropped in place well enough to warrant going back to the Engineering Office in Worcester to proceed. This meant a new set of plans—not as elaborate as the first set, but it does require a new set of plans, much of the information can be taken from the first set and transferred. This set will show where the pump(s) will be and where the connecting pipes will join etc.

At this period of time, two of the original neighbors have dropped out, which leaves 4 of us (one having a double connection) and we will still proceed. We have made contact with the pump suppliers, we have lined up an excavator, who lives 2 houses away from me, also my neighbor Fred Dolan (a participant)— 2 houses in the opposite direction will be the plumber for the job.

There was a lot of 'ground' covered and now

Pumps (4) waiting to be installed.
Photo C. Wells

we're close to opening the drive to bury the pipe. It's November, and I'm uptight about the ground freezing——snow coming and the contractor with the equipment is wasting time— valuable time. I realize he probably isn't just waiting for our job——he may be tied up——nice if he would tell us, IF he was!!

Finally, a backhoe is delivered and a few other pieces and in one day they dug and buried about half the distance from the street down to the split in the drive.

That night, it snowed and snowed some more! Now, we have a mess especially in front of the garage and for a distance from the garage of about 50 feet.

It stayed that way until next spring——the ground froze— it was difficult to plow the snow——the backhoe didn't move for 2- 3 weeks——a general mess!

The four pumps were delivered and stood by themselves ——so we moved them where the wind couldn't blow them over and damage them. They were 8 feet tall and I had a hard time convincing myself they could be buried that deep with a high water table that near the pond.

A COMPLICATION

Now—we had a complication. Each house on the street had a pipe stub from the main pipe to the edge of the property, so the street wouldn't have to be reopened when a 'tie in' is made in the future. This would also give us a place to tie in to the main line. BUT,——the water/sewer department didn't give me a tiein because the Water Superintendent said I didn't own any street frontage. To this I countered I DID OWN PROPERTY FRONTAGE ON THE STREET—10 feet of frontage. In checking the Tax Assessors map——there wasn't any shown!?! And this is where he went wrong. This was clarified by noticing our 200 foot driveway was shown on a different tax assessors map—all by itself.

However, this didn't provide a stub——and to install a stub at the street, would take special equipment——it would have to be buried down 28 feet!!!!

9 Howe Lane after pump installation–can barely be seen lower right edge. Photo C. Wells - 1995.

COMPLICATION CLEARED

Next spring when work resumed—— we REALLY LUCKED OUT by the fact there was a manhole in the street for the sewer line and RIGHT SMACK in front of our driveway. The pipe could be run under the paving and down the side of —what is called a 'chimney'—meaning the stack from the manhole DOWN to the Main pipe. Our pipe would be attached to the sidewall, by the contractor.

My neighbor, as mentioned and one of the four persons, is a plumber——he will work with the excavator/contractor and install each pump, wire it and attach all the plumbing!

Now—NOW —we're in business and with town sewerage—
—now, if I want, I can sell the house —it will comply with
Title 5!

Of course, this cost over 16000 dollars each —— first engineering costs, second engineering cost, excavating cost, pump
and installation costs.

Not cheap and not fun!!

ON THE ROAD

When you drive an average of 1000 miles a week, sooner or
later, an interesting incident or something will come along
which helps to break the monotony.

After spending so much time and so many miles 'on the
road,' this would be a good place to bring out a couple of those
incidents. The time these happened within a year really makes
little difference, so this topic could be inserted most anywhere.

I had finished a service call at Raytheon in Waltham, Ma.,
on Route 20 headed west, and after I had crossed over Route
128 I could now head south. The 'on ramp' came up—which I
took and momentarily I was ready to merge with the south-
bound traffic on Route 128. Really doesn't make much difference what time of day you drive 128—it's always crowded, so
as I came into 128, I was getting up to speed and at about 60, I
was making my way over to the high speed lane by close merg-
ing more than once. As I finally succeeded and changed my
vision quickly from the outside rear view mirror to the windshield—all of a sudden a mouse stuck his head up out of the
air intake vents right in front of the windshield!!!

Stuck his head up and looked right at me—it was so fast
and SO unbelievable, it startled me—how the Hell did a mouse
get in that space—it's sealed from the engine compartment
below when the hood is down.

Anyway, it would duck out of sight and then pop his head
up again and at 60 MPH 'he' was getting quite a breeze!. He
looked in the glass as if to say, "Man, we're really moving"!!!

When I parked at the next customer, I released the hood and left it open enough so if I'm lucky—he'll find a way out—— and he did!!

Another time, I was on Route 128 and amongst the vehicles in the 3 lanes were many cars, trucks, buses—even a horse trailer. As I now had passed all the TV transmitting towers in Needham—traffic had thinned out somewhat and by the time I had passed Canton, it was noticeably thinner. Then I came to a spot where up ahead it looked like there was water in my lane—and enough to be noticeable.

I thought that was peculiar that it rained enough to accumulate but only noticeable in this one lane???? Then as I drove through it——I found out it wasn't rain—rather let's say it wasn't fresh water rain—it was rain as one of the horses had made it!!! AND—it certainly wasn't fresh water, not after being run through a horse first!

My Jolly (sounds like Wendell Eaton), ——I had to get off 128 and find a car wash. It stunk so bad I could easily tell where it came from!!! From that point in time, I now——never follow a horse trailer!!!

Couple years ago—about 2002, I was at an early stage of acid reflux, this was before I recognized what it was, and how to contend with it. As I was driving back from Florida—and to lower my stomach discomfort, I unhitched my belt —opened the britches and even lowered the fly, as I drove.

I noticed, coming down one of the hills approaching Reading. Pa.—my trailer brakes were poor and then I analyzed the plug had probably come out of the socket in the pickup bed—I proved it by looking in the mirror at a side direction light on the trailer. Not a good situation to be in!

Now——approaching a traffic light —this is where I'll fix the plug, even if the traffic is thick——I'm in the left lane almost on the center dividing line ready to go one block and then turn left. I hated to open the door, the cars on the other side are that close——but I opened the truck door—hopped out and as I touched the pavement, my pants suddenly were headed down!— BUT I caught them and then had to pull them up, also walk to the rear, get between the truck and trailer, replug the power cord to the trailer. Here I got the top button in the pants matched to the button hole and as I started back—naturally the traffic light had turned green and I jumped in and got under way. Of course, I had to stop shortly again and get the whole pants thing straightened out before I was again comfortable!!

One night I was making my evening trek home from Stoneham to Northboro, which is about 45 miles. By now, I had multiple routes I could use depending on what the traffic situation was. I normally took Route 2A which brings me right into Concord Center (Ma.), and getting on Main St. means going around a small rotary and then exiting which is now Main St.

As I came around the rotary —looked like a peculiar flicker inside the first store front on the left, which was an insurance office. This got my curiosity up so I pulled into an empty parking spot on the right—— opposite the insurance office—got out, crossed the street and put my hands to the sides of my face for help in looking in a large window. Now I know what the flicker was —there was a fire inside on one of the desks!!!

Another person saw it also and said he would call the fire department——so I went in the Sandwich shop next door and told one of the counter people there was a fire next door ——if they cared to get their customers out!

When I came out—I again looked inside and by this SHORT time—the fire had spread so the entire room was on fire!!!!

Fire engines came shortly— I left so not to get pinned in by fire hoses!!

ONE MORE——

I was driving south on Route 3, a Split Highway, near Lowell (Ma.), when traffic slowed up and as it crawled along I finally passed a State Cruiser stopped on the right shoulder with the roof lights flashing—then another and another and at this point I had slowed to an 'inch along' wondering what was going on when right in front on me ——some guy comes out of the trees and bushes in the median and at high speed was running down the middle of the left lane.

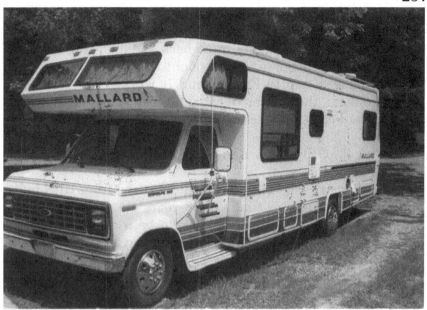

Photo C. Wells - 1995

The astonishing part was ——he was naked as a jay bird (whatever one of those are!!) I could see plainly something was wrong with him——he had a crack in his backside, and I wondered what else may be cracked!!! AND— traffic was moving nearly the same speed as he was running. He didn't run long— — about three State Troopers grabbed him and put him face down on the paved highway, and while he was there spread eagled, they cuffed him!!! While this is taking place and he is face down naked, I should add that this must have been March— it was cold! NOW, I bet he wished he had on at least a loin cloth!!

WE BUY A CLASS 'C' RV

By 1995, we had made up our mind to buy a 'Camper' of some type—and one day when we were in northern Connecticut, we saw one for sale beside the road.

We went back and looked it over on the outside—it was a Mallard 27 foot Class 'C' with a Ford chassis under it. We took down the information and when we were home, I called the number. Of course, this unit had some of the prerequisites that we wanted.

We made arrangements to go back the following weekend —looked it over inside and we bought it.

We made a trip to Florida and it worked out well—one minor problem, the starter solenoid quit—but I could still start it with two heavy duty screwdrivers, until it was fixed.

OFFICIAL RETIREMENT DATE

On February 18, 1996—I officially retired from URS information Systems at this time I'm 68 years old. Time to retire!

However, I have reverted back to be a contractor—so if any or some punch card equipment service calls come in, I will still cover the calls —only now I bill URS and for a different hourly rate than when I was on the payroll as an employee. Of course, NO benefits! — but, I now had Medicare.

SIDELINE SERVICING

In the 1990's, the Worcester Telegram used to have a column called 'Reader's Wants'. Here, readers of the Paper could write or phone a contact and ask for various items, products or services not commonly known, sold or available.

After I had 'officially' retired and in scanning the paper one night, I noticed a reader in Holden wanted someone to fix a Kinsman Organ which they owned. Well, I felt I was able to at least look at this unit——I used to service them on the Cape when I worked for Jim Cullum at Musitronics.

So I called, and the woman was tickled to death I would come out and look at it. I soon found it had a bad 'neon divider' on a note generator board. Then it dawned on me maybe one of the neon's I still had in my possession from IBM parts (to be used in a 604 Calculator)——might work in this Kinsman organ. Of course, Kinsman was long gone out of business, so if this didn't work——the chance of it ever working again was VERY slim!!

I came home, and after some time searching, found a neon, went back and installed it. It WORKED like a charm.

My point here is that this started me dibbling with electronic organs again and in doing so, I met a man who sold dozens and dozens of them in the years past.

Jim Atherton owned a piano and organ store on Boylston Street in Worcester and while the sale of new electronic organs had diminished, he still had used units available in the store and also had many customers calling for service on ones he had sold up to 30 years earlier.

As I became acquainted with him I found Jim to be a man I could admire—he could play an organ AND VERY WELL, even if he didn't play very often— he also was an automobile collector and many other topics which led to a nice acquaintanceship.

On the floor was a BIG Gulbransen Organ which at the time, I didn't realize how big it was, how well it could sound and also how complicated it was inside. There were about 28 LARGE printed circuit boards and utilized electronics to a great depth to achieve some fantastic sounds. Sounds I couldn't hear right now, because it wouldn't work and,——it just sat there. And here, I might add, this had sold for thousands of dollars when new. Jim said it hadn't worked when he took it in trade. He had the service manual for it and I inquired if I could borrow the manual to get a little acquainted with it.

For over a week I used to sit in my recliner chair nights— half watch TV—gab with Bunny and also scan this service manual.

In returning to the store, and with the time available, I got a break by noticing someone had reinstalled an inline 10 contact male plug, one contact group offset, into a 10 contact female plug. THIS—made enough difference so now I had SOME sound!! Anyway, I found about 6 different items that finally brought this back to a GREAT sounding organ! Jim took it home and his wife used it to teach from.

This action brought about many service calls I made at Jim's suggestion. On most of the service calls, he had the service information which made a huge difference and also made it a LOT simpler!

I worked on Baldwin, Wurlitzer, Lowery, Conn, Hammond, Gulbransen, Suzuki, Kinsman and others which I now don't remember the makes!

I also worked for another piano dealer in Worcester—
Sean O'shea——— did his warranty work on keyboards, the most
common of which were imported from Italy. This increased
my service area, and as I analyzed the circumstances I decided to not continue———I wanted my time more than work!

FIND A BUYER

Now that we had a complete compliance with Title 5———
Bunny and I decided it was time to change scenery. By that,
let's find a buyer for the house.

Neither one of us had seen the 'good ol USA' but once, west
of the Mississippi River—this is the time to do it. Neither one
of us was tied to a full time job or any responsibility to anyone
else, I'm sick of this house and the problems associated with
it. With only a couple of small exceptions, the bills are paid
OR will be shortly, we don't owe any money on the house for
the remodeling thats been done———time to go!!!

We took the belongings that we knew the two girls wanted
and passed them on———we had a couple garage sales, we
gave many many items to some people who had given an interest and with that———I started packing the residue in boxes,
liquor boxes. These were readily available, cheap, generally
free. As the boxes were filled, I stacked them in the garage. I
also labeled the contents on the top and one side——— so as
they went into storage, the general contents could be seen.

This process actually started in 1995, knowing this day
would come—it was just a matter of time. It wasn't soon, but
finally anything that could go into a liquor box comfortably———
did and now, we're down to the residue of furniture, bigger stuff
like lawn mower, hutch, and the boxes———all 302 of them!!!!

In August, 1996—I called my friend and Real Estate Broker, Bucky Rogers. He came to the house, we talked and when
he left, we had established a price, a brokerage fee and he had
a listing on the house———he left by noon.

By 2 PM—a car drove down the drive and inquired for me
and about the house—Bucky had notified them the house was
available. They bypassed normal procedure such as appoint-

ment and a showing by the listing broker—liked the house—liked what they saw and left.

Less than 2 hours later——Bucky called and said the house was SOLD AND——to a CASH buyer!!!!

WE had rented 2 ——10 by 20 storage units in Auburn and someway, all the residue went into storage——boxes in one and stacked so I could walk along 3 walls and see what was where plus some islands in the middle of the floor——the furniture and larger pieces went in to the other unit. It was touch and go if the 2 storage units would hold everything—but they did! This left us with a living room TV and not much else in the house.

While waiting for the closing date to come about—Bunny and I slept in the motorhome—the house was empty (except the TV), so our plan was to head to Florida by December.

When I received a phone call from our Attorney—Bob Gabriel, he said I should come up to his office——a deed problem had arisen. This was 2 days before the closing date!

Little did I know what was in store for us as I drove into the office and parked the car!!

DISASTER—FIRST CLASS

In the attorney's office, I learned the buyer's attorney had ordered an 'Abstract of Title'—which was fairly common. A good Real Estate Attorney should do this on EVERY transaction. It's ordered from the County Registry of Deeds—it goes back years and traces the ownership of the property—it also will list any 'encumbrances' meaning liens against the property. Also, registry 'reviewers' will examine the abstract (list)——to insure the deed is passable—'no encumbrances or clouds on the title'.

In 'our' case—a red flag came up which automatically stops a transaction!

I'll give the reason(s) — but I really don't want to spend time or space to give a drawn out explanation.

First—when I had a plot plan drawn by the company in Northboro that mailed it and shortly went out of business—there was a line that went through our living room on an angle by about 2 feet! I noticed it at the time, but I didn't analyze it—
—I knew where the pond side property line was—it was right

at the wall on the edge of the water. This is where it was pointed out before we bought, and the markers were there. I really had no reason to question this 'line' parallel with the water line —and about 15 feet from the water.

Secondly—the second plot plan drawn for use by the contractor for the pump system, had a line at the shore labeled 'High Water Line' which on this plot plan, I also didn't pay attention to—I had no reason to be interested in the water line!!

My attorney also didn't catch any problem —so both plans had now been recorded!!

Once a plan is recorded at the registry of deeds—it's forever—— and a newer plan doesn't necessarily supersede an earlier plan already recorded!!

TO SUMMARIZE —WE NOW HAVE A PROPERTY THAT CAN'T BE TRANSFERRED! (AGAIN).

The problem is we have land that isn't designated on the deed so it must have been 'added' ——filled in, which breaks a law enacted in 1867 and which is not 'grandfathered' meaning the problem doesn't go away within a given time!(IT STAYS) The other problem is the house is built on filled land. How would anyone know that——the house was over 100 years old when we bought it and for general knowledge——we certainly wouldn't build a house over the waterline (in the water)!

THE NEW PROBLEM——the pond is over 10 acres in size—this means any solution will now have to come from the State of Massachusetts and therefore come from within the Department Of Environmental Protection (DEP).

I won't spend the time or space to chase this day by day or even month by month through the process we had to go ——my blood pressure increased to 6 pills per day and I could tell it did!

By now, it was December ——we had moved the mattresses out of the motorhome and were sleeping on the living room floor—didn't know how long it would take to resolve this problem. No one in the DEP would tell us —the guy assigned to clear this (was in Springfield) wouldn't even return the dozen phone calls from our attorney.

It was too cold to stay in the motorhome so we stayed in the house, slept on the floor and waited——and waited. Finally decided to go to Florida——which we did in January 1997.

SLOW PROGRESS

Before we left for Florida——numerous things happened and the most important was that we lost the buyer. There was a 30 day extension built into the 'Purchase and Sale Agreement' to cover unforeseen circumstances such as this. At the end of the extension, practically no progress had been made —
——so we lost that buyer.

I had been acting as a scout, a fact finder for my attorney. One of the places I spent some time and repetitively returned to, was the Tax Assessors Department and the Town Engineers Department for the Town of Northboro.

Soon I was looking at Engineers Drawings for the Condominiums built on the field previously owned by Ray Lemay— (owner of the Grill), also I had chance to study the Engineering plans for the sewer pipe installed in 1984. This plan also covered the topographical elevations of the whole general area.

Here——I found the elevations with regard to the field—
—it showed the existing sluice (Ray Lemay had built) and how it was to be replaced so the pond elevation would be established——and at a level nearly 2 feet lower than it was previously for years. (A sluice is really only a drain, a pipe—it's a drain with an open top in this case. Ray could put boards in between the sidewalls for water control runoff purposes).

In studying the book of Massachusetts General Laws pertaining to the lakes, ponds etc, ——I discovered it was illegal for Ray Lemay to control the level of the pond and he clearly broke the law in doing so. With the new drain pipe installed— that problem had gone away about 10 years back. Of course, Ray had died years before I came into this knowledge.

And one other thing before we left——————we received an indication from the local DEP office that a 'wrap up' should be coming by May ——about 5 months.

That resolution was to be a 'license' ——a document that could be recorded with the Registry of deeds stating there was a problem—the State and the DEP knew about it——steps had been taken to provide a recorded release so the property title would now be clean and transferable, but probably would carry a time limit for some number of years.

THE PLOT THICKENS

In May, we returned from Florida and resumed our position in trying to get this 'license' issued. While in Florida, we had received (and made) many telephone calls to the Real Estate Broker—our Attorney and even to the State DEP office.

I really couldn't see where any ground had been covered or the circumstances changed,—— let alone resolved.

By June, I started to hear that this DEP Office might not be qualified to handle 'this case' and it would be referred to the Boston Office for resolution and the Commissioner's signature. I called the Boston office and developed a contact.

A couple of weeks later——I had a business appointment in Boston —and ironically it was about 2 blocks from the DEP headquarters. So I went into the building—found my contact and he wasn't very optimistic when I could expect a review and a signature from the Commissioner.

SO I said I was going to the Commissioner's office to get an answer. You should have heard the opposition to that! I replied I had waited for months and NOW it was MY TURN for action! Then he realized I was determined to talk to the Commissioner and promised I would have answer about when the signature would be forthcoming by 10 days!

Well ——the Worcester Office could continue, and now I'm told the Governor would have to sign the license!!! And before the Governor would sign this document———it would have to be reviewed by the Governor's Council. This was a team of attorneys who screened documents for the Governor and knowing how some attorneys work ——the whole thing could die right here——just disappear!!

I called the Governors Office and talked with a 'liaison' who promised that as soon as he saw the paperwork come in— —he would 'hasten' its trip to the Governors desk! Yeah —— sure!!!

BUT——within 3 days —he called me and said it had been signed and was on its way back to the Worcester D E P office. I was flabbergasted!!

Shortly, I received a call from the Worcester Office and stated they had the paperwork——I could come and get it,

PROVIDING I paid the 'balance of 600 dollars due. Here I called my attorney and said to him — "if this was a bribe, I would absolutely refuse to pay it!" AND to which he replied—"Don't be stupid——if they issued it—they could easily rescind it! Pay it and then try to get it back——once you have it in your hand —they can't take it BACK!!"

Naturally, he was right. NOW,——this process took about 14 to 18 months. My blood pressure went through the roof but it would start to drop shortly. This was an excursion I wouldn't wish on anybody. It could have been resolved easily and quickly—but wasn't.

My advice to anyone buying property—get a plot plan— get an abstract of title and don't be reluctant——use a good Real Estate experienced attorney!!!

SOUNDS GOOD!!

After I retired from URS and was working on a contractor basis—I found another job —right in Northboro. This was with a sound installation company, my hours were 2 to 6 PM.

I was to be the shipper/ receiver and in charge of all the sound components, amplifiers, speakers, baffles and many other pieces of hardware that had to be 'logged' in and also dispensed for installation.

The first day at work— —there were 465 boxed speakers to be brought in. I should explain—the building wasn't large enough to hold all the stock

Photo C. Wells - 1997

and also to prepare it for various accounts. Anything new would be unloaded on the pavement and had to be brought in.

By now, I had discovered I had a badly worn right knee, so the amount of walking bothered me, but I survived.

I'm sure I started around September and worked through until January when Bunny and I wanted to go Florida for the cold weather.

This company installed large sound systems for stores in malls, free standing stores, offices or commercial applications.

For instance, a system was installed in the Prudential Boston Building which occupied 12 floors and required nearly 300 ceiling speakers. A photo shows the amplifiers within a metal cabinet that was designated for that installation.

IRWIN M. LINDQUIST

Lindy, as he was known, was another of my closest friends. He was also my brother-in-law. Starting about 1951 and over the years, we became well acquainted and shared many incidents and chuckles together.

The Herald obituary printed some of the following, and while I can't improve on it —I'll reprint a few items of its contents. Lindy was 75 the day he passed away on Feb 19, 1998.

He was born in Spirit Lake, Iowa Sept 21, 1922. He was also educated in Spirit Lake and lived there until he joined the U.S. Navy during World War 2.

He married Barbara Day of Randolph November 14, 1945 and enjoyed the rest of his life living in Randolph. During those years they had 3 children —Bonnie (Osmer, now of Orford N.H.), Cindy (Leduc, now of Loudon N.H.), and Randy, now of Bourne, Ma.

He worked at a couple of jobs locally —one being a Route Representative for The Grand Union Tea Co. for over 10 years.

In 1957, he purchased the Randolph Coal and Oil Co. from Gladys Wells, (my mother) and operated the business until he retired in 1977.

Lindy enjoyed many sports, not only as an onlooker, but also as a participant. He also had memberships in many local fraternal and organizations. In addition, he was a partner in establishing Valley Bowl, south of the village, Stirco prefab houses and one of the original members of Pinnacle Skiways, also south of the village.

I, and others will miss him.

FIRE——OF LASTING CONSEQUENCE

In Book—1, one of the topics was about a fire at L.W.Webster's Mill on Pearl Street in Randolph. I think I would be correct in saying it was 1942—and if not, very close. Regardless, that was devastating, without even mentioning the loss of jobs. This was one place that always had job openings and many towns people found employment here ——and some for years!

The mill actually started as Emerson's Mill and next was L.W. (and Kenneth) Webster. Beyond that, it became Branchwood and during this period—it struggled.

In November 1999, the same type of disaster struck again——only this time , the mill was vacant—that is from an employment point of view. Since the fire, the debris has been cleaned up, and all that's left is the tall chimney of the powerhouse——another symbol and the effort of Ed Sault.

200 BOYLSTON STREET,
CHESTNUT HILL, (NEWTON) MA.

Near the beginning of this book (#4), you may recall I worked for Cybertronics (CTI) and in 1967 we initially had a four office suite at 200 Boylston St.Chestnut Hill. About 1972, the offices were subsequently moved to Andover, Ma.

In February 2000, the whole building at 200 Boylston Street, went up in flames. I believe it was so far gone —it wasn't rebuilt.

The remains of the L.W. Webster – Branchwood Mill on Pearl Street. Photo by Barbara Lindquist - 2000.

Photo described in text. Courtesy of Worcester Telegram - Feb. 2000.

TMJ———CONCLUSION

Through the years starting with 1977, I was burdened with the **TMJ** problem. I did get relief from the discomfort, and I could stand the poor effects from this situation for about 12 to 15 months at a time. As time went on, I zeroed in on how to cope, and what to do with improving the circumstances.

After the first year and needing relief from pain now occurring, I made an appointment with Dr. Schaefer and he would rejuvenate my 'plate'. As I used the 'appliance' or plate as I called it, all the chewing and perhaps night grinding———the surface would wear down. Generally, after 12 to 15 months, I would need to have the surface built up. By applying his pulse generator, my jaw muscles would be limbered up or relaxed enough so a 'home position' could be re-established. In mixing up a small batch of acrylic material and then applying it to the plate, subsequent pulses would force the jaw to literally 'pound' this acrylic to the correct thickness my jaw needed, and at which point he would shut the pulse generator off. The acrylic was a rapidly drying material and was very hard when dry.

Generally, some fine tuning and hand filing would put the finishing touches on.

This would give me another 12 to 15 months. I even got to the point where I would measure the jaw distances with a caliper and at 14/64, I was all set—when it had worn down to 11/64, I better make an appointment for a 'buildup'!!

Apparently, I was super critical in regard to jaw spacing—I have seen plenty of people who could chew with no teeth or with their false teeth out.

Over the years, I was doing fine but by about 1997, I could tell the spacing was increasing slightly, which was giving me concern. If the spacing increased and by 'too much', my speech would be slurred—too little, and I would have pain.

By now, I had retired from full time work. My house was completed including the final sewage resolution and Bunny and I were anticipating the future.

In 2001, I was accomplishing things about my jaw that I couldn't do before. I could sleep at night without the spacer in my mouth———soon I found I could eat without it and then—I just left it out for a few hours. Then increasing these hours to all day—so now I do without it for 24 hours. But, after all those years, I had grown thoroughly accustomed to its presence, and it was difficult to overcome the idea I could now close my jaw so no space was left between!

Finally, I succeeded in achieving pain free status——so after 24 years of **TMJ** battle—I'm now out of the woods totally. It faded away as silently as it came on 24 years ago!

If any boxer had to go through what I did for 24 years—I'd bet they would think twice about what the results could be IF the jaw was clobbered with an injury to the temporomandibular joint!

I can only conclude that my 'problem' was caused by —— **STRESS**!!!

In retirement, I still have some residue of tinnitus (ringing in the ears) and a balance problem, but I'm without jaw pain and its now been about 5 years!!!

MODEL TRUCK CONCLUSION

Many topics back, constituting quite a few years, I described a model truck I had made from a kit and then gave this when completed to Armand Dauphinais as a birthday gift. I also mentioned, I would come back to the topic.

After I had 'pulled the plug' on the Motel venture, I diverted some of my Saturday hours to other interests — one being piano lessons.

Sometime in the late 1980's, Armand passed away and due to daytime work hours, my wife and I went to his evening wake in North Grafton (Ma.).

At the funeral home, the parking lot was full and overflowing on to Main Street.

Bunny and I entered a side door and found the room to be well filled. As I made my way into the room, I recognized numerous people and quickly the low buzz of many people talking diminished until suddenly, it was very quiet. As I scanned the room, I noticed the coffin surrounded by many, many flowers and then I noticed that in back of the coffin was a single support arm coming up and protruding towards the coffin front with a single shelf. On this shelf was the model of the concrete truck I had given Armand a few years prior. I also then noticed that many of the people were looking at me — the reason being — word had spread, I was the one who had made and given the model truck to Armand! There it was, right over the open coffin, a very simple gift along with the flowers. Everyone knew that Armand's concrete business was a big item in his life and this was a very touching scene.

SOME STRAGGLERS

In 1999, we traded our Class 'C' Motorhome in and bought a new Class 'A'. With this, we could travel and see more of this huge and wonderful country —— and do it with having to cope with a work schedule on either of our behalf. Those plans never did materialize, the reasons for which I'm going to pass over. And also, I'll pass over the brand of Recreation Vehicle, which not only ate months in time and very noticeably provided numerous examples —— of aggravation. And here, mentioning that time in our life is the same as a blacksmith pulling the cord on his bellows under the forge —which has already fanned the flame of my temper, so with that, I'll conclude the topic!!

So, we visited a huge RV dealership and came away with a fifth wheel trailer and suitable truck as a package. This provided us with a full time place to live for over five years, was less troublesome, but also covered the existing problems of Bunny's health. Meaning, we now just went south in the winter months and stayed in New England part of the summer months.

Before we sold the house in 1998, we thinned out many of our possessions, one of which was my piano. Estimating for this to stay in storage for a variable length of time, under severe temperatures and which would most certainly ruin it, I sold it to my friend and piano teacher, Joe Pulsifer.

In its place about 2002, I bought a keyboard and to be exact, a Technics KN 6000. This unit was an example of years of technology packed into one keyboard with 66 notes. In the approximate 5 years I've owned this, I still haven't explored all its features and capabilities. But, it certainly is providing me with a lot of sounds and interest in my retirement years.

RUDOLF DAY——BETTER KNOWN AS RUDY

I had been visiting Rudy and as I was preparing to leave, I said to Rudy, "See you later, Rudy." With that, he replied, "I don't use that term, but I'm glad to see you!"

Naturally that reply made me curious as to why he said that he doesn't use the term— 'see you later'?

Rudy is a retired undertaker and he said, "As an undertaker, picture me at the Funeral Home standing near the door and as the mourners are passing by to leave,—it really isn't appropriate to say, "See you later!!"

And while we're talking about Rudy Day——his father, Reverend F. Wilson Day was the minister of the Congregational Church in Randolph. Naturally, Rudy was required to go to church each and every Sunday.

One Sunday when he was about seven years old, he couldn't go to church as he had a sore throat, so he stayed home with a sitter.

Later, when his parents returned from church, each had a palm branch and Rudy asked why they had a palm branch. He heard the explanation that when Jesus walked down the street, palm branches were held over his head.

"Darn," said Rudy, "wouldn't you know ——, the one Sunday I don't go to church—he shows up"!!!

AN OLD GEEZER!!

Within one or two topics, I've mentioned I'm now an old Geezer, or I'm now a full fledge member in the Old Geezer Club.

You know you're an old Geezer if————

——You swear the ink in the newspapers you read, must contain ether or something that shortly induces a nap!

——You can remember when you used to sleep all night——now it takes all night to sleepily stagger to the bathroom.

——You look admiringly at some of the females today and cuss your parents for giving you birth 50 years too early!

——Your mind gives you thoughts of things too young, your body gives you thoughts of things too old!

——You remember what happened 75 years ago, but you have trouble remembering what happened 75 minutes ago!

——You remember 'Coke' was a fuel you bought from a coal dealer!

——You went to a bank as a place to save your money—— now you go to a bank to straighten out a mess with your credit card!!

——You also used to go to a bank and 'beg' for a small loan— now you beg the bank not to send any more credit card applications!

Also, you have no trouble recalling——

The Terraplane automobile, along with Star, Maxwell, Overland, Whippet, Willys, Kaiser and Frazier, Chadwick autos, ice cleats, spats, the Cord, Tucker and Duesenberg automobiles, Federal, Diamond T, and Ward LaFrance trucks, vent windows, 'floating power', suicide doors, Socony gasoline, freezer lockers, The Nash Weather Eye, Fels Naptha, union suits, BVD's, lard, Wings cigarettes, Sawyers Bluing, mohair seats, Kay Kaiser, Ish Kabibble, bloomers, tire chains, hand chokes, pant clips, cigarette papers, balloon tires, mustard packs, Raleighs Liniment, castor oil, Big Little Books, Fritzy Ritz— Ernie Bushmiller, Moon Mullins, Betty Boop, Ethyl added to gasoline, innertubes, oilcloth, Tess reins and weights, side arm hot water heaters, punchboards, white oleo, Atwater Kent and Majestic radios, Old Gold cigarettes, hand chokes, Paul Whiteman, Winchester Cathedral, Kirkman's soap, Ivory Flakes, (noisy) knickers, neck wear called 'chokers', The Rainbow Room, Sammy Kaye, side curtains, spark advance, Nancy Drew, Tom Swift, The Kingfish, The Shadow, Gildersleeve, Fibber McGee and Molly, Red Skelton, Charles Atlas, Jack Armstrong —the Belgian Congo, Persia, Siam, Ceylon, George Burns and Gracie Allen, Fred Allen, Milton Berle, The Texaco Hour, Rochester, Jack Benny, Mary Livingston, Dennis Day, Bob Hope, Jerry Colonna, Bowes tire patches, Ed Wynn, Amos and Andy, Chesterfields, methanol, Continental tire 'kits', Marvel Mystery Oil, Cushman's Bakery Products, Kate Smith, Wendell Wilkie, Alf Landon, The

New Deal, CCC organization, Al Smith, Walter Reuther, John L. Lewis, excelsior, and 'hundreds' more!!!!

CONCLUSION

Now that you have come to the final topics within this book and perhaps one or more of the 3 preceding books—I would like to conclude with a couple of trailing thoughts. As you can see, I've had the opportunity to sail through life— or rather my working days of life by pursuing a multitude of jobs. I can't really call any of them, professions because I generally rate a profession as an occupation associated with a college education, which I don't have. As I said early on that I didn't know what in this life I really wanted to do or by what occupation I wanted to a part of. And I might add—I still don't know what the answer is!! But, if I had my life to live over, I can add that I probably wouldn't change much with the exception of maybe doing more house construction or building construction. I like the challenge, the many variations of styles, floor plans and mostly the satisfaction of watching the creation grow—piece by piece.

I also like automobiles, trucks, some small niches of the music world, business management and good food!!

I probably would go after some type of business of my own——if I worked half as hard for myself as I did working for someone else—I'm 99% sure, I could have been successful.

However, I don't have any regrets to the way I chose to live and I've had a tremendous amount of fun and experiences. Naturally, I made numerous wrong decisions and a few of large blunders——all part of life.

As I wandered about from job to job—I noticed that the more I learned —the better I felt emotionally and mentally. This can be attributed to the fact my mind was occupied with experiences and these experiences leave less room for 'trash' —and by trash, I mean thoughts that can't possibly lead anywhere near, or contribute to being near the 'happy land'. I've concluded, the more people you meet and get acquainted with— the more experiences you endure, the more situations you touch on— the greater your satisfaction with life. THIS —is

MARIETTA & CONRAD WELLS

Wells Celebrate 50ᵗʰ Anniversary

Mr. and Mrs. Conrad J. Wells of Rochdale, Mass. recently celebrated their 50ᵗʰ wedding anniversary. Conrad Wells and the former Marietta "Bunny" Day were married June 27, 1953 at the United Church in Randolph. Mr. Wells is the son of the late Alfred and Gladys Wells of Randolph. Mrs. Wells is the daughter of the late Albert Day and Ola Day, also of Randolph.

The couple has two daughters and eight grandchildren. Their daughters, JoAnne Miller of Auburn, Mass., and Lisa Wall of Leicester, Mass., and their families hosted a party for them, attended by 75 friends and family members, at the Randolph Senior Center June 28.

Guests included Conrad's sister, Nathalie Wells, and Bunny's sister, Barbara Lindquist. Other members of the original wedding party who attended were Bertha Stevens, Richard Monroe, Clifford Eaton, Bonnie Osmer, Joan Grey, and Anita Rye.

Mr. Wells is retired from URS Information Systems of Wilmington, Mass., and has recently authored a book on his childhood growing up in Randolph. Mrs. Wells is retired from Lizotte Plastics of Stowe, Mass.

Courtesy of Herald

when you will be happy and the circumstances you are living with, will be the path to that happiness!

In 1998, I developed a problem with the right knee and which I struggled with for ten years. A replacement was done in 2006, and the results I realized, —"should a done' that years ago. It really gave me my life back!!

IN MEMORY

This is a good place to include the following listing. It is a selective and PARTIAL listing comprised of family, relatives, friends and acquaintances. I'm sad to say ALL these people have passed on, (the year is also included).

These people were all important —not just to me, but they are representative of a group that I am proud to have known regardless of where or how we met and where they were living ——even if most are from my hometown of Randolph, VT.

Please note that this is NOT a complete listing of all persons that have passed on within the town or not —— that would take the purpose of it in a different direction from what is intended. (There are people included that haven't lived in town). There are MANY more that I knew their name— knew who they were, but I have to draw the line somewhere within the depth of the acquaintance, so many are not included.

These people I have either grown up with, shared an instance or more with, and with some, worked as an employee.

Many have been previously mentioned in one or more topics within the publications of 'A VERMONT SON' #1— #2— OR — #3.

In more than one case, there may not be a date given, due to the fact the information was not readily available.

I did decide to include the list because I'm more interested in keeping the names around as long as possible —— the actual date is less important than the name.

Many thanks to Barbara Lindquist for her help with the information.

One last thing ——IF you don't see your own name, just remember there IS one DANDY reason!!!!

In Memory
Alfred C. and Gladys H. Wells

Gladys - 1891 - 1977
Alfred - 1878 - 1950

ADAMS, FRANCIS	2001	
ALLARD, CONRAD (CONNIE)	1951	
ALLEN, GENEVA, (BABE)	2005	
ALLEN, GEORGE	1962	
ALLEN, GLEN	1962	
ALLEN, RITA	1971	
ALLEN, WAYNE	1999	
ALLEN, THAD SR.	1961	
ANDERSON, MARCEL (TED)	1999	
ANGELL, ALICE	1994	
ANGELL, DR FRANK	1959	
ANGELL, MARGARET	1986	
ANGELL, PHIL (SR.)	1978	
ANGELL, WILMER (DR. BILL)	1984	
ARMS, DR. BOB	2001	
AUBIN, PAUL		
AUSTIN, BILL	1995	
AUSTIN, DOROTHY		
AUSTIN, VALENTINE	1971	
BAKER, HAROLD (BAKE)	1993	
BAKER, THELMA	1973	
BARCOMB, DAVE	1979	
BARNARD, JOYCE (SIMMONS)	1994	
BARR, HERBERT (HERBY)	1976	
BASHAW, HOLLIS	1990	
BATCHELDER, HENRY SR.	1958	
BATTLES, ALLEN	1962	
BATTLES, GEORGE	1980	
BATTLES, HERBERT	1999	
BATTLES, THELMA	1990	
BEAULAC, ELIZABETH	1995	
BEAULAC, ARTHUR	1982	
BEDELL, ROGER	1981	
BELMAIN, GEORGE	2001	
BERRY, BERNICE	2003	
BERRY, DR. ELIZABETH	1997	
BERRY, DUANE	1991	
BERRY, LAWRENCE SR.	1973	
BETTIS, GRANT	1988	
BILINGHAM, GEORGE	1998	
BIRD, EDWARD	1971	
BLACKMER, DR. JOHN	1957	
BLACKMER, MILDRED	1974	
BOUDREAU, LEO	2000	
BOWEN , ROBERT	2004	
BOWEN, HELEN	1999	
BOWEN, ROBERT (BUD)	2004	
BOWEN, WILBERT	1983	
BOWEN, WILBUR (BUSTER)	2002	
BRAGG, ROY	1975	
BRIGHAM, ESTHER	2004	
BRIGHAM, ISABELLE	1947	
BRIGHAM, LAWRENCE (LARRY)	1970	
BRIGHAM, LEW		

BRIGHAM, STANHOPE	1947	
BROWN, HAROLD	1996	
BROWN, HOMER	1959	
BROWN, LUCY	1945	
BROWN, PRUDENCE (ABARE)	1990	
BROWN, WALTER	1948	
BRUCE, GEORGE	1996	
BULLARD, SAM		
BULLARD, CHARLEY R.	2005	
BURNELL, FAY	1974	
CAMERON, ELMER (BILL)	1968	
CAMPBELL, ALVAH	1971	
CAMPBELL, FRANCIS	1987	
CAMPBELL, KEITH (MUSKY)	2001	
CAMPBELL, MERRILL	1958	
CAMPBELL, RAYMOND	1985	
CAREY, BILL	1966	
CAREY, RALPH	1960	
CAREY, RICHARD	1982	
CARRIER, HAROLD (HAP)		
CASWELL, BILL		
CATLIN, EULA	1985	
CATLIN, GUY	1982	
CHADWICK, NELSON	1986	
CHAMBERS, JIM	1993	
CHAMPLAIN, JACK		
CHASE, HENRY	1985	
CHASE, MARY		
CHAULK, ART	2006	
CHURCHILL, WILLIS	1996	
CLAFLIN, MARJORIE	1970	
CLAFLIN, WAYNE		
CLAFLIN, HUGH	1963	
CLARKE, CEDRIC	1947	
CLARKE, MADINE	1996	
CLARKE, ALICE	1968	
CLOUGH, DANA		
COCHRAN, LEO		
CONANT, EDWARD	2001	
COOLEY, HARRY	1985	
COOPER, RUTH	2002	
CORSE, MAUDE	1988	
CORSE, MURRAY	1985	
COWDREY, FAY	1988	
COWDREY, ROSE	1979	
CURRAN, TOM		
DADMUN, HENRIETTA	1964	
DALTON, JOHN (RED)	1983	
DARLING, ELAINE		
DARLING, LORRAINE (BUNNY)	1990	
DARLING, ROD		
DARRAH, FRANK	1993	
DARRAH, HAZEL	2001	
DAUPHINAIS, ARMAND		

DAVIS, HELEN (HAUPT)	2000	FULLER, FLOYD (GUS)	1997
DAY, BERT	1988	FULLER, GERTRUDE	1975
DAY, BOB SR.	1980	GAIDYS, BILL	1994
DAY, BURLEIGH	1992	GALARNEAU, ARTHUR	1945
DAY, LESTER (SAM)	2000	GATES, OSCAR	1964
DAY, LORA	1958	GILMAN, FLORENCE	1956
DAY, MARGARET (PEGGY)	1996	GILMAN, LESLIE	1961
DAY, MARY	1989	GOODEIL, HENRY	1961
DAY, OLA (DOLLY)	1991	GOSS, MAURICE	1964
DAY, REV. F. WILSON	1943	GOULD, FLORENCE	1994
DAY, RUDOLF (RUDY)	2007	GOULD, MERVILLE	1964
DAY, RUSSELL (BUSTER)	1978	GOULD, STAN	1978
DAY, RUTH	1991	GRANTER, WALT	1997
DIMICK, SHELDON	2001	GRAY, ALLEN (AL)	1965
DODGE, RAYMOND	1986	GRAY, COLIN SR.	1999
DONAT, PETER	1998	GROVER, ALBERT	1945
DREW, GEORGE	1974	HAGGETT, ROY	1971
DREW, HAZEL	1953	HALL, RALPH	1999
DRYSDALE, JOHN	2000	HANCOCK, ALLEN	1990
DUBOIS, DICK	1998	HANCOCK, DOROTHY	1992
DUBOIS, FRED	1970	HANDLY, MARGARET	1994
DUBRAY, TOM	2002	HANNAH, STANLEY	1967
DUCHARME, GLEN		HARDY, HENRY (MIKE)	1966
DUCHARME, BERT		HATCH, JOHN	2005
DUMAS, JOHN	1958	HAUPT, WALTER	1994
DUMAS, ROBERT	1952	HAXTON, JANET (MORSE)	2005
DURKEE, JOE		HAYWARD, FRANK	1999
DURLAND, RICHARD (DICK)	1964	HAYWARD, HARVEY	1964
DUSTIN, ROXIE	1994	HAYWARD, JANET	1993
DUSTIN, CLIFFORD	1986	HAYWARD, HARRISON	2005
DUSTIN, DONALD	2004	HAYWARD, PAUL	1992
EATON, CARRIE	1946	HEDDING, RICHARD (DICK)	1990
EATON, NORMA		HEDDING, DAVE	1945
EATON, WENDELL	1988	HERWIG, WES	2003
EDDY, MYRTIE	1990	HILL, RICHARD (RICKY)	1985
EDSON, DAVID	2003	HILL, WALLACE	1965
ELLIS, CHARLEY (JR)	1991	HOLDEN, HENRY	1997
ELLWOOD, BOBBY	1986	HOLMAN, CHARLEY	1994
ENGEL, REV. FRED	1969	HOWARD, WAYLAND (STUB)	1997
EPPS, FRANK		HUARD, ARTHUR	1989
ERSKINE, SEDRIC	1986	HUDSON, HARRY	1969
ESTABROOK, CLYDE	1984	HUGHES, LORRAINE (TINK)	1986
ESTABROOK, MILDRED	1995	HUGHES, RODNEY (ROD)	2003
FARR, HAROLD	1986	HUNT, CLARK	2003
FASSETT, GERTRUDE	1964	HUNT, TOMMY	2006
FASSETT, OPIE	1972	HUNTLEY, MERWIN	1967
FLINT, ANNE	1982	HUSE, MAY	1979
FLINT, HAROLD	1980	HUSE, STANLEY	1972
FORD, BOB	1994	HUTCHINSON, BOB	1999
FORD, MARY (PEG)	1986	HUTCHINSON, ISABELL	
FORREST, AL		HUTCHINSON, LYNN	
FRINK, ELLIOT	1975	HUTCHINSON, ROGER	1991
FRINK, HOWARD		HUTCHINSON, JIM (RED)	1976
FULLAM, ELBERT	2001	IRION, HERBERT 'BUD'	2005

IRWIN, ELLIS	1954	MCINTYRE, ARENE	1990
JACKSON, ALAIN	1965	MCINTYRE, EDWIN	1978
JAMEISON, JOHN	2003	MCLAIN, BEATRICE	1986
JAMEISON, STEWART	1965	MCLAIN, LEWIS	1980
JAMES, JOHN	1990	MENARD, ELLSWORTH	1979
JARVIS, RAYMOND	1983	MERUSI, DINO	2000
JENNINGS, DR. FRANK	1957	MERUSI, EMIL	1983
JERD, FRED	1952	MERUSI, PRIMO	1979
JOBES, ARIEL	1994	MILLER, LUCILLE	1977
JOHNSON, LUTHER	1963	MILLER, MANUEL	1993
JOHNSON, ROY	1989	MINER, PAUL	1975
JOHNSON, STEVE	1992	MITCHELL, DR. RICHARD	1993
JOHNSON, PHYLLIS (SAVAGE)	1998	MONROE, EILEEN	1996
KENDALL, ROLAND (TINK)	1997	MONTGOMERY, ANNA MAE	1975
KERRY, LEON	1951	MONTGOMERY, ANNIS	1994
KINVILLE, GRACE	1990	MONTGOMERY, ELMER	1959
KNIGHT, BEATRICE	1993	MONTGOMERY, JEAN	1988
KNIGHT, ALFRED (FREDDIE)	1962	MONTGOMERY, JENNESS	1995
LABOUNTY, GORDON	1985	MONTGOMERY, FRANCES	1980
LACAILLADE, FRED		MOORE, JOHN	1981
LADD, ELGIN	1994	MORRILL, DOUGLAS	1989
LAMB, FRANK	1978	MORSE, LESLIE	1968
LAMSON, JOHN JR. (JACK)	2001	MORSE, FLORENCE	1979
LAMSON, JOHN SR.	1964	MORTIMER, WILLIAM (BILL)	1993
LAMSON, PRIMUS	1969	MORTON, MADINE (CLARK)	1996
LAMSON, WILLIAM (BILL)	1985	MOWATT, TOM (JR.)	1991
LANG, WILLIAM (BILL)		MURRAY, AVIS (RICE)	2003
LANG, SHERB		MURRAY, JOHN (JOCK)	1983
LASHWAY, JIM	1968	NORTON, KENNY	1987
LEACH, NORMAN	2006	OLMSTEAD, HENRY	1990
LEADOM, RAY	2001	ORDWAY, RAY	
LEONARD, HENRY	1965	ORDWAY, RICHARD	1960
LEONARD, LAURENCE	1962	ORDWAY, WALLY	
LEONARD, MABEL	1989	OSGOOD SADIE	1973
LINDQUIST, IRWIN (LINDY)	1998	OSGOOD, CARELTON (BUNKY)	2004
LINTON, BILL	1999	OSGOOD, GILMAN	2004
LINTON, GEORGE	1971	OSGOOD, IRENE (BOWEN)	2005
LINTON, WAYNE	2005	OSGOOD, MARK	1959
LITCHFIELD, CORA (WELLS)	1959	OSHA, SEWARD (BUSTER)	1994
LOCKE, RAY	1977	OSHA, JERRY	1981
LYONS, EMILY (STEHLE)	1992	OWEN, DAVID	1997
MALONEY, DICK	1994	PATCH, CLIFF	1995
MANDIGO, MILDRED	1996	PATCH, DONALD	1996
MANNING, GEORGE	1957	PATCH, EUDORA (DOT)	2001
MANNING, KEN	1993	PATCH, HERBERT	
MARSHALL, BOB	1975	PECK, ALICE	2001
MARSHALL, DOROTHY	1974	PECK, THERON	2000
MASINO, ENIS	1996	PELTON, WILLIAM (BILL)	1950
MAZZOLINI, ALFRED	1969	PERRY, MARY	1996
MAZZOLINI, TONY	1987	PHELAN, KAY	
MC GEE, EUGENE (GENE)	1988	PHELPS, HAROLD	1963
MC GEE, FRANCES	1988	PHELPS, MARIAN	1994
MCDOUGALL, PAUL	1984	PHELPS, DICK	2003
MCGEE, ROBERTA (BOBBIE)	2001	PHILLIPS, HARRISON	1999

Name	Year	Name	Year
PICKLE, BERTHA	1978	SARGENT, JOE	2005
PIERCE, ALBERT (MIKE)	1990	SAULT, CONRAD (CONNIE)	1990
PIERCE, CHESTER SR.	1937	SAULT, ED	
PIERCE, RUTH	1992	SAULT, HAROLD	1951
PIERCE, CHESTER JR. (DUD)	1969	SAULT, HENRY	
PIERCE, ED	1994	SAULT, MARGUERITE	1980
PIERCE, ELAINE (OSGOOD)	2000	SAULT, PAT	
PORTER, FRED	1997	SAULT, RUBY	1972
PORTER, LEONARD	1985	SAVAGE, BILL	1975
PRESCOTT, CHARLIE (JR.)	2002	SAVAGE, HELEN	1982
PRIDE, CLIFF		SAWYER, ERNEST	
PRIEST, MARY	1972	SAWYER, CHARLES (BUDDY)	1952
RACE, BERNICE (FARR)	1999	SCHUSTER, BILL	1969
RAINEY, HOWARD	2003	SCRIBNER, ALTON (PETE)	1988
RAINEY, VERA	1993	SCRIBNER, AUDREY	1998
RANSLOW, GRANT (BUD)	1980	SCRIBNER, DELBERT	1960
RANSLOW, HARRIET	2002	SCRIBNER, ELEDA (GRAM)	1995
RATTEE, ARTHUR	1986	SCRIBNER, GORDON H	2001
RATTEE, ERNEST	1970	SCRIBNER, SALLY	1992
RATTEE, EVELYN	1999	SEAVER, EDWARD (EDDIE)	1982
RATTEE, MARY	1997	SEAVER, ETHEL	1977
RAYMOND, JOHN	1976	SEAVER, HUGH	1979
REID, DR. DRISCOLL (DUKE)	1999	SEYMOUR, DOLPH	1987
RICE, PERCY	1980	SEYMOUR, DONNA (UPHAM)	1995
RICHARDS, HENRY JR. (BUD)	2005	SHAPIRO, BARNEY	1948
RIX, HERSCHEL	2001	SHURTLEFF, JOSEPHINE	1957
RIX, WILLIAM	1969	SIMMONS, ASA	1998
ROBB, BARBARA		SIMMONS, HAROLD	1974
ROBB, JACK		SIMMONS, KATE	1945
ROGERS, ALTON	1977	SIMMONS, CAROLYN	1997
ROGERS, BILL	2007	SIVRET, EDGAR	1972
ROGERS, BOB	1989	SIVRET, JAMES JR	1980
ROGERS, BURNHAM B	1994	SLACK, ANNA	1956
ROGERS, GRACE	1966	SLACK, ERROL	
ROGERS, HAROLD SR.		SLACK, PERLEY	
ROGERS, HARRIET (LUCE)	2000	SLACK, THELMA	1998
ROGERS, KEITH	1979	SLACK, LEONARD	1970
ROGERS, MABEL	1996	SLACK, RODNEY	1957
ROGERS, RUTH	1991	SLAYTON, BOB	2006
ROGERS, WOODROW (BUCKY)	1992	SLAYTON, FULLER (TUG)	1966
ROGERS, DAN		SLAYTON, SUSAN	1996
ROGERS, DON C	2002	SMITH, EDDIE	1967
ROGERS, HAROLD JR.	2002	SMITH, GEORGE	1991
ROPPE, GERALD	1989	SMITH, KATHRYN (SOWLES) 'KY'	1966
ROWELL, DICK	1981	SMITH, BOB	1979
ROYCE, ALTON	1999	SMITH, FRED (JR)	2003
RYE, FREDA	2005	SMITHERS, HOWARD	1958
RYE, GEORGE	1983	SMITHERS, MADELINE	2002
SAGER, CLARENCE	1969	SMITHERS, OTIS (OATEY)	1990
SAGER, EVERETT (SPOT CASH)	1970	SMITHERS, STANLEY	1996
SALTER, LESTER	1995	SMITHERS, WENDELL	1992
SALTER, VIRGINA (ESTABROOK)	2001	SMITHERS, ALETTHA (LETTY)	1976
SANFORD, ELMER JR. (SHORTY)	2004	SMITHERS, JACQUELINE	2004
SANFORD, ELMER SR. (SHORTY)	1954	SNOW, HAROLD	1972

SOMMERVILLE, BILL		WELLS, JENNIE (PERHAM)	1968
SOULE, HORACE (BABE)	1982	WELLS, JON	1938
SOULE, MERLE	1976	WEST, GEORGE	
SOWLES, DR. JOHN	1957	WHEATLEY, CAROL	1991
SOWLES, JOHN (JR)	2004	WHEELER, BOB	2004
SPRAGUE, ALLEN	2003	WILSON, BERTHA (TYLER)	2002
SPRAGUE, GEORGE	1967	WOOD, GERALDINE (GERRY)	2004
SPRAGUE, MAE	1986	WOOD, HAZEN	1996
STARK, DELBERT JR.	1988	WOOD, IVAN L (WOODY)	2005
STEELE, 'CHICK'		WOOD, LEYLAND	1994
STELZER, JOHN	1981	WOOD, LYNDAL	2001
STEVENS, ELTON	1974	WOOD, LYNDELL	2000
STEVENS, UNA	1978	WOOD, ROBERT	
STODDARD, THURMAN (TEEP)	1998	WOOD, STANLEY (STUB)	2002
STOKES, MAUDE (EDDY)	1970	WOOD, WALTER	1957
STREETER, FRED	2007	WOODARD, NORM	1992
SWAIN, LEE	1949	WOODRUFF, DR. JIM	1995
TABOR, CHURCH	1991	WOODS, MYRA (SPOON LADY)	1984
TABOR, RALPH	1994	WOOSTER, JANE	1983
TABOR, ROLAND	2005	WRIGHT, MARJORIE	1998
TATRO, HARRY		YOUNG, CHARLEY	2004
TERRY, BILL	1965	ZECCO, PAT	2007
TERRY, FOSTER	1980		
TERRY, MERTON	1991		
TERRY, MYRTIE	1967		
TERRY, BOB			
TEWSKBURY, REGINALD	1980		
THOMAS, GLEN	1985		
THRESHER, AVERY	2001		
THRESHER, JIM	1993		
TILSON, ALICE	1973		
TILSON, HARRY	1962		
TRUE, CHARLES			
TRUE, JEAN	2001		
TRUE, SUSAN			
TRUE, WALTER (PROF)			
TUCKER, DR. RANSOM	1972		
TYLER, EVERETT			
VINTON, LURA (ATTIE)	2002		
VINTON, STILLMAN (SAM)	1998		
VOGHELL, FLORIAN	1992		
WAGNER, ALBERT	1989		
WAITE, DONALD	1999		
WAKEFIELD, ARTHUR	1986		
WAKEFIELD, WELDON			
WALBRIDGE, MARJORIE			
WARNER, FRED	1971		
WASHBURN, BILL			
WASHBURN, JOHN	1988		
WEBSTER, LEON (L. W.)	1965		
WEDGWOOD, LAURA	1983		
WELLS, ALFRED (A. C.)	1950		
WELLS, FAY	1949		
WELLS, GLADYS	1977		

THERE!!!!!

Sometime in the early 1970's Lindy and I were outside his house on Park Street, now known as Wallace Hill Road. I would guess we might be looking at something under the hood of his car. Regardless, it was a nice day—nice comfortable temperature.

Our thoughts or conversation was interrupted by a CRASH which certainly sounded like an automobile—or two—so we looked around and in the direction of the next house slightly downhill and across the street —where David Owen and his sister, Bertha (Owen) Pickle lived.

We could see a car stopped down beyond the house and we could also see David's car stopped as he had backed out of the driveway.

In a very short time ——the very tiny Bertha emerged from the passenger side and as she got her feet under her, she uttered——THIAIRE!!!! And with that—trudged toward the rear of the car to inspect the damage.

I can't spell the word as she exclaimed it due to the fact Bertha had a decisive twang or accent and the word sounded as if she said THI or THAY or better yet a marriage between the two words and, of course it made Lindy and I snicker,—— also, this exclamation was the only word spoken for quite a few seconds.

For many years we would use that exclamation when something happens or is finished!

Now that the last topic of these four books are done —my writing is finished and now I can say ——

THIERE!!!!!!

And said in my OWN, and rather individualistic 'accent!!'